THE PEOPLE OF BAKER BOTTS

THE PEOPLE OF
BAKER BOTTS

J.H. FREEMAN

James A. Baker was elected Captain of the Houston Light Guard in 1879. This portrait is one of a series of the Captains of the Light Guard in the Houston Metropolitan Research Center.

DEDICATION

This book can be dedicated to only one person—Capt. James A. Baker. I do this not just because I worked with him on his financial matters and came to know and admire him. In my 21-year-old ignorance I didn't understand why he asked so many questions: he was teaching me by his favorite method—cross examination. He neither criticized nor complained, and when I left the Firm to enter military service, he was most kind and gracious. That was two months before his death. Although I never saw him again, my memories of this great man remain vibrant and are precious to me.

Nevertheless, the main reason for dedicating this book to Capt. Baker is that he truly is the father of this Firm. In the early 1890s, after the deaths of Peter Gray, W. B. Botts and the first James Baker, Capt. Baker, still a young man, was left alone (except for Robert S. Lovett, who was himself soon to leave). Capt. Baker could have abandoned the legacy he received, but instead he created an institution. Capt. Baker's genius for selecting people built this great law Firm. All through the years he was happy to let others occupy center stage while he remained in the background—though everyone knew he was the most powerful man in the Firm.

Thus, I dedicate this book, and my efforts in assembling and writing it, to Capt. James A. Baker.

– J.H.F.

Design: Peter Layne
Typeset Output: Typografiks, Inc.
Printing: Champagne Fine Printing and Lithographing, Houston, Texas
Bindery: Universal Bookbindery, Inc., San Antonio, Texas

Library of Congress Catalog Card Number: 92-72179

ACKNOWLEDGEMENTS

Dr. Joseph Pratt, Dr. Ken Lipartito, and Dr. Chris Castaneda whose research work for the original history book provided a wealth of material on the partners, and especially to Dr. Pratt who read the manuscript for this book and made numerous constructive suggestions.

Gareth Bahlmann, an associate and amateur historian, who volunteered to obtain photographs for this book. He did far more. Mr. Bahlmann did a vast amount of research and found numerous documents as well as photographs that will be forever valuable in our archives.

Dr. Rita Saylors who acted as editor and put the manuscript in final form.

Charles Szalkowski, the partner coordinator, who gave very careful attention to the final drafts of this book and oversaw its completion, and James Doty, who preceded him in this position.

The Library Staff under Bob Downie's supervision and particularly Trisha Fahugais who always seemed to be able to find any document requested.

My wife, Marion, who wrote her Master's Thesis at Rice University, "Political History of Houston, Texas 1868-1873," and who made a number of trips with me to the Rosenberg Library in Galveston to obtain background material.

The Baker family, and particularly James A. Baker III and Preston Moore, who were always available and gracious in granting interviews.

Margaret A. Sagstetter of Rockport, Texas, a dealer in old books, who supplied a copy of the diary of Peter W. Gray's mother.

E. William Barnett who authorized the writing of this book and the financing of its publication.

Last, but certainly not least, my secretary, Carol Koym, who, despite a full secretarial schedule, supervised the preparation of numerous drafts working with Word Processing at Baker Botts.

– J.H.F.

Someone has said that the difference between an Englishman and a Texan is that the Englishman thinks that 150 miles is a long distance and the Texan thinks that 150 years is a long time. When it comes to the history of modern corporate law firms, the Texan's view is correct. Few of the major firms have histories that reach back into the mid-nineteenth century, particularly when that firm is based in what was until the mid-twentieth century the "outlying" city of Houston, Texas. Baker Botts and Houston have grown together since the founding of the Firm in 1840, only four years after the creation of Houston. Many of the people who fostered the expansion of Baker Botts also played major roles in the expansion of the city.

This is the story of the lives of many of these individuals, the people of Baker Botts. It is told through a series of biographical sketches. Whenever possible, the people have been allowed to speak for themselves through the reproduction of letters, speeches, and excerpts from the Firm's *Office Review*. It is meant to supplement the more formal history sponsored by the Firm, *Baker & Botts in the Development of Modern Houston*. It captures the life of the Firm, the characteristics and quirks of the lawyers who committed their lives to Baker Botts.

Research for the history project generated many of the facts presented in this volume, but the voice of the narrative belongs to J. H. Freeman. Having lived through more than half a century of the Firm's history, J.H. (no name, only initials) is a storehouse of memories about Baker Botts. He first came to the Firm in 1938 to help Capt. Baker[1] — who was 81 years old at the time — keep track of his financial affairs. Upon his return after service in World War II, Freeman helped manage the Firm's affairs while also serving as financial advisor to a number of the partners as well as something of a father confessor to several generations of young associates. As a non-lawyer, Freeman observed the day-to-day life of Baker Botts from a perspective detached from the courtroom or the conference room but much engaged with the individuals who made up the Firm. His is the voice of a lover of history, of people, and of Baker Botts.

In recounting the life histories of those partners who came to Baker Botts before World War II, Freeman gives frequent glimpses of the parallel history of Houston and the surrounding region. He also presents the outlines of the development of the Firm's culture, as well as its client list. But most of all, he gives us a sense of those who have shaped the history of Baker Botts. He breathes life into the half-forgotten names of Firm lore, and for that, we are in his debt.

— Joseph Pratt

---

[1] The abbreviation Capt. is being used throughout this book to reflect Capt. Baker's customary use.

TABLE OF CONTENTS

THE FIRM AND ITS PREDECESSORS

The Firm, through its direct predecessors, dates from 1840, since which time it has been engaged continuously in the practice of law under the following names:

PETER W. GRAY	1840 to 1865
GRAY & BOTTS	1865 to 1872
GRAY, BOTTS & BAKER	1872 to 1875
BAKER & BOTTS	1875 to 1887
BAKER, BOTTS & BAKER	July 1, 1887 to Sept. 30, 1892
BAKER, BOTTS, BAKER & LOVETT	Oct. 1, 1892 to Dec. 31, 1903
BAKER, BOTTS, PARKER & GARWOOD	Jan. 1, 1904 to Dec. 31, 1930
BAKER, BOTTS, ANDREWS & WHARTON	Jan. 1, 1931 to Sept. 14, 1946
BAKER, BOTTS, ANDREWS & WALNE	Sept. 15, 1946 to Dec. 31, 1947
BAKER, BOTTS, ANDREWS & PARISH	Jan. 1, 1948 to Dec. 31, 1953
BAKER, BOTTS, ANDREWS & SHEPHERD	Jan. 1, 1954 to Jan. 31, 1962
BAKER, BOTTS, SHEPHERD & COATES	Feb. 1, 1962 to Dec. 31, 1970
BAKER & BOTTS	Jan. 1, 1971 to date

LOCATIONS OF OFFICES

Baker Botts has had offices in the following cities, listed in order of their opening:

Houston, Texas	1840 -
Kansas City, Missouri	1920 - 35
Mexico City, Mexico	1947 - 73
Washington, D.C.	1972 -
Austin, Texas	1978 -
Dallas, Texas	1985 -
New York, New York	1992 -

The Firm also had offices at one time or another in Kelso and Longview, Washington, and El Paso, Galveston, and San Antonio, Texas, and an earlier office in New York (1920 - 26), but these offices were opened principally to serve the needs of a particular client, or in the case of the Galveston office, admiralty clients generally.

CHAPTER

1

Peter W. Gray, with the Firm 1840 - 1874.

THE FOUNDERS:
1840 - 1877 [2]

When William Fairfax Gray agreed to come to Texas in 1835 to represent two wealthy Washington, D.C. investors, he set in motion a series of events that would result in the creation of one of the premier law firms in America. At the time, Texas was not even a part of the United States; not until the following year did Texas win its independence from Mexico. Gray arrived in Texas at a time of great turmoil, and he and his family quickly took leading roles in the transformation that led Texas into the United States, and the city of Houston into a position of leadership within the state.

William Fairfax Gray was, of course, the father of Peter W. Gray, who began his practice in Houston in 1840. Peter was the first partner in the Firm we now know as Baker Botts (throughout this book we will use the words Baker Botts without punctuation in referring to the Firm). His life was shaped by the history of the Gray family, and he, in

William Fairfax Gray, father of Peter W. Gray.

turn, shaped the early traditions of Baker Botts. William Fairfax Gray was born in 1787 in Virginia and married Mildred Stone in 1817 when he was 30. His parents were from Scotland. He was a publisher, postmaster, and a Freemason. He was commissioned a Captain in the Virginia Militia by Governor James Monroe, and saw active duty in the War of 1812, receiving a Lieutenant Colonel's commission. He did not become a lawyer until 1835 at the age of 48.

At that time, Col. Gray traveled to Texas as land agent for Thomas Green and Albert T. Burnley of Washington, D.C. Since he was traveling on an expense account, he kept a daily diary, which was later published by the family under the title *Diary of Col. Wm. Fairfax Gray From Virginia to Texas 1835-36.* Gray's diary has since become an important historical document since it offers a fascinating account of life in Texas in that period. The flavor of the diary

---

[2] For historical data as to the Firm, see Judge Garwood's history, Appendix to *Office Review*, 6/16/21; Mr. Wharton's history in *Dallas Morning News*, 5/7/33; Mr. Hutcheson's address to Rotary Club, *Office Review*, 1/11/33; "Looking Backward" by Mr. Wharton, *Office Review*, 1/13/27; History as reflected by volumes of Old Legal Directories, *Office Review*, 1/21/26; and Farewell Address, W. A. Parish, Appendix to Vol. 35, No. 1, *Office Review*, 1/28/54.

Republic of Texas Capitol at the northwest corner of Main and Texas, Houston, circa 1857, after the Capitol had been converted into a hotel and the dormers were added to the roof.

is captured in his account of events at Washington on the Brazos on March 2, 1836, Texas Independence Day:

Wednesday, March 2, 1836

The morning clear and cold, but the cold somewhat moderated.

The Convention met pursuant to adjournment. Mr. Childers, from the committee, reported a Declaration of Independence, which he read in his place. It was received by the house, committed to a committee of the whole, reported without amendment, and unanimously adopted, in less than one hour from its first and only reading. It underwent no discipline, and no attempt was made to amend it. The only speech made upon it was a somewhat declamatory address in committee of the whole by General Houston.

. . . A copy of the Declaration having been made in a fair hand, an attempt was made to read it, preparatory to signing it, but it was found so full of errors that it was recommitted to the committee that reported it for correction and engrossment.

An express was this evening received from Col. Travis, stating that on the 25th a demonstration was made on the Alamo by a party of Mexicans of about 300, who, under cover of some old houses, approached to within eighty yards of the fort, while a cannonade was kept up from the city. They were beaten off with some loss, and amidst the engagement some Texas soldiers set fire to and destroyed the old houses. Only three Texans were wounded, none killed. Col. Fannin was on the march from Goliad with 350 men for the aid of Travis. This, with the other forces known to be on the way, will by this time make the number in the fort some six or seven hundred. It is believed the Alamo is safe.

Life was never dull for Col. Gray. Here was a man who had been living comfortably in Fredericksburg, Virginia. He had a large family and was obviously well known and respected. He played the flute and had a library of 250 books. When Gen. Lafayette made a sentimental visit to the United States, he was entertained in the home of Col. and Mrs. Gray. Yet this man was so charmed by his initial visit to Texas that he made an immediate decision to move his family to Houston. His wife, Milly (sometimes spelled Millie), was a very talented lady and also maintained a diary, which is a source of information on life in early Houston. We read from the prologue to the diary of Col. Gray: "Milly Gray was naturally sad on leaving her home in Virginia to move to Houston, Texas, a foreign pioneer settlement. After a one-month sea voyage, she describes in her diary the trip up Buffalo Bayou into Houston. 'The bayou became so narrow at last that I thought it would be no difficult matter to jump ashore from either side of the boat. The water is pleasant but muddy.'"

In May 1837, Col. Gray opened a law office on the east side of Travis Street between Preston and Prairie. His son, Peter Gray, would not join him until January 1840 at the age of 20.

What was Houston like in those days? Here are some entries from *Texas Avenue at Main Street* (Y.A. Pat Daniels, Houston: Allen Press, 1964):

August 30, 1836

A week before the election of Sam Houston as President of the Republic of Texas, the Allen brothers advertise their new 'city' in a local newspaper.

'Nature seems to have designated this place for the future seat of government.'

Sam Houston was elected President on September 5, 1836, winning over Henry Smith, who had been provisional governor of Texas during the revolutionary period, and Stephen F. Austin, 'Father of Texas.' Houston polled 5,119 votes; Smith, 743; Austin, 587.

December 15, 1836

Congress, lured by the Allen brothers' inducements of government buildings, private lodgings for Congressmen, and a city 'handsome and beautifully elevated, salubrious and well watered, and now in the very heart or center of population,' passes an act providing that the capital should be located at Houston until the end of the legislative session of 1840.

John K. Allen was himself a member of the House of Representatives of the First Congress which selected Houston as the capital over 14 rival applicants.

January 19, 1837

First multiple sales of lots are made by Allen brothers in their City of Houston.

This date is called by some historians as the "most reasonable date to mark the beginning of the City of Houston as such."

Somewhat fanciful conception of Houston in 1839, by an artist who obviously had never visited the banks of Buffalo Bayou.

Baker Botts later came into possession of the Allen Brothers' original Town Lot Book, which lists the sale price of all the lots in downtown Houston as well as the names of the buyers. This book was given to Peter Gray in 1870 when the Firm name was Gray & Botts. After Peter Gray left in 1874 to become Associate Justice of the Supreme Court

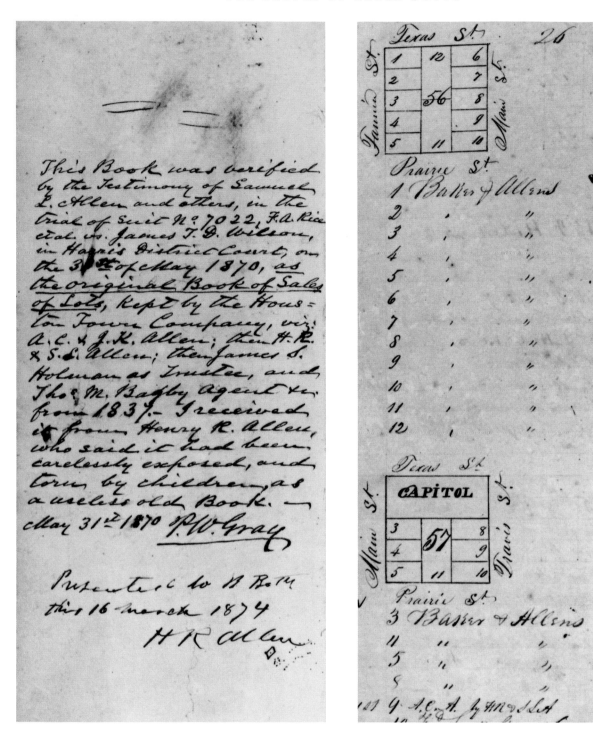

Inscription and extract from the Houston Town Lot Book given to the Firm by the Allen brothers, the founders of Houston.

of Texas, someone in the Firm, being very lawyer-like, went back to the Allen brother who had given the book and had him make it clear that it was a gift to the Firm. (See copy of Peter Gray's handwritten note inside the front cover of the Town Lot Book dated May 31, 1870, on the preceding page.) It remains today, in the Firm vault, a reminder of the close ties between the early histories of Houston and Baker Botts.

The Allen Brothers did not mention one unusual feature of early Houston. According to Young, *True Stories of Houston and Houstonians*, 1913, Houston was remarkable for having numerous large gullies. The largest was on Rusk. It was one block wide at Rusk and Smith, and over two to three blocks wide when Rusk reached Buffalo Bayou.

Texas Avenue at Main Street further describes Houston as the Gray family would have known it:

April 28, 1837

President Sam Houston writing to Robert Irion, Senator from Nacogdoches and later Secretary of State of the Republic, says that Houston has grown tremendously since the time of his last report — January 20, 1837 — and that Houston now has more than 100 houses finished and 1,500 people.

"It combines more advantages and is far superior in every point of view to any situation I have yet seen in Texas for the seat of Government, and commercial and mercantile operations," Houston wrote.

July-August 1838

Millie Gray recorded in her diary "The fever continued to be very fatal and a great many persons died — it is said one third of the population fell victims to it."

Additional history of the Gray family emerges in their connection with the Nichols-Rice-Cherry house restored by the Harris County Heritage Society and now visible in Sam Houston Park from the Baker Botts offices. Here is some of the history from *A Houston Legacy*, Marie Phelps McAshan, Houston: Hutchins House, 1985:

But young Nichols seized his fiddle and struck up a lively, defiant polka.

At that moment, the shape of his destiny waited nearby. A homesick young girl, Margaret Clayton Stone, was leaning on the deck rail of her ship, waiting to land. She had come to Texas with her Aunt Millie Richardson Stone Gray, who would write her famous "Diary" on Texas, and her uncle, William Fairfax Gray, who was to found Christ Church in Houston. Homesick, listening hungrily to the lively music, she vowed to meet the fiddler.

For new arrivals on barren Galveston, introductions weren't hard to come by. More than a jaunty tune across the waves must have drawn them together. On August 7, 1842, Margaret and Ebenezer married. In 1845, Nichols bought the lot at San Jacinto and Congress across from Court House Square. But it wasn't until 1850 that he started building the Nichols-Rice-Cherry house.

Nichols' partner in a general merchandise store was William Marsh Rice. Rice married Margaret Bremond, whose father, Paul Bremond, would build the second railroad in Texas, the Galveston and Red River Railroad. In 1856, Nichols moved to Galveston and sold his house to Rice.

Mrs. Ebenezer Nichols, wife of the first owner of the house, was the niece of Mrs. William Fairfax Gray and a cousin of Peter Gray.

Finally, we quote again from *A Houston Legacy* for evidence of Col. Gray's versatility:

THE FOUNDERS

Name	Birth-Death	Years at Baker Botts
Peter W. Gray	1819-1874	1840-1874
Walter Browne Botts	1835-1894	1865-1894
(Judge) James A. Baker	1821-1897	1872-1897

In May 1837, the first session of the Second Congress of the Republic of Texas was held in the Capitol at Main and Texas. The building was 70 feet wide, 140 feet deep, and painted peach blossom!

Sober voices of lawmakers held steady against shouts of drunk San Jacinto veterans. The cultivated Virginian talked to the escapee from U.S. law, the Methodist minister to the gambler, the U.S. botanist to the illiterate wagon wheelwright, the Baptist to the saloon keeper. Outside, the women, in the best bonnets and dresses they had brought from the States, averted their eyes from a noisy group of prostitutes.

Lawyer William Fairfax Gray, of Virginia, a member of the first session, swung through the doors of the building. Gray had brought his wife, Millie, his flute, and his 250 volume library to the new village. On the east side of Travis, between Preston and Prairie, he set up a law office which today has become Baker Botts (*From Virginia to Texas*, William Fairfax Gray.).

. . . As the aristocrat Gray swung through the doors of the new Capitol, he left behind, for the moment, the smell of mud, horse dung, tar dripping from ox-wagon wheels, stagnant ditch water and the rollicking peal of a Calliope at the foot of Main. An Irish captain preferred it to whistle blowing. Immigrants from France, Germany, Czechoslovakia, Holland, England, the United States, wandered along Main, hopeful, bewildered as to tomorrow. But they spoke with one tongue:

"Long live the Republic of Texas!"

In 1839, within a single month, three Protestant churches were formed in Houston, the first being Christ Church, which William Fairfax Gray is credited with founding (and of which Peter Gray was a founding member), then First Presbyterian and finally First Methodist. All three churches have survived to our day.

Christ Church at the northeast corner of Fannin and Texas, Houston, circa 1890. This is one of several buildings in the same architectural style that have occupied this site. The Grays were long-time leaders of this old Houston institution.

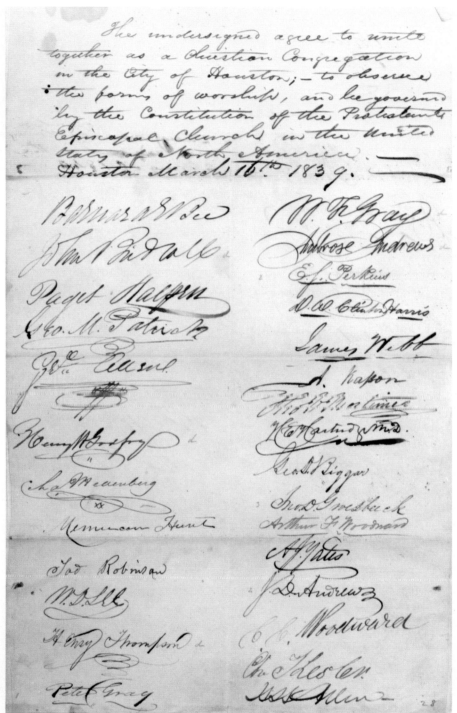

The portrait of Peter W. Gray
shown here hangs in the 11th
District Court, Harris County,
Texas, successor court to the courts
in which he, Judge John Scott
and Judge James A. Baker
were district judges.

Extract from the articles of organization of Christ Church, March 16,
1839, showing the signatures of Peter W. Gray and W. F. Gray.

Peter Gray accompanied his illustrious father to Houston and then followed him into the practice of law. Peter Gray was born in Fredericksburg, Virginia, but came to Houston with his family in 1838, and began the study of law in his father's offices. The next year, at the age of 20, Peter Gray assisted in the removal of the Shawnee Indians from East Texas. The following year he was captain of the 2nd Brigade of the Texas Army and second lieutenant of the Milam Guards during the expedition to repel Rafael Vasquez. What exciting letters this 21-year old must have written to his sophisticated friends in Virginia!

The younger Gray was soon admitted to the bar and began practicing with his father and Judge John Scott in 1840.[3] The following year he succeeded his father as District Attorney (at the ripe old age of 22) and served until Texas was

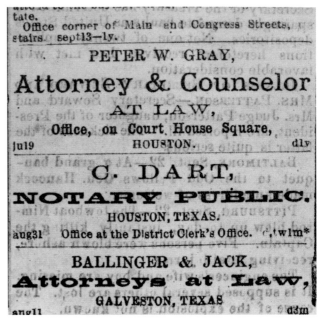

Advertisement from *Houston Tri-Weekly Telegraph*, October 2, 1865, for the law offices of Peter W. Gray.

[3] Peter W. Gray's mother, Millie Gray, kept a diary of her family's move from Virginia to Houston. It includes complaints of her troubles with her ears and her reports on those who are visiting her at the home of William Fairfax Gray, then evidently one of the finer homes in Houston. Her entry of Sunday, January 5, 1840, contains the following:

"We have very few with us now - a Mr & Mrs Manning - A Mr Iken an Englishman - & Mr Tankersley - Judge Shelby came up today - Judge Scott is also here & he & Mr Gray & Peter have entered into a partnership of Law. He is as deaf as I am - & a cripple."

This is the earliest reference found to Peter W. Gray's practice of law. As long believed, he was practicing with his father. However, his mother's description is not of an office-sharing arrangement, as long thought, but rather of a "partnership" with his father and a Judge Scott. Further research produced the following from *The Morning Star*, Tuesday, January 7, 1840:

LAW NOTICE - The subscribers have associated in the practice of the Law under the firm of Scott & Gray. One of them may always be found at the office of W. F. Gray, city of Houston. Their united attention, when necessary, will be given to business entrusted to them.
W. Fairfax Gray.   John Scott.   Peter Gray.

John Scott had come to Texas from North Carolina where he had been a state representative and solicitor general of that state. He was described as a good lawyer and an honest man. The *Telegraph and Texas Register* of December 11, 1839 approved his being named a district judge and stated that the "high standing of Judge Scott as an attorney, and his worth as a private citizen, are the best guaranties that he will ably and efficiently perform the duties of judge." In those days, the district judges of the Republic of Texas were the associate judges of the Supreme Court of the Republic. While he was appointed a district judge in 1839, John Scott soon resigned, apparently because of some doubts about the legal efficacy of his appointment. Evidently, he never sat during one of the term sessions of the Supreme Court of the Republic. He was an unsuccessful candidate for Chief Justice of the Republic of Texas in 1840. The *Telegraph and Texas Register* supported his candidacy: "We know of no man in the country, who unites the essential qualities for a good Judge, in a more eminenet degree of the gentleman whom several papers have mentioned as suitable to fill the important office of Chief Justice of the Republic."

The three-man office of Scott & Gray suffered the loss of Col. W. F. Gray on April 16, 1841. In the discharge of his official duties as District Attorney, he had visited Galveston and contracted a cold which developed into fatal pneumonia. Judge Scott again ran for office and was elected Recorder of the City of Houston in January 1842, but died on June 4, 1842. Peter Gray was thus left to carry on the practice alone.

If one accepts that Peter W. Gray and John Scott joined W. F. Gray's office, the Firm could be said to date from May 1837, when W. F. Gray opened his office in Houston, or even from 1835 when W. F. Gray was admitted to the bar in Virginia.

Masonic Lodge at the northeast corner of Main and Capitol, Houston, circa 1870.
Several of the early Firm lawyers were staunch Masons.

admitted to the Union in 1845. In 1843 he married Abby Jane Avery who devoted, as did he, substantial time to Christ Church Cathedral. He was elected City Alderman in 1841. After Texas became a state, he represented Harris County in the House of the First Legislature, where he authored the first practice act, and in the Senate of the Fourth Legislature. He was elected District Judge in 1854 and served until the outbreak of the Civil War when he was elected to the House of the Confederate Congress. Chief Justice Roberts of the Texas Supreme Court, who had known Gray as a practicing attorney, said of him, "I regard Judge Gray upon the whole, the very best District Judge that ever sat on the district bench of Texas."[4] A man of his talent, however, was not limited to one career at one time. In 1863 during the attack on and successful recapture of Galveston, Gray was an aide on the staff of Gen. Magruder.

After the war, Gray resumed his law practice. Unfortunately, we have little information on his clients. We do know that he represented William Marsh Rice, and we may assume that he represented the Allen Brothers since they made him a gift of the Town Lot Book that they used to record the original lot sales in Houston. There are several indications that he was quite successful:

[4] Hugh Rice Kelly, "Peter Gray," *The Houston Lawyer,* January 1976, pp. 29-35.

FUNERAL OF JUDGE P. W. GRAY.

An Immense Procession.

On Sunday afternoon the funeral obsequies of the late Judge Peter W. Gray were performed from the Episcopal Church. The concourse of people in attendance to pay the last sad tribute of respect and honor to one who was dear to all the people of this city, for his public worth and private virtues, was the largest ever witnessed in Houston. Fully

THREE THOUSAND

people were at the church, the aged and the young, the rich and the poor, all alike bowed in sorrow for a great and a good man, who has passed away from among us forever. Several hundred people, besides the Masonic Order and Bar of the city, attended the remains from the residence to the church.

The body, encased in a metallic casket, was borne by the pall bearers, Messrs. W. J. Hutchins, H. T. Garnett, Cornelius Ennis, W. G. Webb, J. B. Likens, E. W. Taylor, Geo. Goldthwaite and Mayor J. T. D. Wilson, from the hearse into the church, through the uncovered multitude who were unable to find room inside. In the church the funeral services were read by Rev. Albert Lyon, after which an opportunity was afforded the friends and acquaintances of the deceased to look upon the once familiar face for the last time, which was availed of by a large number.

THE FUNERAL PROCESSION

was then formed in the following order:

Music.

Ruthven Commandery, No. 3, Knights Templars.

Gray Lodge No. 329.

Holland Lodge, No. 1.

Pall Bearers. | Hearse. | Pall Bearers.

Members of the Family.

The Houston Bar.

Friends in carriages.

The procession was a very large one, seventy-five carriages joining in it, all filled to overflowing with sorrowing friends.

In Glenwood Cemetery the remains were buried with the impressive and solemn ceremonies of the Episcopal Church, followed by those of the Masonic ritual.

Account of the funeral of Peter W. Gray from an October 1874 issue of a local Houston newspaper. His funeral was the largest that had been held in Houston at the time; the entire membership of the Houston bar is reported to have attended.

1.   The 1850 census listed William Marsh Rice at 32 with a net worth of $25,000 and Peter Gray at 31 with a net worth of $10,000, both substantial sums for that day.

2.   In 1855, he financed Henderson Yoakum's *History of Texas*, which was dedicated to him. This book is commonly referred to as the first history book of Texas.

3.   He left numerous pieces of Houston property to his wife who in turn left them to Christ Church. It is recorded in the Church history that for years after her death each time the Church needed money for capital funds, it sold a piece of the Gray property.

There is also ample evidence that Gray was one of Houston's leading citizens. In 1848, he was a charter member of the Houston Lyceum, forerunner of the Houston Library. In 1870, when the Houston Bar Association was formed, he was elected the first president. After his death, the city named Gray Avenue, and the Texas Legislature named Gray County for him.

It would be interesting to know what discipline Judge Gray maintained in his court. According to the *Houston American Guide Series* WPA, 1941, when Gray was a practicing attorney, he made news one time by being fined $20 for sitting on a table and another $20 for smoking in the courtroom.

We do not know why Gray decided to take Walter Browne Botts as a partner in 1865, but we do know Gray suffered ill health a few years later. It was reported that in 1873 he went to Europe for his health (tuberculosis), came back to Houston, and was appointed a Justice in the Texas Supreme Court in 1874. Bad health

forced his resignation, and he died on October 3, 1874 at the age of 54. Yet, he had lived a full life as a distinguished jurist and lawyer, soldier, public servant, civic leader, and devoted Freemason.

One lasting legacy of Peter Gray was his creation of the law firm that became Baker Botts. As Gray practiced law — first as an individual and then in partnership with Walter Browne Botts — the city of Houston grew steadily. In 1850 after Peter Gray had been practicing ten years, the population of Houston was 2,396, smaller than Bellville in 1980. In 1860, the population was 4,845, smaller than Dayton, Texas in 1980.

Such figures can be read in two ways. Most obviously, Houston on the eve of the Civil War was a very small town in comparison to the sprawling metropolis it was to become in the twentieth century. But it is also noteworthy that this frontier city had more than tripled in size in the two decades after Peter Gray entered the practice of law. Houston had already become an important center of commerce for a broad section of southeastern Texas. It was already a magnet for people with dreams and ambition.

View of the foot of Main Street, Houston, at Buffalo Bayou, and the steamer *St. Clair*, circa 1866. Samuel L. Allen, a brother of the City's founders, operated the cotton warehouse in the background on the current site of the University of Houston-Downtown.

WALTER BROWNE BOTTS

One such person was Walter Browne Botts. He was a member of a prominent family of lawyers from Fredericksburg, Virginia. He was also a first cousin of Peter W. Gray — their fathers had married sisters.

A letter from Barbara Schomp Kirby, custodian of the archives in Dumfries, Virginia (undated but received in April 1986), indicates that W. B. Botts' brother, Lawson, defended John Brown and that Botts' grandfather, Benjamin G. Botts, defended Aaron Burr. This letter indicates that not only Walter Browne's grandfather but also his father and three uncles practiced law. Some quotes from the letter follow:

A few items from my file follow: 8 Mar. 1894 Free Lance Star, Fredericksburg, Va. "A telegram has been received here announcing the sad intelligence that W. B. Botts Esquire formerly of this city but who for many years has been a prominent member of the bar of Houston, Texas died at his home in that place yesterday in the 59th year of his age. The deceased was a brother of Messrs C. M. & A. B. Botts of this city. His wife preceded him to the grave only a few days having departed this life last Saturday, Mar. 3, age 57. They leave 10 children & a large circle of friends & relatives to mourn their demise."

Walter Browne Botts was the son of Thomas Hutchinson & Mary Scandrett (Stone) Botts. His father was a prominent attorney in Fredericksburg, Va. & is buried in the Confederate Cemetery there with three of his children. W. B. Botts' brother Lawson Botts, also an attorney, did indeed defend John Brown in his trial for treason at Harpers' Ferry W. Va. until dismissed by Brown. (Lawson Botts was appointed by the court) Thomas Hutchinson Botts (W.B.'s father) b. 1 Dec 1800 in Dumfries, Va. the son of Benjamin

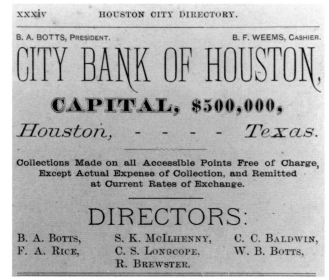

Extract from the *Houston City Directory*, 1879-80. Founded in 1870, Firm client City Bank of Houston was the second state chartered bank, and originally was the banking department of the Houston Insurance Company. W. B. Botts was a director and his brother, B. A. Botts, was president.

Gaines & Jane (Tyler) Botts. Benjamin G. also an attorney b. 29 Apr. 1776 Dumfries, Va. & was one of the team of attorneys who defended Aaron Burr in his trial for treason, "neither asking nor receiving a fee." Unfortunately "the prospects of a brilliant career were cruelly blasted when Benjamin Botts & his young wife met death in the burning of the Richmond Theater on Dec. 26, 1811." Along with Benj. G & his wife was the Governor of the state and over 100 others.

As you can see, W. B. Botts followed a long tradition of law as a profession. His father, Benjamin G. Botts had 4 sons, all of whom practiced law at one time.

Additional information comes from the *Confederate Military History, Vol. XI* published by Confederate Publishing Company, Atlanta, Georgia, 1899:

Walter Browne Botts, with the Firm 1865 - 1894.

July 18th 1864

Robt. E. Lee and G. T. Beauregard will be the Candidates for President in 1867 of so cont...

W B Botts —

Geo Goldthwaite
W D Robinson

Lee may be, Beauregard will not.
G. G. —

Inscription in law book of W. B. Botts dated July 18, 1864, in which he records a wager with a friend that Robert E. Lee and P. G. T. Beauregard would be the candidates for President of the Confederacy in 1867. W. B. Botts, a colonel in the Confederate Army, had returned to Houston after being wounded in the War.

Lieutenant-Col. Walter Browne Botts, a gallant soldier of the Fifth Texas infantry, was born at Fredericksburg, Va., September 7, 1836, son of Gen. T. H. Botts, one of the founders of the Virginia Military Institute. Col. Botts was graduated at this institution in 1854, studied law at Charleston, W. Va., and coming then to Texas began the practice of law at Houston in 1857. At the beginning of the Confederate era he was captain of the Bayou City Guards, a volunteer company, including many of the best young men of that city, and in this capacity he entered the Confederate service, his command being mustered in as Company A, Fifth Texas infantry. At the organization he was elected major of the regiment. He shared the record of his command in Virginia until the battle of Seven Pines, in the spring of 1862, when he was severely wounded. In recognition of his gallantry he was promoted to lieutenant-colonel, but on account of his wound and

a lingering attack of pneumonia he was never able to resume duty. Five of his brothers were also in the Confederate service: Lawson Botts, colonel of the Second Virginia infantry, killed at Manassas; Benjamin A. Botts, captain and quartermaster of Terry's Texas Rangers, and afterward brigade quartermaster and major on the staff of General Wharton; Henry B. and Albert B., of a Virginia regiment; and John Minor Botts, who served with his brother Walter Browne. Col. Botts practiced law at Houston with success and honor until his death on March 7, 1894, only three days after his wife, Martha E. McIlheny, a native of Alabama, had passed away. Eight of their children are now living, and three of the daughters, Mrs. Mary B. Fitzgerald, Mrs. David Rice and Mrs. M. J. Henderson, are members of Robert E. Lee chapter, United Daughters of the Confederacy.

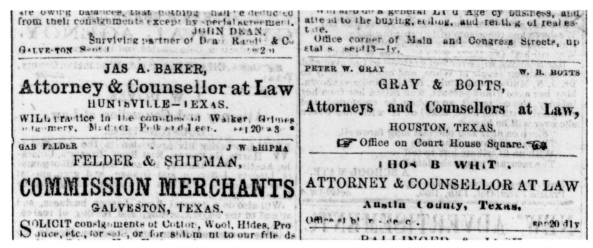

Advertisements from the *Houston Tri-Weekly Telegraph* of October 20, 1865, for both Gray & Botts and the law offices of James A. Baker. This was one of the first announcements for the Firm under its new name. The proximity of the Firm's card to that of Judge Baker's foreshadows their future partnership.

Botts graduated with distinction from VMI, where he studied under Stonewall Jackson. He was a very active Mason, and Mrs. Botts was active in charity work. The last family home was on the corner of Fannin and McKinney.

According to Capt. Baker, Col. Botts represented William Marsh Rice after Peter W. Gray's departure and before Capt. Baker took over this representation. But the relationship between the Botts and Baker families was much closer than a simple legal partnership. After the death of Col. Botts, Capt. Baker took over the guardianship of his surviving son, Thomas Botts. The Capt. later named one of his sons Walter Browne. Browne Rice, who lives in Houston at this time, states that his grandmother was a Botts and married a Rice.

We cannot say with certainty exactly when the partnership of Peter Gray and W. B. Botts began. The cousins agreed to practice law together after both returned to Houston from the Civil War. Firm lore long marked the birth of Gray & Botts as 1866, but newspaper advertisements for the new partnership suggest a date in October 1865. Nor do we know a great deal about the law practice of Gray & Botts in the years immediately following 1866, but it must have been successful,

because in 1872 they induced Judge James A. Baker of Huntsville to join them. As we know now, this was a momentous decision that helped to determine the Firm's future.

The aspiring Firm found itself in a city undergoing upheaval in the aftermath of the Civil War. It is difficult to imagine a man optimistic enough to take in a partner and start building a law firm in a city with such primitive conditions and attitudes, as expressed in *"Houston-WPA Writers Program 1942,"* Anson Jones Press, Houston:

In January, 1866, crowds of idle Negroes daily loitering in the shade of downtown buildings were viewed with alarm by many Houstonians. But civil and economic recovery continued; voters of Harrisburg cast "an unanimous vote for incorporation," and ships brought cargoes of merchandise from the East. Brick buildings rose two or three stories high along Main and Travis Streets, and Massie's Drug Store now remained open all night. Professor Eika's "tonsorial saloon" boasted six baths, equipment for heating water, and eight barbers. Dick Dowling, hero of the Battle of Sabine Pass, reopened his Bank of Bacchus Saloon at the corner of Main Street and Congress Avenue and

Houston Land and Trust Company strategically located on the northeast corner of Franklin and Main, Houston, circa 1895, and the Articles of Organization of Houston Land and Trust Company, 1875, showing the signature and contribution of W. B. Botts.

offered Eau-de-vie brandy, Monongahela Whiskey, champagne and Texas wines, "in exchange for drafts and acceptance." Women began to wear a new type of bonnet called the "Gypsy," described as "a sort of cross between a stove pipe and a soup plate—fits close to the head, like a monk's cowl, and turns up at the side like the eyes of a facetious canary." A newspaper commented that while "other goods may have declined, . . . the rise in hoop-skirts on the streets is, at times, quite startling."

By the end of 1866 twenty-five brick buildings were rising downtown, and in residential sections brick dwellings were going up. Many of the latter were described by the Daily Telegraph as "large, portly, roomy, suburban residences . . . [of] the merchant princes. Others are neat box-houses, or cottages built in the Gothic style, painted in different colors, white predominating.

The municipal election of January, 1867, resulting in the selection of Andres McGowen for mayor, was unmarred by a single fight. The Telegraph on January 9 exclaimed: "What a quiet and peaceable city Houston has become! But few cities of the size and population of Houston can boast such a record the day after a city election." Houston was too quiet for the merchants, who were still suffering from the effects of the war. When yellow fever appeared in neighboring towns, local authorities failed to declare a quarantine; by September the pestilence had become one of the worst epidemics in Houston's history. A story of a supposed victim who kicked the lid off his coffin on the way to his funeral was being told along Main Street while the only doctor in Harrisburg succumbed to the fever. Houston's popular Dick Dowling died, the Daily Telegraph of September 25 commenting: "He will be remembered throughout the country as the hero of the Battle of Sabine Pass, an achievement not only not equalled during the war, but hardly matched by the renowned affairs of Thermopylae.

Card from the *Hubbell Directory*, 1874, for Gray, Botts & Baker.

Harris County Courthouse, Houston, 1869. This was the third county courthouse. In 1869, Peter W. Gray won a major case for First National Bank, for which the Firm received a fee of $1,500.

Advertisement for the Bank of Bacchus Saloon run by Dick Dowling, hero of the Battle of Sabine Pass, from the *Houston City Directory*, 1866.

JUDGE JAMES A. BAKER

During this post-Civil War period, in 1872, Judge James Addison Baker joined Gray & Botts. We have a great deal of information about Judge Baker, but little on his ancestors. This is just as well, since Judge Baker sired a family rich enough in achievements to fill any family's historical scrapbooks. Because all of the Bakers discussed in this volume carried the same name, James Addison Baker, the following chart should be useful for the reader:

THE BAKERS		
Name	*Birth-Death*	*Years with Firm*
James A. Baker (Judge)	1821-1897	1872-1897
James A. Baker (Capt.)	1857-1941	1877-1941
James A. Baker, Jr. (Jr.)	1892-1973	1919-1973
James A. Baker, III (Jimmy)	1930-	none
James A. Baker, IV (Jamie)	1954-	1985-

We will refer to the original James A. Baker as "Judge" both because he carried that title in his day and in order to distinguish him from all the James A. Bakers who followed.

Judge James Addison Baker was born on March 3, 1821, in Madison County, Alabama, near Huntsville. After leaving Madison County at the age of 18, he taught school for two years. Later he became clerk of the chancery court. While clerking at the court during the day, Baker prepared himself for the bar by reading law at night. He was admitted to practice in May of 1843 at the age of 22.

Once admitted to the bar, Baker entered practice with his mentor, Samuel W. Probasco. In 1845, Probasco died and Baker fell heir to the firm practice. Two years later, in 1847, he formed a partnership with Richard W. Walker, who later became a "supreme judge of Alabama."

In May of 1849, Baker married Caroline Hightower (his former partner Probasco had married Caroline's sister). After Caroline Baker died tragically in April 1852, Baker moved to Huntsville, Texas. The two Huntsvilles were sister cities according to numerous Huntsville, Texas, history reports. Many families who settled the town came from its namesake in Alabama. Upon arriving in Huntsville, Baker formed a law partnership with A. P. Wiley. On September 24, 1854, he married Rowena B. Crawford, headmistress for the Female Brick Academy, which was a well-known institution. The Bakers had five children who lived to maturity, James A. Baker, Jr. (Capt. Baker), Robert L. Baker, Mrs. D. M. Parish (mother of Baker Botts partner W. A. Parish), Mrs. George Thompson, and a Mrs. Duncan.

Headstones near Judge Baker's grave in the Huntsville cemetery, which also contains the grave sites of Sam Houston and Judge James Elkins, indicate that at least three other children died in infancy. Infant deaths were not rare in these years in Texas, but three such deaths in rapid succession could no doubt help convince any family to leave an established home for new surroundings.

Baker practiced law with one other person (W. A. Leigh) before being elected to the Texas Legislature in 1861. A year later, while serving in the Confederate Army, he was elected to the 7th Judicial District Court. He served the same court earlier presided over by Peter Gray.

Judge Baker was very active in the community. He was a first decade Trustee of Austin

Judge James A. Baker, with the Firm 1872 - 1897.

College, serving from 1854-58, but was reelected in the second decade from 1864-67 and again in 1873, serving the last time until Austin College moved from Huntsville to Sherman. Judge Baker, along with two other committee members, Judge Abner L. Lipscomb and Henderson Yoakum, was responsible for the establishment of the first law school in Texas as a part of Austin College. Not only was Baker active in the legal community and in higher education, but he was extremely active in the Masonic Lodge. He served three terms as Grand Master of Lodge No. 19. On June 23, 1857, the James A. Baker Lodge 202 was chartered, and his picture remains in the lodge to this day. We have a copy of the 1853 Lodge report, which lists Baker as Worshipful Master and one Sam Houston as an ordinary member.

Judge Baker was an active member of First Presbyterian Church in Huntsville. An item in the *Huntsville Item* of May 8, 1989, noted: "The congregation bought its first church building at 13th and Ave. R in 1856. Judge James A. Baker and Gen. John S. Besser gave the church a bell which is still in use today."

In these years, Huntsville was an important trade center and a well-established city. But by the 1870s, the future of this section of Texas was already evident on the coastal plain, as Houston and Galveston rose to dominate transportation, commerce, and finance. In 1870, Houston's population was only 9,382, roughly the size

Firm letterhead, 1883.

of Sugar Land in 1980. But the city had already established a strong position as the central point of a growing network of railroads serving southeastern Texas. Inland cities such as Huntsville faced an uphill battle in competition with the booming city of Houston. One symbol of the shape of things to come was the steady migration of people from the interior to the coast. Huntsville later proclaimed itself the "birthplace of lawyers," a title which pointed up the fact that Judge Baker, Judge James Elkins, and numerous other noted lawyers once practiced there. But most gained their fame only after making the short trek to Houston in search of greater opportunities.

Advertisement for Firm client Galveston, Harrisburg & San Antonio Railway from the *Houston City Directory*, 1879-80.

Main Street, looking south between Congress and Preston Streets, Houston, late 1870s. This photograph was taken about the time the Firm moved to 45 Main Street, probably the first building on the left. The Masonic Lodge on the east side of Main marked the end of the downtown business district.

Judge Baker's last partnership in Huntsville was with Judge J. M. Maxey before he came to Houston and joined Gray & Botts in 1872. The Firm name at this time became Gray, Botts & Baker. Although still small in absolute numbers, Houston was even then a city of great ambition. Already in 1868, the Houston Ship Channel Co. was organized with Benjamin Botts, brother of Walter Browne Botts, being one of the leading figures. Another form of transportation, the railroads, marked Houston as a coming city, and Judge Baker's expertise in railroad law made him a valuable addition to the Firm.

Only two years after Baker joined the Firm, Gray left to serve on the Supreme Court of Texas. In 1875, for the first time, the name Baker was listed first. The Firm name became Baker & Botts. Although numerous other names subsequently were added, Baker and Botts from that date remained the first two names in the Firm's title and the popular designation for the Firm.

Judge Baker's oldest son, Capt. Baker, read law at the Firm beginning in 1877, became a practicing lawyer in 1881 and partner in 1887, at which time the Firm adopted its fourth multi-partner name as follows:

GRAY & BOTTS (1865 - 1872)

GRAY, BOTTS & BAKER - (1872 - 1875)

BAKER & BOTTS (1875 - 1887)

BAKER, BOTTS & BAKER (JULY 1, 1887)

These Firm designations capture the names of the four partners who are properly considered the founders of the modern firm of Baker Botts. Peter Gray first hung out his shingle in 1840. His cousin, W. B. Botts, and the two Bakers, father and son, greatly expanded the Firm's practice in the decades after the Civil War. By the time Capt. Baker entered his father's law office to begin reading law in 1877, Baker Botts was well established as one of the leading business law firms in the Southwest. Before forming their partnership, each of the founders had built personal reputations as leading lawyers in an emerging new region. Together they laid a strong foundation for the growth of a law firm that would continue to attract lawyers of equal quality.

Judge James A. Baker, shown here in front of his home at 1104 San Jacinto at Lamar Avenue, Houston, watches his grandson, James A. Baker, Jr., being held by a nurse, circa 1893.

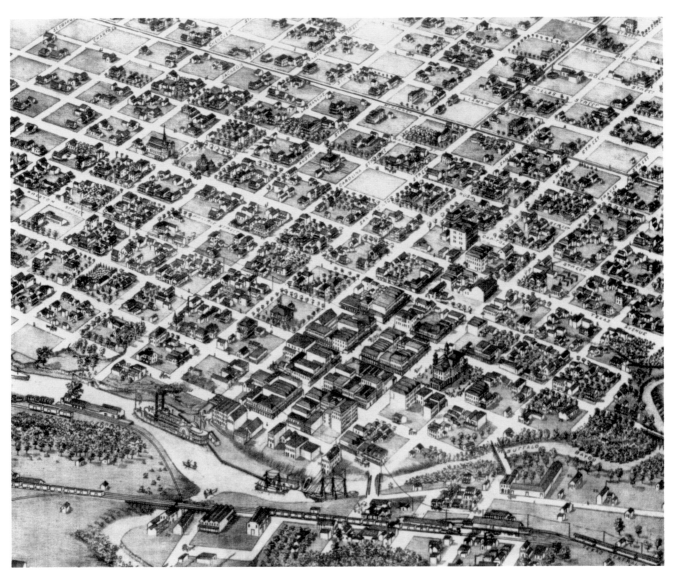

Bird's-eye view of the City of Houston, 1873, by Augustus Koch. This then-popular format
mimicked the view seen from that new sensation, the balloon.

CHAPTER

2

Harris County Courthouse showing Gray's Opera House in the background on Fannin Street, Houston, circa 1884. The second floor of Gray's Opera House was the location of the Firm's offices from 1865 to about 1877.

THE SECOND GENERATION:
1877 - World War I

Of the four founders, Capt. Baker can be seen as a transition figure who bridged the gap between the founders and the second generation of institution builders. The years from 1877, when Capt. Baker arrived at the Firm, to World War I were marked by extraordinary developments within Baker Botts and Houston. If the first four decades of the Firm's history can be seen as the formative years in which several able lawyers established an on-going partnership, the four decades after 1880 were the years in which Baker Botts came of age as an on-going institution and the first modern corporate law firm in its region.

Capt. Baker was at the center of this transformation. He quickly became the symbol of the Firm in Houston. He left his distinct mark on emerging banks and businesses in Houston during and after the late 19th century, and he helped recruit a new generation of lawyers to Baker Botts to handle the legal work of many of these businesses.

A quick look at this second generation of lawyers helps place the Firm's growth in perspective.

THE SECOND GENERATION AT BAKER BOTTS

Name	Birth-Death	Legal Training	Years with Firm	Partner Date	Specialty
Capt. James A. Baker	1857-1941	read law	1877-1941	1887	general
Robert S. Lovett	1860-1932	read law	1892-1904	1893	railroad
Edwin B. Parker	1868-1929	U. Texas	1894-1926	1900	general
Hiram M. Garwood	1864-1930	read law	1904-1930	1904	railroad / general
Jesse Andrews	1874-1961	U. Texas	1899-1961	1906	general
Clarence R. Wharton	1873-1941	read law	1902-1941	1906	trial
Clarence Carter	1869-1936	U. Texas	1907-1936	1909	railroad
Jules H. Tallichet	1877-1937	U. Texas	1909-1937	1915	railroad
Thomas H. Botts	1878-1922	U. Texas	1905-1922	1915	general
Walter H. Walne	1879-1947	U. Texas	1912-1947	1917	general

Note: Both Parker and Carter left the Firm for short periods.

Main Street, looking north between Preston and Congress Streets, Houston, circa 1870.
The building which is fourth from the right is the Van Alstyne Building, 45 Main Street,
on the second floor of which the Firm had its offices during the year 1878.

These ten lawyers all became partners before World War I. Together they built a thriving practice for Baker Botts in the early twentieth century and then provided strong Firm leadership in the 1920s and 1930s.

A benchmark against which to measure the development of the Firm by this second generation is suggested by descriptions of both Baker Botts and Houston around the time Capt. Baker joined the Firm. Clarence Wharton provided one glimpse of the past in an item for the *Office Review* in 1927:

> I learned from Capt. Baker that he graduated from the Texas Military Institute in June, 1877, and obligated himself to teach in the Institute for twelve months, beginning the September following. He taught two months when by agreement he returned to Houston and began reading law in the offices of Baker & Botts, which at that time consisted of two adjoining rooms in what was then

known as Gray's Opera House, which fronted on Court House Square, being immediately West of the Square. The building belonged to Judge Peter W. Gray, and was three stories high. There were roomers on the third floor, one of whom was Mr. W. H. Palmer, who was then practicing law. The Opera House was on the second floor, and adjoined Baker & Botts' offices.

A second view of Houston in this period comes from a historical sesquicentennial edition of the *Houston Post* dated May 2, 1986:

> The Houston Bank & Trust, begun when Houston had a population of almost 12,000, celebrated its 90th birthday yesterday.
>
> On May 1, 1875, there appeared in the front-page classified advertising section of the *Houston Daily Telegraph* (forerunner of *The Houston Post*) a modest notice to the effect that the company was open for business in the Van Alstyne Building in the 300 block of Main.
>
> Its founders were all lawyers: Decimus et Ultimus Barziza, president, W. B. Botts, E. P. Hill, J. C. Hutcheson, J. P. Likens and James Masterson.
>
> Houston's streets then were muddy, its sidewalks wooden. Citizens depended entirely on cisterns for their water, but there were 42 saloons to backstop them in case of drouth.
>
> There were no telephones, no electricity and no public schools.

The legal profession was not highly developed. The recollection of one-time Baker Botts associate, Grover Rees, captures the tone of the times:

Of course, Main Street was paved with brick. The side streets, such as Travis and Fannin were paved with wooden blocks. Every time it rained, those damn blocks would swell and they would pop up. And Main Street was brick only to McGowen, which was not very far. From McGowen on past Rice Institute which had just opened up a year or two before, the road was shell. And in the summertime when people would drive over that shell, there was an awful cloud of shell dust. Hermann Park had just been opened. It was really wild. Along Braes Bayou was countryside.

In 1915, when I was admitted to the Texas Bar, you did not have to go to Austin to take the bar exam. There were a number of examiners, and one of them was John Townes, with the Baker & Botts firm. So, I asked him when I could take the bar exam. He said: "I'm going to be out of town a certain day. If you want to, you can come to my office, and my secretary will give you the examination questions." So I went to his office, and she gave me the questions and I sat down in his office and I answered the questions as best I could. As I remember, it was not a very exhaustive examination. Just three or four days later, I met Mr. Townes in the elevator. I asked him if he had had the opportunity to read my answers. He said: "Yes, Grover, you passed." Now maybe he read my answers, I don't know. But in those days we were all very friendly because there were so few lawyers

Main Street, looking south from Franklin Street, Houston, mid-1880s. The building which is second from the left is the Fox Building, 27 Main Street, in which the Firm had its offices in two rooms on the second floor from about 1880 to about 1892. The Firm paid $40 per month rent for the office space. The Firm's staff expanded while in the Fox Building to include one stenographer and one secretary. The intersection of Main and Franklin was then the heart of Houston's financial district.

John Charles Townes, Jr., member of the Texas Board of Law Examiners and Firm associate from 1909 to 1917. After he left the Firm to serve as an officer in the military during World War I, he was for ten years general attorney for Firm client Humble Oil & Refining Co., president of the Texas Bar Association and, until his resignation in 1947, a partner at Vinson, Elkins, Sweeton & Weems.

in Houston. I belonged to the Houston Bar Association. There must have been no more than 30 or 40 in the Association.

Yet change came quickly to Houston in the late 19th and early 20th centuries. The population surged from 16,512 in 1880 to 27,557 in 1890,

and to 44,633 in 1900 when Houston finally passed Galveston to become the largest city in the state. The rough-edged frontier outpost was becoming a thriving urban center, and it provided excellent opportunities for the growth of a law firm with high aspirations, good connections to the eastern businesses that followed the railroads south, and good leadership.

It might be interesting to review the Firm office locations at the turn of the century. At the time Capt. Baker reported in 1877, the offices were still in Gray's Opera House (formerly owned by Peter Gray, of course), immediately west of Court House Square. The Firm had two adjoining rooms in a three-story building. At some undetermined date during the 1870s, the Firm moved to 45 Main Street near the southeast corner of Congress and Main. In 1880, the Firm moved to one of the Henry Fox Buildings located between Congress and Franklin on Main Street. This building adjoined T.W. House's private bank, which later became The First National Bank Building. The next move, in the early 1890s, was to the Gibbs Building at the corner of Fannin and Franklin. By this time, there were five offices, three for lawyers, plus a library and one occupied by a clerk and stenographer. Clarence Wharton later reported that when he arrived in 1902, Robert Lovett was still there, and his office was in the main Library. "Anyone who used the Library could have at the same time the bene-

Military parade on Main at Congress, Houston, in the early 1890s. The first building on the left is 27 Main Street where the Firm officed for many years. Although entirely speculative, it is possible that the men watching the parade from the windows of that building are Baker Botts staff members.

fit of Mr. Lovett's dictation and his private conferences." Wharton goes on to say:

> John H. McClung was Chief Clerk and attended to the telephone. There were only three desk phones and when a call came for anyone in the office who had no desk phone, he left the receiver down and went into the hall and called loud enough for us to hear him, and we would go down to the telephone in his office and have a conversation.

Wharton goes on to describe working conditions in the Gibbs Building as well as the subsequent move to better facilities:

> When Mr. Lovett went to New York the following year Mr. Parker moved into his quarters in the library. Just about that time Heitmann & Company, whose hardware house adjoined the library, started a series of shipments of steel which would be unloaded from wagons in the alley just under Parker's window and all day long the clash of this steel as it was thrown from the wagons to the pavement would make a horrible noise that would fill the entire building.
>
> However, it never occurred to me that these offices were not all one could desire. I had just come in from Richmond where my office had been in the second story of an old frame building whose lower floor was used sometimes for a grocery store and sometimes for a stable.
>
> The next year the Commercial National Bank began the erection of a new and splendid office building and induced us to take quarters on the top floor. It was finished and we moved into this new and elegant building in the autumn of 1904. It was the very finest in town and at once took rank over the Kiam Building and the Binz Building

The Gibbs Building, 1015 1/2 Franklin Avenue, on the northwest corner of Fannin and Franklin, Houston, 1893. The Firm had its offices in rooms 1-6 in this building from about 1892 to 1904 and paid $75 a month in rent. Wells Fargo & Co., a client of the Firm, occupied the first floor.

which had theretofore been of the first class. We took only the East half of the upper story. The firm of Andrews and Ball, which was organized about that time and which was associated with us in handling the local railway dockets, also had offices on the sixth floor and the remainder of the space was occupied by various persons.

At this point, the "new" firm was ready to take off. With the big three now aboard (a still very vigorous Capt. Baker, a Parker with some experience, and a seasoned Garwood) and with plenty of space in the newest building in town, Baker Botts was poised to expand.

Commercial Bank Building, on the northwest corner of Main and Franklin, Houston, 1913.
The Firm had its offices on the east side of the 6th floor of this building from 1904 to 1927.
The Southern Pacific Building was conveniently located next door. Clarence R. Wharton said
that the offices were still small enough that "if a partner wasn't near one of the phones when it
rang, the office boy went into the hall and hollered for him."

CAPT. JAMES A. BAKER

Capt. James Addison Baker provided the vital ingredients for this expansion. He served the Firm so long (64 years) and was interested in so many areas that it would not be possible to form a complete picture of him from a single source. One person remembered him as a dashing handsome person with a twinkle in his eye (possibly about the time he served as King Nottoc in 1909); a grandson remembers him as a charming grandfather who had the children recite or perform after dinner at his house and rewarded them with small gifts. He also remembered his taking the grandchildren riding in his car and tapping the back of the front seat with his cane telling the chauffeur, "Faster, Alvin, faster." Finally, a witness remembered him in his later years as a very dignified, serious gentleman with the eyes of a banker. This does not even touch his life as a trial lawyer, as a real estate developer, a banker, or an educator. We must consult several sources to begin to appreciate the full life lived by this extraordinary man.

Capt. Baker was born in 1857 in Huntsville, Texas to Judge James A. Baker and Rowena Baker. He moved to Houston in 1872 when his father joined Gray & Botts. He attended Woodall Academy and Austin College (which was then located in Huntsville), but graduated from Texas Military Institute in 1877. He was tendered employment as a teacher but elected to come to Baker Botts to study law.

He married Alice Graham of Waco in 1883, and the children of that marriage were Frank Graham Baker (who died as a youth), James A. Baker, Jr., Walter Browne Baker (named for Walter Browne Botts), Malcolm G. Baker, Mrs. Alice Baker Jones, and Mrs. Preston Moore. Mrs. Baker died May 9, 1932 and Capt. Baker August 2, 1941.

Perhaps the man who knew Capt. Baker best was Jesse Andrews, who practiced law with him for

Capt. James A. Baker, with the Firm 1881 - 1941.

42 years and succeeded him as senior partner (and occupied his office for 20 more years). Following are some excerpts from an article written about Capt. Baker by Andrews for the February 1961 issue of the *Texas Bar Journal*:

> Mr. Baker is remembered as the Senior Partner of Texas first large law firm — as a most successful businessman, Chairman of the Board of Houston's largest trust company, Chairman of the Board of one of Texas largest banks and prominently identified with other business institutions — as one of Houston's first citizens, and, perhaps as much as anything else as the lawyer who managed the criminal prosecution in New York of the murderer of William Marsh Rice, resulting in a conviction of first degree murder, the probating of Mr. Rice's will and the paving of the way for the establishment, under his guidance and direction, of William Marsh Rice University . . . .

No-Tsu-Oh Carnival parade on Travis near City Hall on Market Square, Houston, 1909. Capt. James A. Baker was King Nottoc, monarch of the Carnival, in 1909. The two fanciful names were, of course, "Houston" and "Cotton" spelled backwards.

The indoctrination in military affairs he received at Texas Military Institute possibly accounted for his interest in joining the Houston Light Guards. He was promoted to the highest rank (Capt.); and ever after that throughout his long and varied life, he was known only as "Capt. Baker." During this period the State of Texas was rapidly recovering from the effects of the Civil War and Houston was becoming a commercial center of prime importance. The firm of Baker, Botts & Baker soon took rank as one of the leading law firms of the State,—particularly in the railroad field. It became General Counsel of the Missouri Pacific then commonly known as the "Gould System," which included the Missouri, Kansas & Texas, International & Great Northern, Texas & Pacific and Galveston, Houston & Henderson. A short while later the firm became General Attorneys of the Houston & Texas Central and Houston, East & West Texas.

It would be of interest to know how it was that this firm drew to itself this aggregation of railroad clients. The partners were not especially active or prominent in politics or prominent otherwise except as lawyers and citizens. It can only be concluded that it was because of their reputation as competent and able lawyers and of their standing as citizens in the community that this results.

Judge Baker was a sound and seasoned lawyer; Col. Botts one of the greatest Texas ever had; and Capt. Baker possessed the qualities that attracted men to him and inspired them with confidence in him. Concerning his gifts of this kind, Judge Joseph C. Hutcheson Jr., in his tribute to Capt. Baker in the memorial services in the Texas Supreme Court said, "Combining a vigorous, powerful, firm, almost imperious, nature with exceptional gifts of mind and person, he had a genius for organization and an intuitive sense of the value of cooperation and concert of action. Not only a loyal partisan and a sound and excellent legal adviser, but an exceptionally able man of affairs, he was splendidly equipped to serve his state and section in the crucial years that followed his admission to the bar."

In addition to these traits of character, Capt. Baker possessed another gift,—that of being able, to a remarkable degree, to tell an unusually gifted man when he saw him. Many instances of this might be mentioned. Only three are cited,— Robert S. Lovett, Edwin B. Parker and Edgar Odell Lovett (not related to R. S. Lovett).

. . . While Capt. Baker in his latter years was known primarily as the wise business counselor, in his earlier years he showed himself to be a trial lawyer of consummate skill. Judge Charles E. Ash, at a banquet given in his honor upon his retirement from the District Bench after more than 25 years of service, made the statement that the most brilliant trial lawyer who had practiced in his court

was Capt. Baker. He was of this opinion, he said, because he had observed Capt. Baker's skill in cross-examination. He never attempted to browbeat, threaten or confuse a witness, but appealed to his sense of honesty and fairness,—so much so that he completely disarmed even the most hostile witness and drew from him additional testimony and admissions which greatly weakened, and sometimes completely destroyed, his adverse testimony on direct examination.

As a senior member of the Bar he had an unfailing interest in the young lawyer at the Bar. Many of the lawyers in Houston today will remember his kind words of encouragement when they were young, struggling lawyers, or the words of praise that he bestowed upon them when they had some modest success.

Grand Central Station, Houston, when "Cotton was King," October 1894. In 1894, upon Chas. Tweed's recommendation to Southern Pacific, the Firm was given the charge to handle Southern Pacific's interests in Texas.

Houston Electric Lighting's first power plant, circa 1882.
This predecessor of the Houston Lighting & Power Co. was then a client of the Firm.

Offices of the Houston Gas Company, circa 1890. This predecessor of Entex, Inc. was then a client of the Firm.

36

The most noted case in Capt. Baker's long career involved the murder of William Marsh Rice by his butler. Capt. Baker had represented Rice in a variety of legal matters before agreeing in 1891 to become a trustee for the new institution of higher learning that Rice planned to endow upon his death. As chairman of the board for this institution in the 1890s, Baker began to plan for the successful creation of what all involved hoped would be a model institute in Houston. But such planning was rudely interrupted by the news that Rice had died mysteriously in New York.

The colorful chain of events that followed are described in Capt. Baker's own words in Appendix II. Suffice to say here that Baker journeyed to New York and succeeded in exposing Rice's butler as a murderer and in protecting the endowment promised to the new Houston institute in Rice's contested will. The case made headlines regularly in the *New York Times*, spreading the name of Baker and his law firm in the East.

William Marsh Rice, founder of Rice University, circa 1850. He and his substantial mercantile interests were clients of the Firm for many years. His University continues as a client.

Capt. Baker's work for Rice Institute upon his return to Houston is described in Andrews' tribute:

Then came the gathering up of Mr. Rice's scattered and highly diversified properties, and the creation of an organization to manage them. This organization had its hands full. It soon became an important member of the business community,—lending money, leasing business properties, selling timber, investing in oil properties, etc.

Throughout all this, Capt. Baker brought to play his consummate business ability.

At the proper time, came the laying of the groundwork for the educational institution. No amount of pressing need of it was to be permitted to interfere with the main objective—that of creating a university of the first class. The citizens of Houston might continue to wonder if Rice University was ever to be opened, but the time-consuming thoroughness of planning went on undisturbed.

All the while Capt. Baker was pressing on. The time required to find the right man for President later came to be regarded as inconsequential when compared to the superior qualifications of the man chosen, —Dr. Edgar Odell Lovett, "the dignified scholar and superb gentleman." Under his matchless ability during the 36 years of his administration, Rice University came to be recognized as one of the first scientific schools of the country. Again Capt. Baker had demonstrated that rare ability to recognize the unusually gifted man.

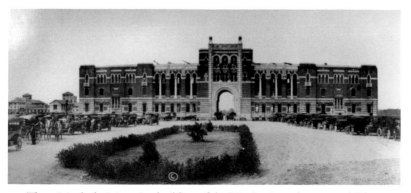

The original administration building of the Rice Institute, later named Edgar Odell Lovett Hall, circa 1912.

Board of Trustees of William M. Rice Institute in 1911, before the opening of the Institute in 1912.
The trustees pictured are, from left, rear: Benjamin Botts Rice, a nephew of William Marsh Rice; Edgar Odell Lovett, president of
the Institute; Emanuel Raphael, president of The Houston Electric Light and Power Company; and William Marsh Rice, II, also a nephew
of William Marsh Rice; front: James Everett McAshan, a Houston banker; Cesar Maurice Lombardi, president of A. H. Belo Company,
publisher of Dallas and Galveston newspapers; and Capt. James A. Baker.

As Chairman of the Board, Capt. Baker, up to the time of his death, gave Rice University his first attention. When founded it had assets of approximately ten million dollars, when he died, upwards of seventeen million, and now, approximately ninety-six million.

Capt. Baker was not a pusher of men — as Edwin Parker proved to be. Nor was he the silver-tongued orator that Garwood became. He preferred to operate quietly behind the scenes for the most part. Capt. Baker fell into a very unusual situation. Although Peter Gray began the practice in 1840, the original three men, Gray, Botts and Judge Baker were all gone by 1897. Near the turn of the century, Capt. Baker found himself senior partner in the Firm at the age of 40 with the need to start building a new firm. As Jesse Andrews pointed out, his ability to select good people and then to engender loyalty and devotion in them proved to be one of his greatest assets.

The Bakers (Capt. Baker, his father, and his son) were always interested in young people. Two examples will suffice. In 1890 Ambrose Worsley was a 21-year old stenographer at the Firm. He worked there only two years but studied law and greatly impressed the Bakers. He did become a lawyer and moved to Chicago. Worsley's letter in 1928 to Capt. Baker is not only of historical interest but offers insights into the Baker family. Much of the letter concerned a case Worsley had taken to the Supreme Court and which Capt. Baker asked him to summarize. We begin in the middle of the letter:

You asked me about my son, and I regretfully inform you that he departed this life on September 25th, 1925, and his wife died about two months thereafter, leaving a little grandson, the only remnant of his family, whose name is Ambrose Douglas Worsley, one of the brightest little chaps there is.

. . . I only wish that I were able to tell you that he is still alive and practicing law with me.

I notice one of your sons is now a member of your firm. I have learned that you lost your oldest boy which I regretted very much, as I can remember him. - I think his name was Graham. I remember him as a little fellow. At least, I remember your little girl. She must be quite a woman, as it is a long time since I left Houston.

. . . I must also acknowledge to you that I received great inspiration from the life of Judge James A. Baker, Col. Botts and James A. Baker, Jr. Col. Botts had the greatest memory of any man I have ever known and was a wonderfully interesting conversationalist, and a great lawyer. Judge James A. Baker, of course, was one of our ablest American lawyers and was respected by everyone far and near. Will I ever forget how much he thought of you? He simply adored you, and I am glad to remember that you never misplaced his confidence, nor did you ever misplace the confidence of anyone else. I was in your office for years and I never knew of the least shadow of wrong on the part of any member of your firm during that time, with your immense practice, and what a large practice you had.

. . . I know that you still continue to carry on with that same high standard as well maintained when your dear father and the lamented Col. Botts were connected with the firm.

I must tell you another interesting thing, and one which I can never forget, which shows how much your father thought of me.

During the world's fair Judge Baker called on me in Chicago. I did not know he was even to visit our city. He called on me one afternoon and found me located at Room 1007, Teutonic Building (now Roosevelt Building) where I am still located. I had an office about 4 x 6, no carpet nor rug on the floor; a little unvarnished desk and a small chair.

Judge Baker looked me over, and I know by the way he appeared that he saw I was in need. He asked me how business was and I frankly told him it might be better, and so it might have been. We spent the afternoon together and I took him around, as best I could, and showed him the "loop". He was amazed at the high buildings, and I remember taking him up in one of the highest; it was so high that he wanted to come down and did not wish to retrace his steps in any other high building.

But this is what I want to get at: Judge Baker said to me: "Mr. Worsley, do you need any money?" I said: "No, Judge, I think I can get through." He wanted to give me some money and was going down in his pocket, when I said to him: "No, Judge, I don't want any money." When he left me, he said to me: "Now, Mr. Worsley, I think you need some money." I said: "No Judge, I will get through all right." He said: "Well, now I am going home and I want you to draw on me." Now don't forget, draw on me when you need any money, and don't forget to draw for enough." I thanked the Judge, but I never drew for any money although many times I felt as though I could have used some money.

Of course, I have gotten by all this time, but I will never forget that Judge Baker was one of my best friends in this world, and I know that he would have done anything for me that was in his power.

Like his father, Capt. Baker was very interested in young lawyers. When a very young associate was out of state for Christmas in 1940, Capt. Baker wrote a Christmas letter stating among other things: "Your parents have every reason to be proud of your accomplishments, and their well deserved pride will increase with their declining years." Just to indicate that he knew what the young lawyer was doing, Capt. Baker cited three cases the lawyer was handling that he wished to discuss with him. This letter was so treasured that it was found in the personal effects of the young lawyer's deceased parents many years later.

Among some of Capt. Baker's other activities were The Houston Light Guard, which was formed in 1873 with Peter Gray's brother as first

Captain. It was primarily a social organization that specialized in drill competitions. There were reports that when the Light Guard paraded in full-dress uniforms, young ladies were known to swoon on the streets. According to *Chronicle* reporter T. E. Bell, under Capt. Baker the drill was elevated to a lofty art. The team brought back so many trophies from drill competition that they were finally banned from contests. Being Captain of the Light Guard was obviously a great honor. This was the source of the title "Capt." that Baker carried proudly for the remainder of his life.

Capt. Baker was also involved in real estate development. He owned several parcels of land, including the block bounded by Main, Clay, Travis, and Bell where he once lived. He was

Composite photograph of the Houston Light Guard in 1888, by C. J. Wright. By this time, Capt. James A. Baker had relinquished the command. The Light Guard organization encompassed the scions of Houston's leading families. Its membership included the professional, business, and political leaders of the day. The unit was absorbed into the Texas National Guard as part of the 36th Infantry Division, and fought with distinction in the Spanish-American and later wars.

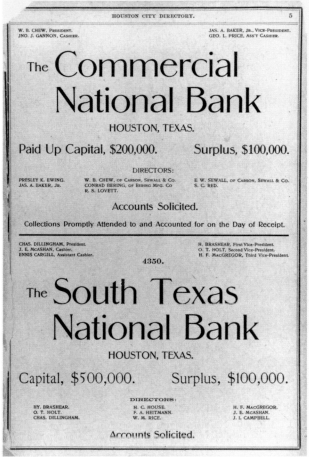

Advertisement for Commercial National Bank and South Texas National Bank, from *Houston City Directory* of 1900.
The interior photographs were taken in 1911. Both banks were clients of the Firm. They merged in 1912 to form the South Texas
Commercial National Bank, one of Houston's two largest banks for many years, and a predecessor of Texas Commerce Bank.
The largest shareholders of the newly created bank were the Ripley family, primary owners of South Texas National Bank,
and Capt. James A. Baker and Rice Institute, primary owners of the Commercial National Bank.

engaged with others in subdivision development. A brochure on Woodland Heights dated 1910 lists him a director. Many Baker Botts partners lived on North and South Boulevards after a group headed by the Baker family developed Broadacres. For those interested in architecture, in the archives we have the drawings for 22 Courtlandt Place with the statement that it was a wedding gift from Capt. Baker to his daughter, Alice (Baker) Jones.

Heading the Rice Trust with millions of dollars to lend was a natural role for Capt. Baker as he was also a banker for most of his life. He remembered old friends. Austin College, which he had

attended as a youth, needed $30,000 in 1912, and Capt. Baker had the Trust make the loan. It was repaid in full.

Capt. Baker served not once but two times as head of the Houston Bar Association, one time because it was to host the American Bar Association, and it was felt that Capt. Baker was particularly qualified to be the host President. He was one of the organizers of the Texas Bar Association in 1882. He also served as Vice President of the American Bar Association.

In 1918, Capt. and Mrs. Baker established the Graham Baker scholarship at the Rice Institute in

Home of Capt. James A. Baker, 1416 Main Street (corner of Bell Avenue), Houston, circa 1900.

View of "The Oaks," located at Hadley and Baldwin, Houston, circa 1913. Originally built and owned by Edwin B. Parker, The Oaks was purchased by Capt. James A. Baker in the 1920s. Upon his death, Capt. Baker bequeathed The Oaks to Rice Institute, which later conveyed it to become the first home of the M.D. Anderson Cancer Institute.

memory of their son. It was given to the undergraduate with the highest academic standing. Upon his death, Capt. Baker also left his home, The Oaks, and seven acres of land at Hadley and Baldwin to Rice. The Oaks was almost a Firm institution. It was built by Edwin B. Parker, who sold it to Capt. Baker when Parker went to Washington. For years, Firm meetings held in the basement were considered command performances for the Baker Botts lawyers. They were all very familiar with this magnificent home. For a time after it was deeded to Rice, the Oaks served as the first home of M. D. Anderson Hospital. Sadly, all that remains today of this landmark home is a vacant lot with the faint markings of a driveway and a foundation.

Capt. Baker's work in building his other "home," Baker Botts, proved much more durable. As illustrated above, one lasting legacy was the selection of an able second generation of lawyers. Another important legacy can be seen in the Firm's list of clients. Capt. Baker was on the boards of an array of important Houston companies. He also

developed and maintained close contacts with the eastern-based firms that grew in importance to Baker Botts in the 20th century. Capt. Baker lived in New York for six months after the Rice murder and became acquainted with numerous bankers and lawyers. The media also did a great deal to spread his name and the name of the Firm. (See "The Patrick Case," Appendix II.) He subsequently maintained a summer home at Bass Rocks, Mass., and often entertained there.

While his extended family vacationed there each summer, he often commuted into New York City to work. The word "rainmaker" had not been invented, and Capt. Baker would not have claimed such a title, but no one did more to spread the Baker Botts name in legal, business, and financial circles in Houston, in Texas, and in the East.

No one more embodied the values, the work ethic, or even the image that Baker Botts hoped to convey than Capt. Baker. He was a central figure in the coming of age of both his law firm and his city.

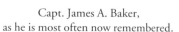

Capt. James A. Baker,
as he is most often now remembered.

ROBERT S. LOVETT

Even among the outstanding lawyers in the early Firm history, Robert Scott Lovett stands out as a legendary figure. He grew up in rural San Jacinto County and never finished high school (one report was that he never wore shoes until he dropped out of school and went to work). He was a day laborer for the railroad, but someone inspired him to read law and obtain his license. Then, as he began handling small railroad matters in East Texas, he caught the attention of both Judge Baker and Capt. Baker, and the rest is history. From being a barefoot boy on a farm in East Texas to being the most powerful man in the railroad industry in the United States was truly a Horatio Alger performance.

Even though he was a partner only eleven years, Lovett remained a friend and a client of the Firm for life. Along with Capt. Baker, he helped to spread the name of the Firm in New York and the East. As a highly visible railroad executive who took a leading role in his industry's affairs, Lovett served as a potent symbol of the talent and the professionalism housed in the "outlying" city of Houston, Texas, in the offices of the law firm of Baker Botts.

One version of Lovett's first big break in the practice of railroad law is provided in Ambrose Worsley's letter to Capt. Baker in 1928 (as cited previously):

> I was in Judge Baker's office the afternoon when he *made* the Honorable R. S. Lovett. Judge Baker and I were working on the Houston East and West case, when "Bob" Lovett, who was then a young lawyer at the Houston Bar, walked into our office and the conversation was about as follows:

> "Hello Judge." "Hello Bob."

> *Judge Baker:* "How are you getting along, Bob?"

Robert S. Lovett, with the Firm 1892 - 1909.

Lovett: "Well, I guess I am getting by, but that is all."

Judge Baker: "Say, Bob, I was up to Dallas the other day, and in talking with Governor Brown he said to me: 'Judge, have you got any young man in your office who may have studied law some and is able to look up the law and answer some legal questions? I believe it would be a good thing for me to have a young man of that kind in my office in your (Judge Baker's) absence.'"

Judge Baker: "Well, Governor, when I get back to Houston I will try and find some young man who will answer your purposes."

44

BAKER, BOTTS, BAKER & LOVETT.

JAS. A. BAKER.
JAS. A. BAKER, JR.
R. S. LOVETT.
E. H. PARKER.

HOUSTON, TEX.

Firm letterhead, 1895.

Judge Baker: "Bob, do you think if I sent you up there you could fill the bill."

Lovett: "Well, Judge, I would be tickled to death to try."

Judge Baker: "All right, Bob, you get your duds together; get ready to move and I will send you up there tomorrow."

Lovett: "Thank you Judge, I will be most pleased to do that."

Whereupon Judge Baker and Bob Lovett retired to the outer office and went down the stairs. I think I know where they went. Judge Baker returned to his office in a short time, and the next I heard of Bob Lovett he was in Dallas writing letters to the firm of Baker, Botts & Baker.

The above is the manner in which one of our great railroad men and lawyers received his start toward prosperity and success. There is no doubt but what other young men similarly situated would have succeeded as well, but you must give Bob credit for taking advantage of the opportunity.

Jesse Andrews picks up much of the remainder of Lovett's story in his previously cited reminiscences in the *Texas Bar Journal* in 1961:

Born in the adjoining county of San Jacinto and grown to young manhood without educational opportunities except of the most rudimentary kind, young Robert Lovett had come to Houston to read law in the office of a lawyer. His license obtained, he returned to his native county to practice law. But he had fallen under the observation of Capt. Baker. By the latter he was given employment in a minor way on the HE&WT Railroad which ran through his county. The young man grew on Capt. Baker and not long afterwards was invited to come to Houston and take a place in the Houston office. His work, after, was principally for the railroad clients.

When, subsequently, because of certain litigation it became necessary for the Gould Lines to move their headquarters to Dallas, Mr. Lovett moved to Dallas to be Assistant General Attorney of the T & P, the firm in Houston retaining the position of General Counsel. But it suited Capt. Baker's and his purposes best for him to return to Houston. He resigned from the T & P and, on January 1, 1894, came to Houston to become a member of the firm, the firm name being Baker, Botts, Baker & Lovett. (Editor's Note: Lovett actually became a partner on October 1, 1892.)

Greater things, however, were in store for Mr. Lovett. He remained a partner in the firm until 1904. His work was still that of the railroad clients, for the most part. Among those chiefly receiving his attention were the Southern Pacific Lines in Texas. By 1904, E. H. Harriman, that greatest of all railroad builders, had become Chairman of the Board of the Southern Pacific as well as the Union Pacific, the latter company holding large interests in many railroads. The Southern Pacific Lines in Texas at the time were having trouble with the regulatory authorities of the State. This fell to Mr.

View of the Houston General Electric Company and a car of the Houston Electric Street Railway Company, both clients of the Firm, circa 1891. Robert S. Lovett negotiated a significant compromise with the City of Houston on behalf of Stone & Webster, managers of the street railway company, to keep the streetcar line privately held.

Lovett to handle. In this way he and Mr. Harriman became acquainted. This acquaintance ripened into such an admiration of Mr. Lovett by Mr. Harriman and respect for his ability that he prevailed on him, finally, to come to New York and be General Counsel for both the Union Pacific and Southern Pacific Systems.

More than that, having the power to do so, he directed that, after his death, Mr. Lovett should succeed him as Chairman of both systems. Thus the lawyer from San Jacinto County, tapped by Capt. Baker, became so great in the railroad world that, in a hearing before the I.C.C., on one occasion it was said, "Mr. Lovett holds more railroad power in his hands than any man that ever lived."

It is amusing to note that when Lovett's son, Robert A. Lovett, died in 1986, *Time* referred to him as being "very patrician" and "a symbol of the so-called Eastern Establishment." The son was an outstanding investment banker at Brown Brothers Harriman and served numerous presidents in various capacities from World War I through the Kennedy Administration. The article did not mention that his father began his career grubbing stumps for a railroad in East Texas.

When Lovett left the Firm, the name was changed on January 1, 1904, to Baker, Botts, Parker & Garwood. The two men whose names were added, Edwin Parker and Hiram Garwood, became dominant figures at Baker Botts in subsequent decades. The two men presented a study in contrasts. Parker was the Firm's first graduate of a law school. He was much concerned with organizational matters and was an office lawyer at heart. Garwood had read law and practiced politics before joining Baker Botts at the age of forty. He was a powerful speaker and an outstanding trial lawyer. Garwood was the dreamer who spun a persuasive vision of the Firm's potential; Parker, the nuts and bolts man, made that vision a reality. Along with the other members of the second generation of Baker Botts partners, these two joined Capt. Baker in building a permanent institution of high quality.

Robert S. Lovett resided at this home at 2017 Main on the corner of Gray Avenue,
Houston, until he moved to New York in 1900.

Before he built "The Oaks," Edwin B. Parker resided in this home at
1010 Hadley Street on the corner of Fannin, Houston, 1900.

EDWIN B. PARKER

Edwin Brewington Parker was the first lawyer who came to the Firm as an associate rather than a partner, if we except Capt. Baker who read law in his father's office and eventually became a partner. He became the first modern managing partner at Baker Botts before leaving Houston and the Firm to undertake important work in Washington, D.C. in 1917.

He was born in Shelby County, Missouri on September 7, 1868, and attended Central College in Fayette, Missouri. His uncle, Alsdorf Faulkner, a Texan, took an interest in him, and this apparently determined his future. He left the farm to obtain a law degree at the University of Texas and graduated in 1889. Upon graduation, he needed more income than he could obtain by practicing law, in order to pay off the debt incurred in obtaining his education. He took a position as secretary for the Vice President of the Missouri Kansas and Texas Railroad at Sedalia, Missouri, and in 1893 became Assistant General Passenger Agent.

In 1894, Parker was employed by the Firm; in 1900, he became a partner. He showed drive and initiative early on. Indeed, Firm records indicate that Parker was still an associate when he took responsibility for hiring Jesse Andrews in 1899. Parker was not a timid man.

As an indication of the Firm's standing in the community as well as how highly Capt. Baker regarded Parker, we quote from the history of The Houston Club. This is in reference to the founding of the Club in 1894, the year Parker was

Edwin B. Parker, with the Firm 1894 - 1926.

employed as an associate:

Houston had only one "skyscraper" (a six-story walk-up) and 32,000 residents, when the club was chartered by its founders, all young business and civic leaders. The original executive committee members were Ed B. Parker; Capt. James A. Baker, Jr.; A. S. Hall; George W. Heyer; and B. J. Parks. O. T. Holt was elected president of the Club, and would later be elected mayor of Houston.

BAKER. BOTTS. PARKER & GARWOOD

COMMERCIAL BANK BUILDING

JAMES A BAKER
EDWIN B PARKER
H M GARWOOD
JESSE ANDREWS
C R WHARTON
C L CARTER
J H TALLICHET
THOMAS H BOTTS
LAMAR SMITH

HOUSTON, TEXAS

Firm letterhead, 1910.

Parker was a manager at heart, an autocrat by nature. He showed a strong interest in the administration of Firm affairs, taking it upon himself to bring a measure of business-style efficiency to the growing Firm. In 1911, he put forth the first Plan of Organization in a sixteen-page memorandum to "All in the Office." Here are some paragraphs selected from this long document. This is vintage Parker, and he continued to write inspirational messages during his entire career.

This memorandum, which I have not had an opportunity to read over after dictating, is submitted for your consideration and criticism. It represents substantially my idea of the most effective manner of handling our business. Under it I am burdened with a good many responsibilities and details which I would very willingly relinquish; at the same time, as I see it, it is to the interest of the business that I should be so burdened. I want every one in the office, from Capt. Baker to the office boy, to feel entirely free to offer any suggestions that may occur to them. I have absolutely no pride of opinion in this matter and what we all want is to get the best results.

We who today, and such of us as shall in the years to come be responsible for preserving the reputation and holding and increasing the volume of this firm's business, have a great responsibility resting upon us. Our first care must continue to be, as it ever has been for more than forty years past, to maintain the good name of the firm for integrity, fair dealing and legal ability. All the rest amounts to nothing unless this reputation is preserved and deserved. Those who have gone before us have set us a high standard and we must live up to it. We cannot stand still, but must go forward or backward. With the impetus which we now have it is comparatively easy for us to go forward, provided every man does his full part in an effective way under an organization which will insure perfect "team work". To the younger men, especially those who have been but a short time at the bar, I want to emphasize the necessity of being self-reliant and resourceful. Do not be afraid to admit that you do not know, and if necessary, ask. On the other hand, never admit that you can't. Practice "Christian Science" in your mind. Make up your mind that you will and you can.

Whatever is worth doing at all is worth doing well. The little business which we take for our clients often leads to big business, and in order to hold the big business, we must take the little with the big, and having undertaken it, must give it just as careful and painstaking attention as if a large amount were involved, even though we lose money by so doing.

Bear in mind that we are all working not as individuals, but as a firm. The individual must be subordinated to the firm. It is through consolidation of effort and ability and concentration of energy that the best results are obtained. We have now a very complete, efficient and effective organization. We are, and must continue, a happy family, and to that end let each treat all the others, no matter what his or their position may be, with consideration and courtesy, and bring into the office only happy faces and kind words.

Sporting a beard, spats, and a cane, Parker looked the part of a Wall Street lawyer, 1920s-style. He went about the task of bringing to Baker Botts the more highly structured organization then coming into favor with the larger Wall Street firms. More centralized management was instituted. All letters and all fees had to be approved by Parker. Secretaries worked not for a particular lawyer but the Firm. The Plan of Organization set out in detail the duties of each person in the office. Not only were there non-lawyer people in management positions, but whereas Capt. Baker's duties required a half page, the duties of the Administrator and the Financial Manager each required substantially more space.

Main offices of Firm client, Houston Lighting & Power Company, 1905, at 620 Main, Houston.

Perhaps Jesse Andrews in his fiftieth anniversary speech (*Office Review,* December 29, 1949) best summarized Parker's contribution to the Firm:

Baker, Botts, Baker & Lovett was then made up of two partners, Capt. Baker and Mr. Lovett. Mr. Parker was not even a partner; he did not become a partner until the following year. There was no other lawyer in the office except one who confined his work exclusively to work in the library. Many of you here knew these three men intimately. Capt. Baker was the business lawyer. Mr. Lovett was the great corporation lawyer. Mr. Parker was the builder of the Firm.

I would not imply from this that Mr. Parker, too, was not a great lawyer. He indeed was. His ability as a lawyer in the later years of his life received international as well as national recognition. But the work for which he is best known in the offices of Baker Botts today is his work in building the Firm. He had a new concept for Baker Botts of what a law office should be. The custom at that time was for lawyers, two or three, sometimes four, to associate themselves in a partnership and let the work done by the partnership be done by them alone. Mr. Parker's conception was that the partners should employ young lawyers of capacity and ability to attract business to the law firm on their own account. This has become the commonly accepted practice, and in all cities, particularly in the great cities of the East, will be found large law organizations the majority of the members of which are employed lawyers.

But this was not by any means the sole contribution that Mr. Parker made. He was an indefatigable worker himself. He was a man of vision and courage. He was not afraid to move into larger and better offices or to add more men from time to time. He was careful to see that no client's business was neglected and that the office was run in a business-like way. He took an active part in the affairs of his city and was a leader in many organizations.

He contributed in this way for more than a quarter of a century after my admission to the Firm. When he resigned, because of certain international obligations he had assumed, his interest in the welfare of the Firm did not cease. It continued up to the date of his death.

In 1917, Parker was called to government service. From the memorial to Parker we read:

In the early days of the war when the War Industries Board was being formed, Judge Lovett was called to be an organizing member. In July, 1917, he wrote the firm:

"The country needs upon the War Industries Board a man combining the qualities of legal ability, sound business acumen and indefatigable industry, who is willing to serve without compensation. I know of no man who combines these qualities in such high degree as E. B. Parker. Will he serve?"

Three days after the receipt of this letter Judge Parker was on his way to Washington, where he entered at once upon his duties with the War Industries Board. When in August following Judge Lovett left the Board to become Director of Capital Expenditures for the Railroad Administration, Judge Parker took his place as Priorities Commissioner. He remained until after the Armistice.

In the great task of increasing our army from 200,000 to 4,000,000 men, equipping it and hurrying it overseas at the rate of 225,000 per month, the War Industries Board and its Priorities Commissioner played a significant part.

Parker was not finished with government service. We had equipment overseas for the supply of over 2,000,000 men and supplies, and equipment costing over $3,000,000,000 had to be liquidated. In February 1919, Parker was made Chairman of the United States Liquidation Commission. The work of this Commission was completed in less than two years.

In 1920, Parker returned to Houston, and a great dinner in his honor was given by the Hous-

The Texas Company's Port Arthur Plant, showing the revolutionary Holmes-Manley stills, circa 1925. Edwin B. Parker served as general counsel of Texaco, as The Texas Company was often known.

ton Bar Association. A few months later, Parker was appointed General Counsel and a member of the Executive Committee of The Texas Company, with offices in New York. He would also have an office in The Texas Company Building in Houston and would remain as Managing Partner of the Firm. As a matter of fact, it could be said that the Firm had a New York office in 1920. In a June 1, 1920 release prepared for the use of Legal Directories, it was stated that Mr. Parker at his office in New York would be available to handle general business for the Firm and its clients.

Although Parker's prominent positions with a major oil company brought the Firm both prestige and income, the arrangement inevitably caused tensions. A "commuting" managing partner was a luxury that many in the growing Firm did not think could be afforded.

In May 1923, Parker's involvement in matters outside the Firm increased with his appointment as Umpire of the Mixed Claims Commission, which was created by an agreement between Germany and the United States to settle claims arising under the Treaty of Berlin signed August 15, 1921. Some 12,400 claims asking for $1,480,000,000 were handled. As a result of his government service, Parker was given numerous awards from foreign governments and the Distinguished Service

OPINION IN THE LUSITANIA CASES.

MIXED CLAIMS COMMISSION, UNITED STATES AND GERMANY.

Established in pursuance of the Agreement between the
United States and Germany of August 10, 1922.

EDWIN B. PARKER, *Umpire.*

CHANDLER P. ANDERSON,   WILHELM KIESSELBACH,
American Commissioner.   *German Commissioner.*

Extract from the official opinions of the Mixed Claims Commission, of which Edwin B. Parker was Umpire, in the case of the sinking of the *Lusitania.*

Medal from the United States.

In January 1926, Parker felt that he could no longer lead a double life and resigned from the Firm. He was busy now as Commissioner of the

Tripartite Claims. Judge Parker never learned to say "no." In 1927, he became Chairman of the Board of the U.S. Chamber of Commerce. He also served as Trustee for Carnegie Endowment for International Peace, on the board of George Washington University, and on the Council on Foreign Relations.

There are indications that some of the older individualistic partners were not convinced that they should submerge their personalities to the institution of Baker Botts and were not enthusiastic about Parker's "It's all in your mind" lectures. One of the more typical Parker memos is dated July 31, 1916. Those "enjoying" a long hot Houston summer without air conditioning found themselves suffering through Parker's memo "To All in the Office":

> While Chicago and the middle west particularly, and the whole country generally, is, to a greater or less extent, prostrate because of the intense heat, we who are here are enjoying delightful summer weather. We have but to keep busy, be regular in our habits and determine not to worry in order to be well physically and mentally, efficient and ready for any emergency.

Wharton's handwritten note appears in the margin:

> Andrews, you will see from this Weather Bulletin that our Mr. Parker in addition to his other manifold duties has taken over the work heretofore performed by Dr. Brunerymyer. We may expect regular Bulletins and much temperatures during the next 60 days.

Yet Wharton, Andrews, and the rest of the partners learned to live with Parker's many demands, as well as his somewhat officious tone. The Firm was growing rapidly. When Parker came to Baker Botts in 1890, there were three lawyers; when he left in 1926, there were 25 — 10 partners and 15 non-partners. Someone had to take responsibility for developing better means of managing the hiring and the work of the Firm. Parker volunteered for the job; his colleagues seemed willing to tolerate his memos in exchange for being relieved of the necessity of managing a growing Firm.

Parker died in Washington on October 30, 1929, and was buried in Glenwood Cemetery in Houston. He was survived by his wife but no living children. Attached to Parker's Memorial are numerous letters from prominent Washington figures including several Supreme Court Justices. Chief Justice William Howard Taft referred to him as "my neighbor." Indeed, in the years before his death, Parker had been rumored as a possible appointee to the Supreme Court.

Apparently, Parker accumulated a substantial estate. After providing handsomely for his wife, he left his estate "to establish or maintain a graduate school of international affairs." In typical Parker fashion, he set out in considerable detail how the Trustees should proceed. Some idea may be gained of the circles in which this onetime farm boy moved by the Trustees he named in his will. Among them were Harlan F. Stone (Chief Justice of the U.S. Supreme Court), Henry L. Stimson (later Secretary of War), William D. Mitchell (Head of the F.B.I.), and Harry T. Klein (President of The Texas Co.). In 1931, the Trustees of the Estate selected Columbia University as the site of the school and founded the Parker School of Foreign and Comparative Law, which is still in existence.

Parker was ahead of his time in many respects. At least a generation before the Firm began recruiting nationally, Parker hired Maurice Epstein, a Jewish Columbia Law graduate, who was with the Firm in 1924 when Malcolm Lovett arrived and

To my friend S. R. Bertron Jr. with the sincere regards of
Washington
June 2 6th 1924.
Edwin B. Parker

This photograph of Edwin B. Parker, inscribed to S. R. Bertron, then president of client Houston Lighting & Power, was taken two years before Edwin B. Parker left the Firm.

remained for many years. Parker was also employing women lawyers in the 1920s. In this respect, a memorandum from Charles Szalkowski found in the Firm History file and dated November 9, 1983 is of sufficient interest to reproduce:

Regarding the obituary which appeared in the *Texas Bar Journal* for November, 1983 of

Dorothy C. Most:

In that obituary, it states that after admittance to the Texas Bar, she became associated with our Firm. Because she received both an LL.B (University of Texas, 1925) and a J.S.D. (St. John's University, 1931), it was not clear when she had been at the Firm. You reported that you had not heard of her.

I spoke with Mr. Lovett about Ms. Most. He said that she was the lady law graduate referred to in the famous letter "offering" him a position at our Firm. She came to the Firm in about July, 1925, and succeeded him as Firm Librarian. Her duties included supervising the library and preparing legal memoranda for the senior lawyers (there were very few young lawyers).

She was evidently not happy at the Firm, and left prior to our move from the Commercial Bank Building at Main and Franklin to the Esperson Building on December 31, 1926. Mr. Lovett recalls that vividly because he spent New Year's Eve moving the library.

One point of interest is that Ms. Most was not the first Baker, Botts woman lawyer. Mr. Lovett succeeded Doris Connelly as the young lawyer who was also in charge of the library. She had been at the Firm several years; he is not sure how many. Ms. Connelly was daughter of the Clerk of the Texas Supreme Court, and left the Firm to return to Austin on the death of her mother.

After she left the Firm, Ms. Most attended the Julliard School of Music and was a director of the Brooklyn Opera Company.

Edwin Parker seems always to have been a man on the move from his adolescence in Missouri to his death at the age of 61. He moved a great distance in his eventful life. More than half this life was spent as a lawyer at Baker Botts. During those years, he also moved the Firm a considerable distance in its evolution from a small partnership to a large modern law firm.

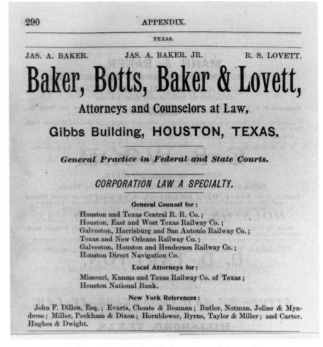

Baker, Botts, Baker & Lovett card from the *Hubbell Legal Directory*, 1898. Even then, the Firm claimed "corporation law a specialty."

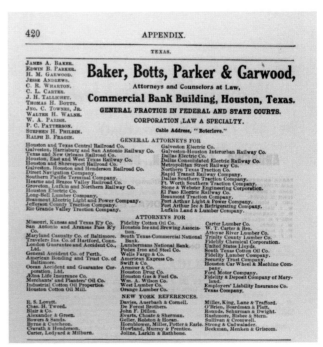

By 1916, the date of this card from the *Hubbell Legal Directory*, a majority of firm clients were non-railway companies.

HIRAM M. GARWOOD

When E. H. Harriman hired away railroad specialist Robert S. Lovett to be General Counsel of Southern Pacific and Union Pacific, the Firm found itself in a difficult situation. There was no experienced lawyer to replace Lovett. The problem was solved by inviting forty-year old Hiram Morgan Garwood to join the Firm. The Firm desperately needed Garwood, and apparently Garwood did some hard bargaining for himself. The Firm name immediately became Baker, Botts, Parker & Garwood on January 1, 1904, a name it would bear for 27 years. Garwood was the last person to join the Firm as a name partner.

Hiram Garwood was born in the town of Bastrop, Texas on January 11, 1864. He attended Excelsior College there. He obtained a B.S. at the University of the South in Sewanee, Tennessee, and then studied law under Joseph N. Sayers of Bastrop. He married Hettie Page and had three children, Calvin B., St. John, and Louise. Both boys became lawyers and both worked at Baker Botts before nepotism was ever discussed. One of the sons, St. John Garwood, later served with distinction on the Texas Supreme Court.

Garwood showed an early interest in politics, serving in the Texas House two years, then as County Judge back home. In the 1890s, he spent a term in the Texas Senate, where he took an active role in the debates over the creation of the Railroad Commission of Texas. He practiced in Bastrop fifteen years, LaGrange, Texas for two years, and in Houston two years before he joined the Firm. He was a very successful trial lawyer and an able lobbyist in Austin. He was also very effective in matters pending before the Railroad Commission of Texas.

Upon his arrival at the Firm, Garwood succeeded Lovett as General Attorney in Texas for Southern Pacific Lines and as a director of the Texas and New Orleans Railroad Co. It was said

Hiram M. Garwood, with the Firm 1904 - 1930.

that for the next 25 years not a single important railroad case was decided that he did not participate in, directly or indirectly. He was active and well known in Houston and across the state. For example, he was Vice President of Second National Bank, served as President of the Harris County Bar Association and the Texas Bar Association, belonged to numerous clubs, and was an active Episcopalian and Mason. He was awarded an honorary Doctor of Law degree by the University of the South in 1922. He was a member of the Council of the American Law Institute and served on the Board of Regents of the University of Texas. The town of Garwood, Texas was named for him.

Garwood was apparently a spellbinder as a speaker. One of our partners commented:

I first knew Judge Garwood while I was studying law at the University of Texas. At that time, one of his nephews was a fraternity brother of mine and

Judge Garwood accordingly came to lunch at the fraternity house on Sundays. After lunch, the entire chapter and their dates would gather around the Judge attracted by his brilliant conversation and his evident love for and understanding of mankind. It was not unusual for him to keep his audience spellbound for several hours.

Clarence Wharton commented on a speech made by Garwood before the Louisiana Bar Association honoring a deceased Chief Justice:

THALIAN CLUB, HOUSTON, TEXAS

Thalian Club, at the corner of Rusk and San Jacinto, Houston, circa 1909. Houston Society stratified after the Civil War. The dashing young men of the Light Guard perpetuated the martial spirit of the Confederacy with snappy uniforms and competitive drills. Later, it was membership in the ZZ Club that marked a young man's acceptance into Houston society. A break in the ZZ's ranks in July 1901 brought forth the Thalian Club. The second president of the Thalian Club was Robert S. Lovett; the seventh president was Hiram M. Garwood. The Thalians built this elegant clubhouse in 1907, at a cost of $40,000. For a few years, it was the scene of elegant balls and social functions, but by 1917 it had become the Elks Home.

One reading McCauley's Essay on the Earl of Chatham or Warren Hastings, is divided in his admiration between the subject and the essayist, and those of us who have read Judge Garwood's address delivered before the Louisiana Bar Association last week, discussing the life and character of Judge White, are filled with mingled admiration for the greatness of the late Chief Justice, and the splendid style and expression of the essayist.

Frank Andrews, senior partner of another Houston firm (later Andrews & Kurth) made the following statement at Judge Garwood's memorial service (he died May 15, 1930):

I think of him now as the most scholarly and polished gentleman in all avenues of cultivated attainment that it has been my good fortune to intimately know. He knew accurately more of the world's history, of its important events, of its philosophy, than anyone with whom I have ever come in contact. Its biography, its civilization, its development, causes as related to effect, were thoroughly mastered by him and formed a strong background for a liberal education of this cultured and accomplished gentleman. And, while he never tried to specialize in history, he became, through the process of omnivorous reading and intelligent acquisition, a great historian. In literature, ancient and modern, he was a great master. He knew and loved the great and scholarly books of the ages and the great scholars who wrote them as a man knows and loves his personal friends and associates. He knew the characteristics of the great authors, and therefore understood them better and admired them more. So thoroughly versed was he in history and literature that he could deliver, as he frequently did, an instructive and accurate lecture of the highest literary merit with the briefest preparation.

Merchants & Planters Oil Company, Houston, circa 1918. Capt. James A. Baker served as vice president of this client, whose business was cottonseed oil.

Texas Portland Cement Co., circa 1918. Around 1916, Baker Botts assisted in the purchase of property on the banks of the Houston Ship Channel for the construction by Texas Portland Cement Co., a Dallas based company, of a cement plant. Texas Portland Cement Co., a subsidiary of International Cement Corporation, an international corporation producing cement and cement products in North America, Europe, and South America, remained a client for many years.

Katy yards, Houston, 1916. Prior to Judge Baker's arrival at the Firm in the early 1870s, Gray & Botts acted as general attorneys for the Missouri, Kansas & Texas (Katy) Railroad. When Jay Gould acquired control of the Katy through a leasing agreement, the Firm was, in effect, working for him. In the mid-1890s, the Katy was paying the Firm a $2,500 retainer for handling litigation in Harris County, and its then parent, Southern Pacific Corporation, provided a steady $5,000 biennially for the Firm to lobby in Austin.

57

Garwood, possibly because he didn't arrive on the scene until he was 40, could more fully appreciate the Firm and thus developed a stronger emotional attachment to it than did many of his partners. This was reflected in his many speeches. He dreamed dreams of what the Firm meant and what it could become. Here are the opening paragraphs of a speech he made in December 1913:

Among the forces which assert a controlling influence upon the destinies of mankind in the individual and in the mass, there is none greater than tradition.

It is the memory of deeds done rather than blood or stock that counts in families. As long as there is the hope of producing one great man, no nation is lost. Where an appeal to the past can be made, that hope is never wholly extinguished.

So when the present of a life or a business grows logically out of its past and as logically prepares for its future, it rises above the dignity of an episode and becomes an institution. Extending in an orderly and intensely practical way beyond the brief day of its immediate activities, it becomes a part of an orderly systematic and permanent development.

In an institution thus linked with the past and looking to the future as a continuation of that past, the dignity of each daily task is infinitely added to. Each great case won, each great problem solved, each daily task however small in itself, becomes a part of a permanent and comprehensive scheme of development and adds strength and beauty to a structure which shall live beyond the brief day of those who have taken part in that development and which yet shall always be a part of all that was best in all of the builders.

We are, each of us, a part of an organization that has borne a not unworthy share in the life, and especially the legal life, and in the history of a great Commonwealth.

This firm is now almost half a century old. I have always thought of it, not as a mere temporary association of individuals, however pleasant or profitable, but as a permanent institution, just as Harvard or the Bank of England is an institution, with a strength, a life and individuality made up from, yet greater than, all or any of its members in that the accumulated knowledge and achievements of its members, past and present, becomes the common capital of all to preserve, increase and transmit to those who shall come after us.

For more than a quarter of a century, Hiram Garwood helped build a tradition of forceful eloquence which became a part of the "common capital" of all subsequent trial lawyers at Baker Botts.

Hiram M. Garwood received Houston's most prestigious social honor when he was selected King Nottoc in 1907. Shown with the Queen by his side (Alice Graham Baker, Capt. Baker's wife), Hiram Garwood presides over his court.

JESSE ANDREWS

Jesse Andrews, like Capt. Baker, served the Firm for so long (62 years) that he bridged several generations. Although he entered the Firm in the 19th century, there are lawyers now in the office who knew him well. Some remember him as an oddity within the Firm, a liberal Democrat in an organization not known for its enthusiastic support of Ralph Yarborough. Others remember him as a man who continued to work hard at his profession well into his eighties. Of course, this man who bridged several generations had many other identities to his colleagues in the early decades of the century.

Andrews was born on April 9, 1874, in Waterproof, Louisiana. His parents were Mark and Helen Andrews. The father was a horse-and-buggy doctor. He attended Jefferson College in Mississippi from 1887 to 1889, and for two years worked in the "hardware industry." In 1891, he enrolled at the University of Texas and graduated from the law school in 1896. No one who knew this tall, slender, dignified lawyer in later years would guess he was a starting guard on the first football team at the University of Texas (a team which, incidentally, played without protective equipment).

Andrews set up his own practice in Houston and was barely making ends meet when he worked with Edwin B. Parker of Baker Botts on a case. Parker was impressed with Andrews and tendered him employment with the Firm in 1899. This was common practice at a time when the Firm still recruited practicing lawyers on the basis of their observed performance in court instead of recent law school graduates on the basis of their academic performance. Andrews gladly accepted the $75 a month position, little dreaming that this would occupy the next 62 years of his life.

Andrews married Celeste Bujac on Nov. 8, 1900, and they had one son, Mark Edwin, also an

Jesse Andrews, with the Firm 1899 - 1961.

attorney. Andrews became a partner in 1906. The Firm name was then Baker, Parker & Garwood as it would continue to be until Garwood's death in 1930.

Andrews was active in numerous business enterprises. He helped organize the South Texas Cotton Oil Company in 1910 and served as its President until 1932 when it was acquired by Wesson Oil. In 1912, he became a director of a bank later to become Second National Bank (and still later MBank) until he moved to Kansas City. He was a director of Guardian Trust Company and when it merged with Second National, he later again became a director and member of the Executive Committee. He was a director of American General Life Insurance Co. and Foley Brothers Dry Goods Company until it merged with Federated Department Stores. He was the personal attorney for Robert Welch and served as Trustee of the Welch Foundation.

Second National Bank, Main Street, Houston, circa 1923. Organized in 1907 as Lumberman's National Bank, this long-time client changed its name to Second National Bank in 1923, and to Bank of the Southwest in 1956. It was merged into the Mercantile Bank holding company of Dallas to create MBank in 1983. Second National had merged with San Jacinto National Bank in 1944 and with Guardian Trust Company in 1945. At one time, Capt. James A. Baker was president of Guardian Trust Company, and Hiram M. Garwood was vice president of Lumberman's.

Despite all of his accomplishments in law and in business, fate determined that Andrews' name (as was the case with Capt. Baker and William Marsh Rice) would always be associated with the Long-Bell Lumber Co. The company was not even originally his client. For a time, Edwin Parker was the Firm lawyer for Long-Bell. The company owned substantial timber interests in Texas (as well as the West Coast) and had offices in Kansas City. After Parker's move to Washington in 1918, Andrews was spending so much time in Kansas City that in two years Baker Botts opened an office there with Andrews in charge. Not all the partners were happy with this decision and some never became reconciled. When Long-Bell suffered severely during the Depression, Andrews went to Washington and was instrumental in writing and securing passage of Section 77B of the Bankruptcy Act. This saved not only the Company but the Long fortune, and he was thereafter ever a hero to the Longs.

There were other clients of that office such as Union Electric Light & Power which employed the Kansas City Office of Baker Botts to complete much of the legal work for its Bagdell dam project, which created the Lake of the Ozarks in central Missouri. At times Houston partners, including Walter Walne and Tom Davis, went up to Kansas City to assist in litigation. The office itself grew to a peak of 55 lawyers, but these Kansas City lawyers never became full-fledged participants in Firm governance or finances. There was continued pressure from Houston to close the office (the days of branch offices had not arrived). Andrews steadfastly refused. Only after given an ultimatum to choose between Kansas City and Houston did Andrews return to the "home office" on December 31, 1935. The Kansas City office reorganized as Lombardi & Robertson and continued its operations unaffiliated with Baker Botts.

Andrews' close association with Long-Bell nonetheless continued, and in 1952 he was elected Chairman of the Board and continued to serve as General Counsel. He had a leading part in steering the Company into a very profitable merger with International Paper Co. in 1956. He was pleased to recount that the fee for this work was the largest

BAKER, BOTTS, PARKER & GARWOOD

JAMES A. BAKER
HIRAM M. GARWOOD
CLARENCE R. WHARTON
JULES H. TALLICHET
WALTER H. WALNE
RALPH B. FEAGIN
JAMES L. SHEPHERD, JR.
JAMES A. BAKER, JR.
BARKSDALE STEVENS
HOMER L. BRUCE
WINSTON CARTER

EDWIN B. PARKER
JESSE ANDREWS
CLARENCE L. CARTER
THOMAS H. BOTTS
PALMER HUTCHESON
RODMAN S. COSBY
YORICK D. MATHES
CARL D. MATZ
FLAVEL ROBERTSON
CONRAD J. LANDRAM
CALVIN B. GARWOOD

COMMERCIAL BANK BUILDING
HOUSTON, TEXAS
511 R. A. LONG BUILDING
KANSAS CITY, MISSOURI

GENERAL COUNSEL

The Long-Bell Lumber Company
Kansas City, Mo.

KANSAS CITY, MISSOURI

The Firm's Kansas City letterhead from the early 1920s.

single fee ever collected by the Firm at that time.

Andrews became very interested in city planning and when he returned to Houston served on the City Planning Commission for 19 years, 16 as chairman. A likely reason for his interest in city planning is that while he was in Kansas City, Long-Bell founded and laid out all the plans for the new city of Longview, Washington. He had a very heavy hand in all the planning. The Firm even maintained an office in Longview for a time.

Andrews was a proponent of zoning. While he was chairman of the Planning Commission, the city's area increased from 73 to 349 square miles and the population from 385,000 to 1,000,000. Improvements credited to the Committee under his leadership were a park and parkway system, a major street plan, a permanent policy of subdivision development, and a blueprint for Houston's freeway system.

Possibly because of the Long-Bell situation and possibly because of his nature, Andrews believed in going his own way. City planning was not popular in Houston, and in politics he was allied with the liberal wing of the Democratic party. The media reported that he was one of the national figures supporting President Roosevelt for a fourth term. Even in his personal investments, he was different. While most of the senior partners owned downtown real estate, Andrews was a stock and bond man and maintained an apartment at the Warwick rather than owning a home in Houston. Very late in life he did buy a modest home in River Oaks.

In an interview with the *Houston Press* on May 6, 1960, he was asked his philosophy of life. "A man ought to work hard, be diligent, and be economical." The *Press* observed "he is of Scottish descent and abhors waste." Andrews followed his own advice. He kept what he called his little black book and after he returned from his Kansas City trips, he was pleased to show anyone his neat entries such as newspaper 5¢, shine 5¢, cigar 10¢, etc. He kept these for years. On the other hand, he

The R.A. Long Building, Kansas City, Missouri, 1928. The R. A. Long Building served as headquarters for Long-Bell Lumber Company, the Firm's primary client in Kansas City, and as the Kansas City office of Baker Botts. This office opened in 1920 and closed in 1935. At various times, the Firm was on the fifth and thirteenth floors of the building.

was generous with his family and in-laws even though he lived a very frugal life personally. He did not believe in retirement. He kept 8-5 hours until the time of his last illness and retained a full senior interest.

What was Andrews like personally? He was tall, lean, dignified, courteous, and quiet. He had the reputation of being a tough negotiator among his equals, but in the lawyer interviews all the young lawyers reported that he was gentle, kind, and helpful to them. He was popular among the young lawyers. He could be very charming.

The Firm opened an office in Kelso, Washington in 1922 to serve Long-Bell Lumber Company. C. E. Lombardi of Dallas was employed by Baker Botts to open the office. With the development of the Long-Bell company town of Longview, Washington, the Firm moved into this building in Longview. Jesse Andrews officed here during his routine visits to Longview with R. A. Long. The Longview office was expanded to include additional attorneys who, upon the closing of the office before the end of 1935, remained in Longview.

One would have to know Andrews and the dignity which surrounded his office to appreciate this, but on Christmas Eve, it was his custom in his later years to bring a bottle of liquor down, and he and Baker, Jr. would drink a quiet toast to one another. (There was no drinking allowed in the office.) One year, Andrews dropped the bottle in his office and it smelled like a distillery. There were many happy grins among the lawyers and secretaries but not a word was said.

Andrews was very proud of and interested in the Firm history. Although the memorandum quoted below struck many in the office at that time as being a bit odd, it was Andrews' way of inserting some history into the Firm records. He no doubt realized that some day his memorandum would be quoted:

December 1, 1953

To the Lawyers:

Fifty-four years ago today I entered the employ of Baker, Botts, Baker & Lovett. There were then two full partners and one limited partner. The employed persons consisted of a lawyer to investigate authorities, a chief clerk, and three stenographers. Houston then had a population of about 50,000; had four banks, two of whom the Firm represented; was known as the "City where 17 railroads meet the Sea." Of these, the Firm represented eight. My beginning salary was $75 a month. I got my first raise, $25, January 1, 1901.

– Jesse Andrews

Finally Andrews made a specific request on December 27, 1957, and this is to comply with that request:

December 27, 1957

It might be of interest to someone in the future, writing a history of the Firm, to have this clipping from yesterday's "Houston Press", since it gives a

Looking towards Buffalo Bayou on Main Street, Houston, 1927. Foley Brothers, a long-time client of the Firm, hangs its new electric sign. Lawyers from the Firm, including W. Alvis Parish, Jesse Andrews, and John T. McCullough, assisted in the acquisition of Foley Brothers Dry Goods Company by Federated Department Stores, Inc. in 1945.

picture of the [Gibbs Building] in which the Firm had its offices for a number of years. Its offices were there in December, 1899, when I was first employed.

The building stood at the northwest corner of the intersection of Fannin Street and Franklin Avenue. It faced on Franklin Avenue. About midway of it was a broad stairway, not enclosed, extending straight from the sidewalk to the second floor.

The Firm's offices were on the second floor. Capt. Baker's office was at the southeast corner, his desk sitting almost in the balcony window. Adjoining his office, facing Franklin, was a larger room which served as the general office. In it was a long table. At the end next to Capt. Baker's office was a desk and a chair in which sat John H. McClung, who was the bookkeeper and the detail man. Between McClung's desk and Capt. Baker's wall sat the latter's stenographer, Miss Eula Gray. At the far end of the long room in on the wall, was a telephone, the only one in the office.

Passing out of the door of the larger room and proceeding in the hall in a westerly direction around the stairway, one came to another large room, facing Franklin, from which a smaller room had been partitioned off. In the smaller room was the desk of Mr. Parker, always stacked high with files. In the other part of the room was Mr. Parker's stenographer, Smith, and in this room, also at a small desk near a window facing Franklin Avenue, I sat.

The room adjoining Capt. Baker's office, with a window looking out on Fannin Street, was again a large room, in which Mr. Lovett had his desk and in which was also the library. In it was a long table at which sat a lawyer who preceded me in the organization, J. M. Patterson, but whose work was limited to investigation of authorities. There was no partition between the library and Mr. Lovett's office. Before him was a table, to his right was a desk, and at his left was a revolving bookcase on which there was a set of Texas Reports. Behind him was the window. In the library sat his stenographer, Miss Solomon.

Jesse Andrews in his later years after he returned to Houston from Kansas City.

Elsewhere in this building, and I think on the same floor, were the offices of Frank Andrews and W. T. Burns, both practicing law which had a close relationship to the law work of the Firm.

Frank Andrews, who had been an Assistant Attorney General when C. A. Culberson was Attorney General, had come to Houston to live prior to my being employed by the Firm. The reason for his coming was that he was to be the attorney for the T. W. House Bank and attorney for the Houston & Texas Central Railroad Company. The T. W. House Bank was the prominent bank in Houston at the time. Frank Andrews was a close friend of Col. E.

M. House, the brother of T. W. House. In this way that employment was arranged. The H&TC was one of the railroads of which the Firm were General Attorneys. It was one of the group known as the Sunset-Central Lines, embracing, among others, the railroads from New Orleans to El Paso, in which the Southern Pacific Company had a dominant, but concealed, interest. Mr. Andrews was to try the cases for the H&TC in the District and Appellate Courts.

W. T. Burns was employed to represent the H&TC and some of the other Sunset-Central Lines in the Justice and County Courts. Strange to say, he, though a Republican and always a Republican, was the State Senator from this district and seemed to have no trouble holding office from term to term. Mr. Burns, as is well known, subsequently became U.S. District Judge, being the first one appointed to that position in the Southern District.

When Mr. Wharton was employed, which I think was in January, 1902, he was given a small office across the hall from me, not facing on the street.

The Firm remained in this building until the completion of the construction of the building for the Commercial National Bank, called, according to the name above the door, "The Commercial Bank Building". Into this building the Firm moved in 1904, I think.

Jesse Andrews died in Houston on December 29, 1961, at the age of 87. After 62 years of work for Baker Botts, he deserved a rest.

CLARENCE R. WHARTON

Clarence Ray Wharton, although small in stature, was a giant among men. He was a scholar and a historian, but first of all, he was an aggressive, able trial lawyer who gave no quarter. Although he was never Managing Partner, he had a strong hand in all major decisions made while he was a partner.

Wharton was born October 5, 1873, in Tarrant County, Texas, to Frank B. and Ella Ray Wharton. Wharton's father fought in the Confederate Army and in the Indian wars which followed. The younger Wharton attended a country school until he was 15 and then for four years was a country school teacher. He studied law and was admitted to the bar in 1893 when he was 20. He first practiced in Decatur, Texas and then in Richmond, Texas, from 1897 to 1901. At a large community meeting in Galveston, it was said that Wharton was standing on a chair (in order to be seen) and making a fiery speech when Edwin B. Parker heard him and hired him, setting the course of Wharton's life. His remaining years were spent with the Firm. He became an associate in 1902 and a partner in 1906.

Wharton married Adele Spoonts in 1902, and they had three daughters and one son. Outwardly Wharton was gregarious and had a great sense of humor, but there was tragedy in his family life. This was most evident in a very touching story he wrote called "Three Portraits," which gives a sense of the inner man. It is the story of the tragic deaths of Wharton's father, his brother, and his teenage son, all of whose portraits were hanging in Wharton's home.

It is interesting to note that the Wharton home on Baldwin was across the street from "The Oaks," the original Parker home. It was referred to as the "cottage" where Parker lived when the big house was under construction. Wharton apparently loved the place and obviously could have lived in more substantial quarters had he chosen to

Clarence R. Wharton, with the Firm 1902 - 1941.

do so. Although boarded over, it still stands.

Wharton tried lawsuits for the Firm's most important clients. By all accounts, he was a fiery trial lawyer who relished combat in the courtroom. Wharton's reputation as a trial lawyer was such that one substantial company reportedly put the Firm on a retainer so that Wharton would try no more cases against them. Within the Firm and the city, he also was highly visible. He was an expert on utility rate hearings; he trained many of the partners; his counsel was sought on many important Firm matters; he was the first chairman of the Community Chest; and he furnished leadership to the Red Cross during World War I.

The following *Office Review* article by Mr. Parker on January 11, 1923 indicates Mr. Wharton's confidence in himself and his attitude toward work:

At times it appears doubtful whether or not each of us has and maintains the proper attitude towards

Railway Station, Houston, 1914. There are five firm clients represented in this photograph: at left, a building of the Hughes Tool Company, a client normally represented by Frank Andrews but which in special situations turned to Baker Botts for counsel; carriages of the Houston Transit Company; a delivery wagon of American Express Company; an engine of the Missouri, Kansas & Texas Railway Company; and in the background, a building of F.W. Heitmann & Co.

his work. True it is that often times we have referred to us some small task which is the source of much annoyance as well as having to devote to it much more work than the matter apparently should require. These, however, must come along with the larger and more important matters, and it is up to each of us at all times to grapple with any problem, whether large or small, and carry it through to the end. In revising our Plan of Organization for 1923 we passed to Mr. Wharton a statement outlining the work and clients he would look after. In returning this statement Mr. Wharton writes:

I have gone over and am returning herewith the suggestion about my work as it shall be written in the plan of organization for 1923, and it is entirely satisfactory with me, nor do I have any changes to indicate.

My view of our office work is this: I have little preference as to what I do. I am both ready and willing to do anything from the trial of a case in the County Court, up or down, as the case may be. I like to examine abstracts, and when possible will do abstract work.

My experience in handling will litigation and suits involving trusts, has been considerable and I have had occasion to study the cases upon these topics and can be helpful in such litigation.

My experience in handling cases involving oil leases has been considerable and I have had

El Presidente

A sketch of the life of

General Santa Anna

By
Clarence R. Wharton

PUBLISHED BY GAMMEL'S BOOK STORE
AUSTIN, TEXAS

The Isle of Mal Hado
and Other Sketches

*Three Hundred and Fifty Years
of Texas History*

By CLARENCE WHARTON

No. 7162

IN THE SUPREME COURT
OF TEXAS

STATE OF TEXAS

VS.

STANDARD OIL COMPANY

ARGUMENT SUPPORTING MOTION FOR REHEARING
CALLING THE COURT'S ATTENTION TO THE
CHICAGO BOARD OF TRADE AND APPALA-
CHIAN COAL DECISIONS OF THE SUPREME
COURT OF THE UNITED STATES AND
ASKING A MODIFICATION OF THE
LANGUAGE USED IN THE FOR-
MER OPINION OF THE
COURT

C. R. WHARTON
Attorney for Sinclair Oil & Rfg. Co.

IT MAY TAKE A THOUSAND
YEARS

Address Delivered by

C. R. WHARTON

at the 93rd Annual Commencement of

BAYLOR UNIVERSITY

at Waco, May 30, 1938

Clarence R. Wharton was a prolific writer, as represented in this small selection of publications.

occasion to study practically every American decision upon this subject, and I can be helpful in that character of litigation.

My experience in trespass to try title is second to that of Mr. Carter, and I can be helpful in that kind of litigation.

My experience in rate litigation has been considerable, and I can be helpful in such controversies as may arise in that domain. In fact the best part of my last twenty years has been spent in considering decisions and rules of procedure that affect the right of utility companies.

I am ready to be assigned any work that comes during the year 1923 within the limitation only that I can find time to do it.

The spirit thus manifested is that which we should all have towards our work, and it is the problem of each to see that this spirit is carried into any and all matters that may be referred or come to him.

Clarence R. Wharton in later years. He delivered the address at the dedication of the San Jacinto Monument in 1936.

Wharton was an avid history reader and developed a hobby of writing history. In addition to many articles, his published works include *The Republic of Texas* (1922), *El Presidente* (1924), *San Jacinto, the Sixteenth Decisive Battle* (1930), and *History of Texas* (1939). In 1930, he edited a five volume Texas history called *Texas Under Many Flags*. One of his books, *History of Texas*, was used as a textbook in the Texas public schools for a time.

In his later years, Wharton was a short, stout man with an owlish appearance. He was a very forceful individual and could not be intimidated. He mellowed into being a character. He had an office in the Library in the Niels Esperson Building overlooking the Esperson Garage. There was no air conditioning and the windows were open. To clean out his files, he would sit in his office in his rocking chair, wearing houseshoes, humming a happy tune and rip the unwanted portion of the files apart and toss them out of a window to the garage roof.

Although one of his specialties was land title work, he was bored with detail. On one occasion, he rolled up an abstract, looked through it with one eye, and dictated to his secretary, "I have looked through your abstract and approve same."

On another occasion, he had minor surgery and received an enormous bill because the doctor knew he was wealthy. Wharton was aware that the doctor had charged someone else a fraction of the amount. He wrote the doctor complaining that the fee was outrageous. Back came his letter with a notation: "Pay this or nothing." Wharton added a notation "Thanks very much," signed "C.R.W.," and mailed it back to the doctor.

Wharton died of cancer in May 1941, only three months before Capt. Baker. Their deaths marked the end of an era.

CLARENCE L. CARTER

Two of the second generation of Baker Botts partners, Clarence Leon Carter and Jules H. Tallichet, specialized in railroad law. This was hardly surprising; at the turn of the century, approximately half of the Firm's billings still came from railroad work.

Clarence Carter was born in Homer, Angelina County, Texas, on November 23, 1869. His parents were Joseph John and Eleanor Agnes Carter. He acquired his basic education in East Texas, and in September 1889, he entered the law school of the University of Texas, graduating with a law degree in June 1891. That September he began his career as an attorney at Livingston, Texas. During 1892-93, he served as county attorney of Polk County; he was district attorney of the Ninth Judicial District from 1894 to 1899. Carter was a member of the firm Feagin and Carter, engaged in general law practice at Livingston from 1899 to 1902.

After moving to Houston, he was division attorney of the Southern Pacific Railway Lines from 1902 to 1906, and from 1906 to 1907 he was engaged in a general individual practice. In 1907 he joined the Firm and in 1909 became partner. During his 29-year stay at Baker Botts, Carter also was vice president and director of the Groveton, Lufkin and Northern Railway Co. and also of the Union National Bank. He was honored with election as president of the Harris County Bar Association in 1908.

Carter married Miss Alice Lyle Winston at Moscow, Texas on January 11, 1893. One of his sons, Winston, was an attorney and junior associate at the Firm. The other children were Mrs. A. J. Casperson, Mrs. T. M. Murray, Miss Ruth Carter,

Clarence L. Carter, with the Firm 1902 - 1936. This photograph is from the eulogy prepared by Union National Bank.

and Ernest T. Carter. For several years Mr. Carter acted as Managing Partner of the Firm. If managing partners were to be described as active or passive, Carter would be in the passive category. Carter was a kind, gentle, modest person. Partner Frank Coates said of him that he was a "saint."

It is interesting to note that Carter had originally joined the Firm in 1902 to work on railway cases. But just after three years of grueling work for damage suits against John Lovejoy, Presley Ewing, John W. Parker, and other stalwarts, he left Baker Botts to open his own law office. In 1907, Wharton suggested that the Firm hire someone to assist him because his trial docket had become very heavy. Wharton recommended Carter, who was not interested initially because he remembered the drudgery of his late railway docket when he had worked for the Firm. Wharton, however, urged him to return, promising him a lifetime association with the Firm.

Clarence Carter was a brother of W. T. Carter and part of the family that owned very substantial timber interests in East Texas, and that was a significant client of the Firm for many years. It was brother W. T. Carter who advised Clarence to accept Wharton's offer. He stayed with the Firm until he died in 1936 at the age of 66. For most of his legal career, he remained a specialist in railroad law.

The Carter home on South Blvd. was designed by Birdsall Briscoe and was among those shown by the Rice Design Alliance in 1990.

JULES H. TALLICHET

The Firm's second railroad specialist, Jules Henri Tallichet, was born in Austin, Texas, on April 20, 1877. His father was professor of Romantic Languages at the University of Texas. He attended Austin public schools and the University of Texas, and started practicing law at Austin in 1899. Tallichet was married to Miss Estelle Montelin of Austin in 1904. They had three daughters and one son.

Tallichet's career before he joined the Firm was noteworthy. After he graduated in 1901 with a law degree, he entered the law office of Judge Sam R. Fischer at Austin and began specializing in railroad work. He was trial attorney for the Southern Pacific Lines in Austin and West Texas for eight years. In 1909, he moved to Houston and joined the Firm. As general counsel for Southern Pacific, he represented them during the shop strike of 1915 and was counsel in the famous railway clerks' case which resulted in the setting up of a federal railway code.

He joined the Firm of Baker, Botts, Parker & Garwood in 1909. On January 1, 1915, he was made partner, and in July 1917, when Edwin B. Parker left the Firm to assume the first of his many governmental duties during World War I, Tallichet assumed responsibility for what was then one of the Firm's most important clients, Southern Pacific in Texas. He continued to serve in that capacity until his death.

Tallichet, affectionately known as "Tally" to his colleagues, was a tall, imposing individual. A handsome and strong man, he was interested in outdoor sports but was also an avid reader. In addition to his other outdoor interests he was an ornithologist. He was noted for his ready wit and profound knowledge of Texas history. As a collector of books with an interest in history, Tallichet helped Wharton in the latter's collecting books about Texas history. An avid hunter all his life, he became interested in boating in the later years of

Jules H. Tallichet, with the Firm 1909 - 1937.

his life. He was commodore of the Houston Yacht Club.

Tallichet was a man of strong emotions, given to outbursts of temper and frequent profanity; the latter his colleagues remarked he had perfected to near art. For this reason, the Firm assigned him a male secretary. Tallichet was known to rip his phone off the wall and throw it out the window in a fit of temper.

Tallichet was fiercely loyal to his client, Southern Pacific. It was said that when the railroad unions went on strike, he would strap on a pistol (some said two) and go down to monitor the picket lines. He handled the merger of a number of railroads controlled by the Southern Pacific into the Texas and New Orleans Railroad Co., which became the railroad operated by the Southern Pacific in Texas and Louisiana.

Tallichet died in Houston on November 23, 1937.

The Houston Yacht Club clubhouse, pictured here circa 1936, the year Jules H. Tallichet was elected as Commodore.

The *Sunset Limited*, flagship train of Firm client Texas & New Orleans Railway, leaves the Houston station, circa 1935.

THOMAS H. BOTTS

Thomas Hutchinson Botts was the son of Walter Browne Botts and was the last of that name to practice law with the Firm. He was born July 8, 1878, joined the Firm in 1905, became a partner in 1915, and died at the age of 43 in 1922. He was an office lawyer as opposed to being a trial lawyer, and since he died at such a young age, we know little of his clients. We learn more about Thomas Botts from Capt. Baker's memorial tribute than from any other source.

Capt. Baker seldom let down his guard and gave vent to his feelings, as he chose to operate quietly behind the scenes. But his tribute to Thomas Botts delivered before the Harris County Bar Association on June 5, 1922 indicates how deeply Capt. Baker felt about both father and son:

Mr. Chairman and Gentlemen:

Death is no respecter of persons or of rank. He lays his icy finger upon the babe in the crib, upon the boy on the playground, upon the young manhood and young womanhood when they first cast their lives on the broad expanse of human activities, upon men of middle age before they reach the maturity of their power of usefulness, and in the evening of life when our faces are turned toward the setting sun. And in whatever form it comes it tears our hearts and wrings our souls. Whether it comes in one form or another, we are never prepared for it.

I am doing today a service which in the nature of things I expect my boy to do for me.

I knew Tom Botts from infancy to the day of his death. I grasped the hands of his father in congratulation when he had blessed his home. I cheered him in his boyish sports as he grew up before me from year to year. I stood by his side at his mother's bier, and in two days afterwards I held his hand as he wept at the grave of his lamented father. It was then that I began the relationship to

Thomas H. Botts, with the Firm 1905 - 1922.

him that we sustained the balance of our lives - almost that of parent and child.

Under my advice he went off to Virginia to a preparatory school, from there to finish his course at the University of Texas, and when he graduated there I can see him now as he came into the office smiling and happy, and I extended to him the hand of welcome, as he came to fill the place and he worthily filled the place that his honored father sustained in our firm. From that day to this our relations have been more near that of parent and child than associates in business.

There was never a time when he did not respond with alacrity to duty's call. There was never a time when he neglected the interests of the client or forgot the courtesy or kindness due from a young man to an older one. He filled worthily the shoes of his honored father. I remember soon after I went into the firm I said to Col. Botts, the father of Tom, "I want to ask you what I should do under these circumstances - what is the ethical thing to do?" He said "Jimmie" - he called me "Jimmie" - "why do you ask me?" And I said "Col., because I have a doubt about it." He said "You have answered your own question. The fact that you have a doubt about it, my boy, is sufficient answer to your question, - don't do it." That was the life that Col. Botts led, that was the standard he established among those who knew him. He was rarely in the court house. I never knew him to try or assist in the trial of more than two or three litigated cases, and yet there was no man within my knowledge, or those who knew him, who enjoyed the confidence and respect of the bar and the bench greater than Col. Botts, and so the boy came along with no inclination for the life of the advocate, no peculiar qualities for the rough and tumble contests of the courts, but he entered the field of practice, staying in the quiet of his office, making examinations of authorities, delving into decisions, ever mindful of the rights of his clients and applying the correct legal principles to the rights of his clients. I have never known a young man who filled that place and that responsibility with any greater responsibility than our deceased friend.

His disposition was ever cheerful. His father was always an optimist. "Everything, Jimmie, is coming out all right. It looks gloomy today, the sky is overcast - I see you are disposed to look discouraged. Wait until tomorrow, the sun will shine again and everything will come out all right." Always bright, always cheerful, always hopeful, and the only man I ever knew to die of a broken heart. I never knew a closer relation between husband and wife than that between Col. Botts and his wife. He left for his office every morning about eight o'clock, drove down in his buggy, carried his lunch in his pocket, ate it at one o'clock and went back at 6 o'clock. He was little indisposed. Had he been sick a number of days, we would have thought different, but he was even without temperature, but when death laid its icy finger upon the good wife,

he also laid it over Col. Botts' heart, and without the rise of temperature, without any apparent cause of death, in two days he joined her in that home beyond the skies.

Tom was a duplicate of his father. A duplicate of those qualities that go to make up a lawyer and a man - strong in his friendship, loyal in his friendship, true to his duty, loyal to his duty, true to his family, loyal to his family, he set an example worthy of emulation not only by the younger members of the profession, but the older ones as well.

Having lost his parents in early life, having been afflicted as he was, so that he had to discontinue writing with his right hand and learn to write with his left, this, as has been said of him, instead of dampening his ardor or diminishing his energy, seemed to cause him to redouble his efforts and he achieved a reputation in this community, not only among you, as brother members of the bar, but throughout the community at large. I have lived here for more than forty years, and I do not believe I ever saw a greater tribute to any man of his age than was paid to that young man yesterday by the entire citizenship of the city.

I could hardly trust myself today to attempt these remarks, but it is a pleasure to me to stand here this morning to attest to his wonderful character, and to say that in my judgment he has set an example worthy of emulation by all those who knew him and loved him.

Thus did the Firm's second Baker eulogize its second Botts. The words expressed much about the depth of feeling that had bound the founding generation together in a close-knit partnership. The task of the second generation had been to develop strong ties to further cement such personal bonds in the growing Firm. It then had to recruit a third generation and instill in these young lawyers the values and traditions of Baker Botts.

From Buffalo Bayou looking up Main Street, Houston, circa 1910. In the background are the Harris County Courthouse, Houston Land & Trust Co., First National Bank, and Commercial Bank buildings.

Celebration for the opening of the Houston Ship Channel, 1914. Notice the band playing on the barge, the sculling, and the large crowd gathered on the banks of the channel. Capt. James A. Baker delivered the address at the opening.

CHAPTER

3

Firm Christmas party at the Brazos Hotel, probably 1929. Unfortunately, precise identities have been lost. Modern observers have reconstructed some identities, as follows: Left to right: unidentified, Jesse Andrews, Mrs. Jesse Andrews (Celeste), H. Malcolm Lovett, Mrs. James L. Shepherd, Jr. (Marguerite), Calvin B. Garwood, Miss Ruth Andrews, unidentified, unidentified, unidentified, Clarence L. Carter, unidentified, Palmer Hutcheson, unidentified, unidentified, James L. Shepherd, Jr., Walter H. Walne, unidentified, John P. Bullington, Homer L. Bruce, Mrs. James A. Baker (Alice), Capt. James A. Baker, Mrs. Alfred H. Fulbright (Margarette), Alfred H. Fulbright, unidentified, unidentified, unidentified, John T. Garrison, Mrs. Brady Cole (Ann), unidentified, James A. Baker, Jr., Mrs. Clarence R. Wharton (Adele), Clarence R. Wharton, Miss Willie A. Rowell, W. Alvis Parish, Mrs. Homer L. Bruce (Clara), Hiram M. Garwood, Mrs. James A. Baker, Jr. (Bonner), Jules H. Tallichet, Mrs. W. Alvis Parish (Beth), Barksdale Stevens, Mrs. Palmer Hutcheson (Eleanor), Winston Carter. Standing Rear: Rodman S. Cosby, unidentified, unidentified, unidentified, unidentified, Brady Cole, unidentified waiter.

THE POST-WAR BOOM:
1917-1929

By the time of World War I, the second generation at Baker Botts recognized the need to add more lawyers. The regional economy boomed after the opening of the ship channel, and the Firm's practice prospered. With the return of normalcy, Baker Botts entered a new era, one marked by the arrival of a cluster of young lawyers who would come to maturity before World War II.

The list of the nine lawyers who entered the Firm between 1914 and 1927 and later became partners is impressive, as shown below.

This cluster shared certain characteristics. They were by and large honor graduates from the University of Texas law school, although two were Texans who went off to Harvard Law School before returning to Houston. As a group, they spent a longer period as associates than any similar group in the history of Baker Botts: 10-12 years to partnership was the norm. Reflecting the needs of the Firm's clients, this group tended to become more specialized.

NEW MEMBERS, 1914 - 1927					
Name	*Birth/Death*	*Law School*	*Years with Firm*	*Partner Date*	*Specialty*
Ralph B. Feagin	1891-1946	U. Texas	1914-1946	1921	corporate/utilities
Palmer Hutcheson	1887-1966	U. Texas	1919-1945	1921	general
W. Alvis Parish	1887-1959	U. Texas	1910-1953	1923	utilities/corporate
James A. Baker, Jr.	1892-1973	U. Texas	1919-1973	1927	general
James L. Shepherd, Jr.	1892-1973	U. Texas	1917-1964	1929	oil/gas
Homer L. Bruce	1892-1979	Harvard	1920-1979	1931	tax
Brady Cole	1901-1953	U. Texas	1923-1953	1935	patents
John P. Bullington	1899-1948	U. Texas	1927-1948	1935	trial/railroad
H. Malcolm Lovett	1902-	Harvard	1924-	1938	corporate

Note: Both Feagin and Parish left the Firm for short periods.

Bird's eye view of Houston, 1926. The Esperson Building and the Rice Hotel addition are both under construction.

They pursued their legal careers in a great place to practice law — Houston in the 1920s. No decade in Houston's modern history has since matched the expansion of these years. Already by 1920, Houston's population was 138,000, roughly the size of Beaumont in 1980. In 1930, this figure had surged to 292,000. For the city, the symbol of prosperity was the hosting of the Democratic National Convention in 1928. For the Firm, the symbol was the move in January 1927 into the newest and finest building in town, the Niels Esperson Building.

Information from the 1920 City Directory is of interest since it gives one an idea of how far Houston had spread at that point:

- James A. Baker, Jr. lived with his father at 1416 Main. (Capt. Baker owned the block.)
- Thomas H. Botts - 301 Webster
- Ralph B. Feagin - 209 Webster
- Hiram M. Garwood - 3404 Montrose
- Palmer Hutcheson - 4111 Main
- Edwin B. Parker - "The Oaks" on Hadley at Baldwin (For those not familiar with Houston streets, Hadley and Baldwin intersect just south of the current Bland Cadillac dealership)
- James L. Shepherd, Jr. - 4111 Austin
- Jules H. Tallichet - 3229 Fannin
- Walter H. Walne - 3823 Brandt (one block from E. O. Lovett - Rice President)
- Clarence Wharton - 2204 Baldwin
- Miss Willie A. Rowell (then Chief Clerk) - 404 Tuam

WALTER H. WALNE

The transition figure between the second generation and the World War I-era partners was Walter
Hillman Walne. He was the last lawyer hired by
Baker Botts without a completed law school
degree; he later became the driving force in the
move toward a meritocracy in hiring based primarily on academic performance in law school.

Walne was born April 10, 1879 in Clinton,
Mississippi, worked his way through Baylor, and
attended the University of Texas Law School, but
didn't graduate. He withdrew because of a death
in his family, but under existing rules, he was able
to pass the bar examination and qualify to practice without a law school degree.

Here Walne himself picks up the story in an
interview published in the *Office Review* in
September of 1946, on the occasion of the change
in the Firm's name to Baker, Botts, Andrews &
Walne:

Walter H. Walne, with the Firm 1917 - 1947.

> The son of a Baptist minister, Thomas Jefferson
> Walne, the attorney says he entered the legal pro-
> fession because he had the "wholly mistaken
> notion it would afford him the opportunity to
> make speeches."
>
> He was always a member of the public speak-
> ing and debating classes at Baylor University
> where he was graduated and the University of
> Texas law school because "I like to argue," he
> frankly admits.
>
> It was Mr. Parker who talked a polite but
> declining Mr. Walne into joining the firm. At the
> end of his second year in law school, Mr. Walne's
> father died and explained Mr. Walne, "I took the
> bar examination and went home to take care of
> my mother and sister. You see today, with my
> qualifications, they wouldn't take me into this
> firm." And he said, pointing to the pictures of the
> six on the wall, "some of them couldn't get in
> either. But times have changed."

Claim Agent in Dallas
For three years he worked for utility companies in
Dallas and gave himself the title of claim agent,
but in fact he was trying cases. He later joined a
law firm and because he was interested in the work
he spent his evenings briefing cases for the older
lawyers. "You know," he explained, "an older
lawyer is always glad to find a young one who will
do the work."

One day young Mr. Walne walked into the
courtroom to do the chores for one of the older
lawyers. The older lawyer said, "Walne, you are
going to try this case." It was a damage suit. "I
tried it and I have been trying cases ever since,"
Mr. Walne said.

Then after seven years in Dallas came the
offer from the then known firm of Baker, Botts,
Parker and Garwood. "The offer came in a letter
and I couldn't just write a letter back and decline,

BAKER, BOTTS, PARKER & GARWOOD

COMMERCIAL BANK BUILDING

JAMES A. BAKER
EDWIN B. PARKER
H. M. GARWOOD
JESSE ANDREWS
C. R. L. HARTON
C. L. CARTER
J. H. TALLICHET
THOMAS H. BOTTS
JNO. C. TOWNES JR.
WALTER H. WALNE

HOUSTON, TEXAS

Firm letterhead, 1914.

I had no intention of taking the position because I was well satisfied in Dallas. I was working with two fine men who gave every opportunity to young men, but I thought I should make a trip down here to say no. It was fortunate that I did."

Parker Great Salesman
"E. B. Parker was a great salesman as well as a great lawyer. He offered me $200 a month and took a piece of paper out of his desk drawer to show me how much the partners were making.

All of them were making so much more than any of the partners in the law firm in Dallas I couldn't refuse. You couldn't refuse such an opportunity."

Mr. Walne was told, "You are being chosen as material for this firm." His work was supervised by the partners who sat behind him in the courtroom coaching, prompting. Among the prompters, Mr. Walne said, was Jesse Andrews.

Seek Honor Students
"We began after I came to the firm to seek out the

The Houston City Auditorium, on Louisiana at Texas, Houston, was built in 1910 and torn down in 1963. The Houston Symphony orchestra played here. Walter H. Walne was president of the Symphony for six terms during that era.

Walter H. Walne in his later years.
He was the Firm's first "hiring partner."

honor students of the University of Texas law school and other nearby law schools." Mr. Walne explained.

"We seek men of the highest intellectual attainments. Since law is an intellectual business, we want to find men of high quality."

Walne's importance in the total Firm history was not fully understood until outsiders wrote the Firm history. He was not a warm and lovable person, and some of his contemporaries regarded him as tough and brusque, but he had vision and set high standards for the Firm. Even though he never graduated from law school, he felt that the Firm should employ only the top honor graduates of law schools and that it should broaden its search for the top talent in the state. His hiring in 1929-30 of Frank Coates, Gaius Gannon, Tom Scurry, and Tom Davis from the Dallas-Fort

Worth area, which created quite a stir in the Firm, was his opening salvo in broadening the base of the Firm's hiring. His lasting influence may be best illustrated by Shepherd's comment thirty years after Walne joined the firm that Walne had hired every partner still in the Firm in 1947, except for Baker, Andrews, and Parish.

Walne chose the legal profession because he thought it would give him an opportunity to make speeches and he liked to argue. As a lawyer he would be described as pugnacious and tenacious. He left no stone unturned in preparing a case, and one young lawyer who left the Firm after two years gave as one of his reasons that he got tired of briefing for one man on one case. This was an exaggeration, but he did try very large cases and insisted on being extremely well prepared.

Walne was married to Margaret Butler of Austin, and their three children were Walter Walne, Jr., Mrs. Whitfield Marshall, and Mrs. Charles Snead. His wife helped interest him in the Houston Symphony, which was struggling to survive in the 1920s and 1930s. Walne's enormous energy and his great attention to detail went into the rebuilding of the Houston Symphony, which he headed for six terms. One employee of the Firm stated, "Although I was a youngster and had never heard a symphony orchestra, I was so carried away with Mr. Walne's enthusiasm that I bought two season subscriptions." Walne himself professed to care little about classical music, but he cared about Houston, and he felt the city needed a good symphony. His leadership helped place the symphony on a firm financial footing.

The Walne home on South Blvd. was designed by Birdsall Briscoe and was one of the show homes on the list of the Rice Design Alliance in 1990.

Walne died May 6, 1947 at the age of 69. He helped instill in Baker Botts a strong commitment to excellence in hiring. For that, he deserves to be long remembered.

RALPH B. FEAGIN

Ralph Bayard Feagin was the last Firm managing partner of the old school. His contemporaries who knew his contribution to the Firm called him tough, and young lawyers fresh out of law school often described him as intimidating.

The following biographical sketch of Feagin, written by the Editors National Press Syndicate, was obtained from Mrs. Cad Willeford, the granddaughter of Feagin:

Ralph Bayard Feagin, one of Houston's successful young attorneys, was popular at college, active in the war and is now a participating member of the law firm of Baker, Botts, Parker and Garwood.

Mr. Feagin was born in Livingston, Texas, on March 12, 1891. His father was Judge James Columbus Feagin and his mother was Nannie Elizabeth Josey.

He graduated from the Livingston Texas High School in 1908 and in the fall of the same year entered Baylor University at Waco, where he attended college until 1911. In 1911 he entered the University of Texas and was graduated from there in 1914 with the degree of L.L.B. During high school and college days, Mr. Feagin worked as stenographer and abstractor and studied law in a law office at Livingston, Texas. He took an active part in journalistic work both at Baylor and at Texas University, where he established and was editor for the first year of the Daily Texan, the first college daily newspaper published in the South. During his senior year at Texas University, he served as quiz master in the Law Department and also lectured during part of his senior year while one of the professors was on a leave of absence.

On July 6, 1914, Mr. Feagin entered the service of the law firm of Baker, Botts, Parker and Garwood. He remained with this firm until 1917, when he was given leave of absence to do wartime Red Cross work.

Ralph B. Feagin, with the Firm 1914 - 1946.

He served as secretary of the Red Cross Committee, of which Judge R.S. Lovett, Chairman of the Board of the Union Pacific R.R. Co., was chairman, in New York from July to September, 1917. When Judge Lovett went to Washington in September, 1917, to be commissioner of priority shipments, Mr. Feagin was taken with him as secretary. Later he became executive secretary of the priorities committee of the War Industries Board, with Judge Lovett as chairman and later with Edwin B. Parker of Houston as chairman.

In May, 1918, Mr. Feagin was commissioned as First Lieutenant and went immediately to the American headquarters in France. He was later commissioned Captain of the General Staff of the A.E.F. He served on the General Staff until April, 1919, at which time he was discharged from the army in France at the request of Edwin B. Parker of Houston, who had come to Paris as Chairman of the American Liquidation Commission, charged with the responsibility of disposing of all properties and equipment owned by the American Army in Europe and of settling claims between the U.S. War Department and the Allies. He served as assistant to Mr. Parker in this work until he returned to the United States in June, 1919.

In July, 1919, Mr. Feagin returned to the firm of Baker, Botts, Parker and Garwood, of which firm he later became a member and managng partner, with offices in the Commercial Bank Building.

In addition to his law activities, Mr. Feagin is a member of substantial corporations including the Houston Lighting and Power Co., Johns-Manville, Inc. of Texas, and the Texas State Rice Milling Company. He is President of Magnolia Dairy Products and President and Trustee of the Houston Ice and Brewing Association.

In July 1919, Feagin returned to the Firm as a partner and was made Assistant Managing Partner in 1920, when he was not yet 30. This is an indication of Feagin's ability, Parker's influence, or both.

Only eight years after he returned in 1927, Electric Bond & Share Company made Feagin such an attractive offer that he moved to New York as a Vice President of the company. He also became President of United Gas Corporation when it was organized in 1930. In May 1933, he returned to the Firm and served as Managing Partner until his death on April 3, 1946.

No one doubted Feagin's administrative ability. He had the drive of a Parker and used the stick while dispensing with the carrot. He was all business and not known for small talk. It could be said that although he may not have been loved, he was respected. As a result of his six years with Electric Bond and Share, he became an expert in public utility-related issues and not only carried a heavy load of practice in this area but was called on to testify before congressional committees.

Feagin kept notebooks, some of which are still available. At year end he required partners to send him a memorandum summarizing their accomplishments for the year as well as their failings and their plan for overcoming these failings. Capt. Baker must have surely been amused as he wrote his report (he was 34 years Feagin's senior), but reply he did. He often asked partners for reports on clients for which they were responsible, and at year end he assigned clients to certain partners and held them responsible for maintaining relations with these clients. One of his partners noted that Feagin had an uncanny faculty for long-range planning with patient willingness to bend his attention to every essential detail.

No one has ever attempted to trace the number of important clients which came out of Feagin's six years in New York, but two quickly come to mind. United Gas was spun off by Electric Bond and Share in 1930 when Feagin was president. He later took HL&P public in 1943. These became very substantial clients in their revised form.

We have mentioned that Feagin helped create and was first editor of the *Daily Texan* while still on the University campus. According to the 1921 *Office Review,* he was also instrumental in raising funds for the creation of the *Texas Law Review.* The greatest debt we owe Feagin, however, is for his editorship and very great interest in the *Office Review.* He was Parker's protege, so we don't know whose idea it was, but clearly the *Office Review* became Feagin's project, and he served as editor for many years even when he was Managing Partner. Had it not been for his vigorous editorship of the *Office Review,* the writing of the Firm histories would not have been possible.

Feagin married Paula Garrison after he returned from World War I and became Managing Partner. He died in 1946, and was survived by Mrs. Feagin and two children, Ralph B. Feagin, Jr. and Betty Jane Feagin.

Office of Houston Gas Company, circa 1886. Founded in 1866, this forerunner of the Houston division of the United Gas Corporation turned on a supply of manufactured gas, the first in the South, in 1868. The United Gas System was first conceived by Ralph B. Feagin. He made it a reality in 1930 through the incorporation and formation of the United Gas Corporation. Ralph B. Feagin served as United Gas Corporation's first president between 1930 and 1933, when he moved back to Houston from Louisiana. United Gas Corporation was a holding company for more than 40 separate companies in Texas, Louisiana, Mississippi, Florida, and Mexico.

The Houston Ice and Brewing Company's Magnolia Brewery, established in 1892, was located north of Buffalo Bayou on either side of Washington Avenue between 4th and 5th Streets. Later, additional facilities were added south of the Bayou. A 600-foot concrete roadway covered the Bayou from Franklin to Milam, unifying the complex. A 1935 flood seriously damaged much of the brewery. Rising flood waters behind a dam of debris lodged in the narrow channel at the brewery destroyed property throughout the lower business district. As a result, the Harris County Flood Control District was created in 1937, and the Addicks and Barker Dams on the head waters of Buffalo Bayou were built. A portion of the main brewery still stands at 401 Washington, a derelict warehouse is located at 110 Milam, and a small two-story portion of the Magnolia office building has been restored at the corner of Franklin and Milam. In the early 1920s, almost every senior partner of Baker Botts served as a trustee for this company.

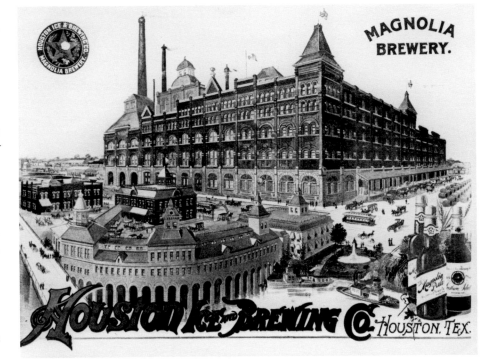

PALMER HUTCHESON

William Palmer Hutcheson, or "Pam," retired from the Firm on December 31, 1945, to practice law with his sons, but because he was a very active senior partner for many years and this Firm has been so closely related to the Hutchesons, no history would be complete without mention of William Palmer Hutcheson.

Hutcheson was born January 1, 1887, in Houston, the son of Capt. Joseph C. Hutcheson, a prominent lawyer in Houston, and Bettie Palmer Hutcheson. Both the Palmers and the Hutchesons were early Texans, Judge Edward Albert Palmer having come to Texas in 1847. The Hutchesons were always conscious of duty to country. An uncle was killed while leading a company of Hood's Brigade in the Confederacy. Palmer himself volunteered in World War I as a private, became an officer, and was later twice decorated for service in combat. All three of his sons served overseas in World War II. Palmer attended Hill School, Princeton, and the University of Texas Law School. He first practiced from 1911 to 1916 in the firm of Hutcheson & Hutcheson, with his father and his brother, J. C. Hutcheson, Jr. The latter subsequently served as Mayor of Houston and, for many years, as Chief Judge of the Fifth Circuit Court of Appeals.

Upon his return from the war, Hutcheson became an associate at Baker Botts on October 1, 1919 and a partner on January 1, 1921.

Mr. Hutcheson's letter to the Firm on the occasion of his withdrawal tells us a great deal about the Hutchesons and the Firm of that day. A portion of this letter is reproduced:

> Now that you as my present partners and I, with the joinder of my future partners, have announced my approaching withdrawal from this firm to enter the general practice of law with my two sons, Palmer, Jr., and Thad, and with Mr. T. S. Talia-

Palmer Hutcheson, with the Firm 1919 - 1945.

ferro, under the Firm name of "Hutcheson, Taliaferro & Hutcheson", I desire to write a farewell message and for this purpose I am taking the liberty of using for the first time the stationery of my new firm, which will become effective January 1, 1946.

As that date nears, I am filled with mixed emotions of sorrow over leaving this firm and my valued friends here, and of happiness over the coming association that I will have with my sons in a small family firm. Perhaps it would not be inapt to say that my sentiments resemble those of the son who is leaving the parental home to establish a home and fireside of his own, or perhaps, it is more accurate to say, returning to his father's home after a long and pleasant sojourn with other friends.

Of course, as most of you know, I practiced law here for a number of years with my father, now deceased, and my brother, Judge Hutcheson. When I returned to Houston in 1919, my father had virtually retired and my brother was on the federal bench. This firm was then kind enough to extend to me an invitation to become a member, which I accepted with mingled emotions similar to those which I have expressed above about my approaching departure.

. . . I shall always value the many years of pleasant association that I have had in this firm, not only with the partners, but also with those young men who have labored long and earnestly to make the partnership a success. Perhaps it was my fondness for them and my interest in their development that led me to realize, at the end of World War II, the joy that would come to me from a similar contact with my sons. I shall hope that my sons will always have the privilege of intimate association with the fine young men in this organization who will doubtless constitute in a large part, the backbone, and the front ranks of its future. Naturally, I am pleased that my nephew, Joe Hutcheson, has become a member of the firm and I feel that he will always constitute a link between me and my boys on the one hand, and the partners and the younger men of the organization on the other hand. Naturally, also, I shall hope to continue the same pleasant personal relations that I have had with each member of the organization.

I cannot close without referring to three occasions which stand out particularly in my mind in connection with this association. The first was the occasion in 1919 of my coming over to join the firm at the old offices in the former Commercial Bank Building. Mr. Andrews and Judge Garwood had concluded the arrangements with me, so, of course, I went to call first on them and then on my other dear friend, Capt. Baker. They assigned me to an office where Ralph Feagin kindly conducted me and discussed with me my new field of work, for even in those days he was acting as an associate managing partner, his natural ability in that respect having already come to the attention of the firm. I have always been glad that the association which

began with Ralph then continued so pleasantly over the years when we were both members of the firm.

The second instance that is outstanding in my mind is the occasion in 1933, when the firm was kind enough to designate me to address the Rotary Club of Houston, with the firm as the honor guest, representing all of the organizations in Houston that had existed here for more than half a century. The importance of this occasion to me was not at all self-pride, but pride in the firm of which I had come to be a member and the tradition for which that firm stood. I have turned to the summary of that address contained in Volume 14, Number 1, of our *Office Review* and have noted some things that I take the liberty of quoting as follows:

". . . Col. Botts, once Grand Master of the Masonic Order in Texas, was once a partner of A. S. Richardson of the same rank, and the latter was once a partner of Judge E. A. Palmer (my grandfather on my mother's side), whose commission from Sam Houston I hold before me here, so I can claim to have been a 'Virginia cousin' to the firm even then."

". . . Capt. Baker - and his father before him - and later his son after him; my father learned to love the first two through his associations, and I to love the last two through mine."

". . . It is for the lawyer to so practice his vocation that the law and justice will ever walk hand in hand and it is for you other vocationalists, as clients, to see that your lawyer is aided in doing so whether it helps or hurts your cause."

Hutcheson died in Houston in 1966, but only after seeing his oldest grandson join the Firm, with the result that a Hutcheson has been a partner at the Firm continuously since 1921. He was survived by his wife Eleanor, his sons Palmer Hutcheson, Jr., Thad T. Hutcheson, Sr., and Edward C. Hutcheson.

Photograph taken by Miss Willie A. Rowell, secretary to Capt. James A. Baker, between 1910 and 1922 from the Firm's offices in the Commercial Bank Building. On the left is the First City National Bank after its expansion, the Fox Building at 27 Main Street (in which the Firm officed for many years), and the South Texas National Bank prior to its expansion.

W. ALVIS PARISH

He was known to his contemporaries as "Al" and to some of the younger lawyers as "Big Al," but no one who met Al Parish could ever forget him. The Texas Senate resolution adopted on February 2, 1959 best gives a summary of the career of Walter Alvis Parish:

WHEREAS, Almighty God, in his infinite wisdom and mercy, did on January 24, 1959, call to be with Him, Mr. W. Alvis Parish, leading Harris County lawyer and chairman of the board of the Houston Lighting & Power Company; and

WHEREAS, Mr. Parish was born in Huntsville, Texas, in 1887, attended Winchester Normal College in Winchester, Tennessee, Texas A&M College and the University of Texas, obtaining his law degree in 1910; and

WHEREAS, he was associated with Baker, Botts from 1910 through 1919; with Jones and Parish from 1919 through 1920, and with the then legal firm of Vinson, Elkins and Wood and later he rejoined Baker, Botts, which became known as Baker, Botts, Andrews and Parish; and

WHEREAS, in 1914, as a young lawyer, Mr. Parish was named counsel for the Houston Lighting & Power Company, became a director in 1917, a vice president in 1927, a member of the executive committee in 1935, president in 1953 and board chairman and chief executive officer in April of 1958, having had a major role in the success of the company; and

WHEREAS, Mr. Parish was a powerful influence in Houston's business development and its community life during the past fifty years; and

WHEREAS, Mr. Parish was a member of the Board of Governors of Rice Institute, a director of Southwestern Drug Corporation of Dallas and the Houston Terminal Warehouse and Cold Storage Company; and

WHEREAS, Mr. Parish was an elder in the

W. Alvis Parish, with the Firm 1910 - 1953.

First Presbyterian Church, a member of the American, Texas and Harris County Bar Associations and of Phi Delta Theta social fraternity, a member of the Houston, Houston Country, Petroleum, Ramada, Cork, International and Champion Golf Clubs and the Bankers Club of New York, Shreveport and Petroleum Clubs of Shreveport; and

WHEREAS, Mr. Parish is survived by his wife, Mrs. Beth Hoffman Parish; a son, Robert Underwood Parish of Houston, Texas; and two step-daughters, Mrs. June Hoffman Kangeiser of Topeka, Kansas, and Miss Barbara Hoffman of Houston, Texas; and

WHEREAS, it is the desire of the Senate to pay tribute to the memory of this fine public spirited citizen and outstanding businessman who had the mental capacity, the forcefulness and self-reliance that is given to few men and who contributed so much to his state and especially to the city of Houston; now, therefore, be it

RESOLVED, by the Senate of Texas, that we extend sincere sympathy to the family of Mr. Parish; that a copy of this Resolution be sent to each member of his family; that a page in today's *Journal* be devoted to his memory; and that when the Senate adjourns today, it do so in his memory.

There are many interesting facets of Parish's life. He was a nephew of Capt. Baker, but that was not a factor in his career at Baker Botts. It is not known why he left the Firm earlier in his career for a period and then returned. He surprised many by leaving again late in his career to accept a position with a client.

Parish was a tall, impressive individual who exuded power and tended to dominate all those with whom he came in contact. His decisions may not have always been correct, but they were made with conviction and usually carried the day. Even though he had left the Firm at one time as indicated, in his later years he had strong convictions regarding the Firm. He felt that one's first loyalty was to the Firm — not just eight hours a day, but in all his activities twenty-four hours a day.

For years, Parish was in charge of the Houston Lighting & Power financings. The closings took place in New York. Young lawyers who trained under him reported that Parish would engage a

The Houston Lighting & Power Company headquarters at San Jacinto and Capitol Streets decorated for Christmas in 1914. In 1909, there were ten workers officing on the first floor of the headquarters, including among them the President and a lawyer from Baker Botts.

suite of rooms in New York for a
month and act as perpetual host. All
those involved not only attended
breakfast in his suite but made themselves available at all times as he was the
stage manager for the month of activities. Parish considered Houston Lighting & Power his personal client, and
although he allowed young lawyers to
work for the company, he was jealous
of his relationship. More than one
senior partner felt his sting when they
became too close to top management.

The Firm had no departments in
his day, but since he handled corporate
financings, he selected and trained
John Mackin and Baine Kerr, who so ably headed
the Firm's corporate practice for many years.

Parish was 66 years of age when he became
President of HL&P and 71 when he was made
Chairman of the Board and CEO. In the HL&P
history, much of the book is devoted to the first
three presidents, Edwin B. Parker, Sam Bertron,
and Hiram O. Clarke. Parish was described in
that publication as "stern and unbending but also
generous and gregarious," as a free spender with
his personal income but a tough business man.
The HL&P history then states that, "Parish also
avoided such modern conveniences as typewriters
— every personal letter was handwritten — and
airplanes — he always travelled by train, engaging
a compartment so he could surround himself with
reading and writing materials." Finally, the
HL&P history recites that during a period of
much public discussion over rates, Parish had a
stock answer to critics he met in social situations.
"If you don't want your bill that high, just don't
turn on the switch." This was vintage Parish.

One Parish incident is worth reporting, but
one would have to see Parish explode to appreciate it. He had a limousine and a driver at the
Light Company. There was a noise in the glove

W. Alvis Parish in his office at Houston Lighting & Power Co.
He left the Firm in 1953 to become President of HL&P.

compartment door which bothered Parish, and he
ordered the driver to take it by the dealer immediately with him in the car. The mechanic reported
that he couldn't find the cause but said "Mr.
Parish, if you will just hold your hand on the
glove compartment door while you are in the car,
it won't happen." Parish's language can't be
repeated, but he had the driver take the car over to
a competitor and trade it in on a new limousine of
a different make. He never had trouble making up
his mind.

He was a showman and a teacher. One young
lawyer did some work for a corporate client and
asked Parish about billing. Parish asked the young
lawyer what fee he would suggest. The answer was
$2,500. Parish then called the client, with the
associate sitting in the office, described the service
and stated, "I want to do something I seldom do.
I want you to set the fee." The reply was $5,000.
The moral as far as Parish was concerned was that
there was an art to charging a fee as well as to
practicing law.

Parish had another side to him. He liked the
tough, blustery, bull-of-the-woods image, but he
had a soft side. He had a maiden aunt school
teacher who he felt might have financial needs in

90

the future. Although he was not a wealthy man and never tried to accumulate wealth, he set up a trust fund for the aunt, and only one person in the office was aware of it. He was so generous with his funds that often on December 31 he would take out loans in order to make substantial gifts to charities and repay the loan out of the following year's income.

On December 31, 1953, Parish recorded in his daily work record that he was leaving the office at 4:35 p.m. and left this message:

This is my final daily record of work with the Firm, generally, respectfully, admiringly, and, with me, affectionately known as the "Baker, Botts" Firm. With the history of the past, the hopes of the future, and the knowledge of the great men who have adorned and blessed our Firm in days gone by, I bid my partners and my associates farewell, a long, a last adieu as a member of the Firm and an active practicing member of the legal profession.

At the close of this day, December 31, 1953, I retire from the practice of the law, having practiced forty-three and one-third years. I feel that I am retiring while in full vigor of mind and body. A lawyer should be remembered by those with whom he has mingled professionally as he was in his prime - at his best. At the end of my professional career I have no cause to be vain, for the result of my hard work for a lifetime seems very small. It is difficult for one to realize that a lawyer could work so long and so faithfully as I have done and yet accomplish so little. I can say but little in my behalf, only this, that I have devoted my life to my profession and to my clients. If I have ever done an unprofessional act, I do not know it, and think I can safely say that I have at all times tried to hold high the standards of my profession - not by talk but by my conduct as a lawyer. I have never sought the so-called honors of this world, have never cared for them. I have always disliked notoriety. I have never been money-mad. I never thought myself a great man, never had a suspicion I could be one, and thus have saved myself much trouble and my friends, it may be, some annoyance. I confess, however, that I have at all times desired the respect and friendship of those of my profession who have known me well.

Although there is much drudgery in the general practice of the law, yet it is my judgment, formed from long experience and observation, that it is the noblest of all professions, more in it to develop a man who loves it and lives for it alone. While it demands greater sacrifices in order to succeed than any other, yet if one could have the good fortune, as have I, to be a part of the Baker, Botts Firm and spend his professional life in association with the high type of men who have constituted the Firm, I believe that if he were to live his life over again, he would choose to be a lawyer.

I am glad that I have practiced law in the times during which I have been a member of the legal profession. I have been blessed with health and strength during a practice of more than forty years and have had many opportunities, my share of them. I have had as much success as I have expected and fully as much as I have deserved. My professional career has been a pleasant one. My associations with members of Baker, Botts, and all others in the organization, from top to bottom, have been happy and at all times most enjoyable. I know of no better test of a man than his possession of the affection of those most intimate with him. I hope and pray I have the affection of each member of the organization. You have mine.

Richly cherished in my memory until my earthly time is spent will be Baker, Botts, and my association with the lawyers and others in its organization. God richly bless each of you and keep you well, strong and happy will be my constant prayer.

JAMES A. BAKER, JR.

James Addison Baker, Jr. is in the unenviable position of being the son of Capt. Baker, who was with the firm 64 years and a leader for most of that time, and the father of Secretary of State James A. Baker, III, who has made quite a name for himself in government service. Baker did not try to rival his father, and most of his son's success came after his death. Since Capt. Baker, the father of James A. Baker, Jr., was also really James A. Baker, Jr. but never used the title, the man we know as "Baker, Jr." was actually the third James A. Baker.

He was born in Houston on November 3, 1892 and died May 21, 1973. He graduated from Hill School and then Princeton University in 1915. He served overseas as a Captain in the 90th Infantry Division in World War I. The difficulties and even the injustice of being the son of a famous father is perhaps best illustrated by one simple fact: "Capt." Baker carried a lifetime title from his time as head of the Houston Light Guard while his son – a real captain – carried the name "Junior."

Baker joined the Firm as an associate on June 1, 1919. He became a partner on February 1, 1927. He tried cases successfully early on as did almost all new lawyers at that time, but, at Capt. Baker's request, developed an office practice and devoted a great deal of time to managing the family properties. For years, the Graham Realty Company (a Baker family company) owned the block bordered by Main, Clay, Travis, and Bell. There were numerous stores on the block and a large sign advising those wishing to rent to "call Mr. Baker at CA 4-9441" (the Firm's main number).

In college, Baker was quite athletic and was both intercollegiate wrestling champion and pole vault champion. He was an excellent tennis player and competed with much younger men until an injury in his mid-50s slowed his game. He then

James A. Baker, Jr., with the Firm 1919-1973.

took up golf and became a good golfer.

Baker was a modest man. He and his wife (Bonner Means) made their home at 1216 Bissonnet and never moved. Mrs. Baker lived there until the time of her death in April 1991 at the age of 96. The Bakers could have lived anywhere else in Houston had they chosen to do so.

In all the interviews of men who were young associates during his days as a partner, the universal description of Baker was that he was the kindest, most generous, and most thoughtful person they ever knew. The memories of one of the young lawyers who worked with him serves as a reminder of the powerful influence of the "personal touch" in creating a family atmosphere at Baker Botts:

Mr. Baker, Jr. was one of the kindest and most gracious people I have ever known in my life. He went out of his way, he and Mrs. Baker, to do nice things for the young lawyers in the Firm. Mr. Baker would invite the young lawyers to lunch on a frequent and regular basis, often down in the dining room at Texas National Bank. When there was a new baby, the Bakers always had a nice present, usually a piece of sterling for the baby. He loved to take young lawyers to the Rice football games. That was then in the new stadium. He would always take us to one of the country clubs for a meal before the game and hardly ever made the kickoff, especially with Mr. Baker's driving, which was notoriously poor. Mr. Baker had some of the thickest and most unusual eyeglasses I can remember and he must not have been able to see very well. He kept a number of us young lawyers busy handling his automobile wrecks. One time he collided with a car driven by a lady. He was very embarrassed. He got out and acknowledged that it was his fault and expressed his regret. He handed her his business card, and she looked at it and read it. Oh, are you related to Browne Baker? That made Mr. Baker feel good because that was his brother. He said oh yes, that's my brother. Do you know him well? She says, no, not very well. You see, he hit me last week. I liked to work with Mr. Baker. He was a wise tutor, mainly in the ways of how to get along with people, how to charge bills.

He brought his lunch to the office in a black lunch kit similar to those used by school children. One day he had an unexpected business luncheon and invited his secretary to eat his lunch. She was the only secretary to eat pheasant under glass that day.

This was still the time when much of the Firm's business came from the East Coast. On a number of occasions, business would be referred to the Firm by the Chairman of the Board of some large national corporation who remembered "Jim" from Princeton days.

James A. Baker, III remembers his father as a good family man, but a disciplinarian. [The Secretary of State was known in his youth as "Jimmy." Capt. Baker also reported that Col. Botts always called him "Jimmie" (Capt. Baker's spelling)]. Jimmy recalled being awakened on some slow mornings with a glass of cold water in his face. Baker, Jr. often worked on weekends and took Jimmy with him. Many years later, Jimmy recalled how he enjoyed that, and he still remembered where all the partners' offices were located in those days.

One of the great losses for the Firm (but possibly not for Jimmy's career) was that because of the anti-nepotism rule, the Firm could not consider hiring Jimmy because his father was still a partner. Yet this rule did not come into effect primarily because of the Bakers. By the 1920s, the hiring of close relatives of various partners was creating debilitating tensions within the Firm. The partners decided that such tensions were not compatible with the Firm's often stated commitment to hiring and promotion based solely on merit.

Among Baker's obligations, in looking after both the family and Firm business, was serving on the Texas National Bank Board. He had served on that Board (including its predecessor bank) 35 years when he was made Chairman in 1955.

As his father had been, Baker was a member of the First Presbyterian Church and was also a member of the Houston Club and the River Oaks and Houston Country Clubs. His son in Washington comes by his love of hunting naturally since Baker was an active member of the Eagle Lake Rod and Gun Club and once served as its President.

Baker died at age 80 in 1973 after having been inactive in the Firm for about six years. He was survived by his daughter, Bonner, his son, James A., III, his wife, Bonner, two sisters, Mrs. Alice Baker Jones and Mrs. Preston Moore (Ruth), and a brother, Malcolm.

JAMES L. SHEPHERD, JR.

James Leftwich Shepherd, Jr. was born on January 22, 1893 in Huntsville, Texas, a city that has sent many outstanding lawyers to Houston. He grew up in Colorado City, Texas. He attended the University of Texas and obtained his law degree in 1916. Shepherd showed his early versatility by tutoring Latin and working as a grocery clerk to pay his tuition.

He entered practice with his father in 1916 but the next year was tendered employment by Baker, Botts, Parker & Garwood. He became a partner in 1926 and continued until his death on October 8, 1964.

Shepherd developed an early interest in oil and gas law and was designated by the Firm to keep up with all developments in the field. He became an outstanding specialist in the fields of oil and gas, real estate, and water rights. He did not limit his practice to these fields but also carried on a general practice.

Shepherd loved people, enjoyed parties, and was a great storyteller. He became interested in Bar work early on and was a natural for it. He was President of the Houston Bar Association in 1945, the State Bar Association in 1946-47, Chairman of the Mineral Law Section of the American Bar Association in 1937, and Chairman of the House of Delegates of the ABA in 1957-59. He felt very strongly that Firm lawyers should take an active part in American Bar work and was instrumental in the Firm's developing a program to encourage attendance.

Shepherd was a tall, slender, distinguished looking gentleman who smoked cigarettes in a long holder and wore a soft felt hat. He was a favorite target of the associates in their New Year's Day skits because of his great sense of humor and the fact that he was so easy to identify in the skits. His popularity both among the associates and the partners cannot be overemphasized. He was one

James L. Shepherd, Jr., with the Firm 1917 - 1964.

of those rare people who could be strong without being controversial. Shepherd had great stature in the Firm, but never took advantage of his position by asserting himself except when he was consulted.

Shepherd was married to Marguerite Street in 1919. She lived until 1958. His second wife and widow, Helga Jacobsen Shepherd, survived him on his death in October 1964. The two children by the first marriage were James Leftwich, III and Cecelia Cambias.

One of his partners had this to say about Shepherd:

Jim's talents, achievements and contributions to the Firm and his profession were not limited to the field in which he gained outstanding nationwide recognition. His record and recognition at law school as a student and scholar (election to membership in Chancellors, Order of Coif and Phi Delta Phi Legal Fraternity) set the course for his intellectual interest in all fields of the law

The signing ceremony for Rice Institute's purchase of its interest in the Rincon Oil Field, December 18, 1942. Standing, left to right: A.S.Cleveland, Tom Martin Davis, C. A. Dwyer, Palmer Hutcheson, John Freeman, James E. Elkins, County Judge Roy Hofheinz, Alfred H.Fulbright, John Q. Weatherly, and Harry Hanszen. Seated: James L. Shepherd, Jr., Benjamin Botts Rice, and John T. Scott. This investment proved to be an important one for the Institute, laying the foundation for its endowment to vault to new heights.

Construction of the Sinclair Oil Company plant, east of Manchester, circa 1915. The Firm, employed initially by the Sinclair Companies in 1918, was counsel for the Sinclair Companies in Houston and the surrounding territory, which included Galveston, Portland, and Beaumont. In 1922, the Firm was given general authorization to make litigation settlements in an amount up to and not exceeding $350.00 in any case.

James L. Shepherd, Jr. He was president of the
Houston Bar Association and the State Bar of Texas and Chairman
of the House of Delegates of the American Bar Association.

during his years of practice. He followed in one of the finest traditions of the Firm, excellence in scholarship and in performance of the task at hand. In addition to the load he carried in his stewardship of the Oil Department of the Firm, he handled or supervised the handling of the affairs of many other clients in various types of businesses, such as the Bank of the Southwest and its predecessors, and financial, loan and investment clients of all descriptions, The Borden Company, various estates and trusts, matters in receivership and bankruptcy, clients whose affairs involved water rights, United Gas Corporation and the corporate, antitrust and fair trade problems of our clients generally. He became and was a lawyer's lawyer as well as a business lawyer of imagination and exceptionally practical achievements.

HOMER L. BRUCE

Homer Lindsey Bruce, like Wharton, was definitely one of the more colorful partners. Any time there is discussion of Firm personnel over the last forty years, there are sure to be some Homer Bruce stories. One young lawyer remembered him as follows:

> Mr. Bruce was eccentric, and at times he was irascible, but he could be very kind and charming. After North Texas he became a Rhodes scholar. The story that I've heard is that on the way to Oxford he stopped by Cambridge, Massachusetts and spoke to Dean Roscoe Pound of the Harvard Law School and took with him to England the first year books for Harvard Law School. A year later, he wrote Dean Pound and asked for the second year books. Then World War I broke out and Mr. Bruce was in the army in France. After the war, the story is that he went to the Harvard Law School, called on Dean Pound and said he was ready to take his first and second year exams and enter as a third year student. The story is that was arranged and he spent only one year at the Harvard Law School, whereupon he was graduated and he came to this Firm. A lot of us thought of Mr. Bruce as a tax lawyer but if you said that to him he would flare. He considered himself to be a lawyer and he didn't want to be limited in any way. In many ways he was a renaissance lawyer. He was a brilliant mathematician. He always had in his office a number of books on higher mathematics and 1 of those 2 calculators that the Firm had was kept in his office.

He was a brilliant lawyer. One of his tax partners prepared the following tribute shortly after Bruce's death.

> Homer Bruce's background of accomplishment when, in August 1920, he was employed by the Firm as an associate, foretold that he would ener-

Homer L. Bruce, with the Firm 1920 - 1979.

getically discharge his responsibilities, and augured for success in his endeavors. Homer in his way became a legend in and out of the Firm. More so than many, he remained a solitary figure within our group, but his membership in the Firm was priceless to him and he was ever alert to the maintenance of Firm inputs consistent with his regard for it. His ingenuity and prompt dispatch of their work impressed and attracted important clients.

The effect of the federal income tax laws as a modifier of business transactions led Homer to devote many of his best efforts to the mastery of that field of law. He argued causes involving federal income tax matters before the Supreme Court of the United States three times, and in two of those causes, Letulle v. Scofield, 308 U.S. 415 and Kirby Petroleum Co. v. Commissioner, 326 U.S. 599, principles were enunciated which became basic to the supportive law surrounding the statutes. His interest as a lawyer, however, was in devising means

Sugar Land sugar refinery and railroad yards, circa 1910. The Firm obtained the charter for Imperial Sugar Company in 1925. In 1929, Homer L. Bruce spearheaded the issuance of a convertible preferred stock for Imperial Sugar Company — blazing a new trail in corporate law. In 1988, Baker Botts was involved in the acquisition of Holly Sugar Corporation by Imperial Sugar Company.

to achieve the legitimate business aims of his clients, and he shunned limiting himself to any one field of legal endeavor. Some of his determination and ability as a legal generalist is reflected by his appearances in matters involving constitutional law before the Supreme Court of the United States in Group No. 1 Oil Corp. v. Bass, 283 U.S. 279 (1931) and Rickert Rice Milling Co. v. Fontenot, 297 U.S. 110, the latter having been with United States v. Butler, 297 U.S. 1, the companion cases which overturned the 1933 Agricultural Adjustment Act. In a matter involving realty easements, the decision of the Texas Supreme Court in Anderson v. Tall Timbers Corp., 378 S.W. 2d 16 (Tex., 1964) framed Homer's tenacity in the pursuit of a cause he championed.

The tenacity which spurred his brilliance occasionally poured over into a quixotic penchant for lost causes and projects. Many of us are familiar with the case of King v. Bruce, 201 S.W.2d 803 (Tex., 1947), but that case had its role in leading to the 1948 Texas constitutional amendment permitting the partition of community property. Many are unaware of Homer's impetus upon the work of Dean Griswold of Harvard Law School which led to the joint return and marital deduction amendments of the Revenue Act of 1948, and to repeal of the community property penalties imposed by the Revenue Act of 1942.

Homer had his human foibles. The corridors sometimes pulsated with electricity from his broodings. He was impatient with dullness, and he was not always charitable in his respect for opposing viewpoints. But an unfailing kindness stretched out from Homer to any of us who had troubles which were not entirely of our own making. For years he was one of the real lawyers within our Firm; other members of our organization constantly sought his assistance in unwinding the knotty problems of their clients' affairs. His work in the case of Calbert v. U.S., 281 F.2d 507, was a mighty pitch-in at a time when he was distraught from Clara's illness and death.

Beyond his work as a great and imaginative lawyer of his time, the objective facts we knew of Homer when he came with the Firm remained largely the ones we knew of when he died. To a background largely implanted through private tutoring from his mother and father (Dr. William H. Bruce, an early president of what is now North Texas State University, Denton, Texas), Homer added a distinguished scholastic career at the University of Texas (B.A. 1913, mathematics and classical studies majors) embellished by the award of athletic letters as a quarter-miler, membership in the Friars Society, the oldest and most highly respected service organization at the University, and selection as a Rhodes Scholar. At Oxford, his B.A. degree in 1915 was with honors in history and French. While pursuing those studies, his bicycling trips through Southern Europe with Harold Carmichael, later President of the University of Alabama, were among his happiest memories. In 1917 he returned to the United States to join the United States Expeditionary Forces, and in August consummated through marriage a long understanding he had with Clara Chrisman. As an artillery captain in France during World War I, he drafted an artillery manual that became a basic with the U.S. Army, and reputedly guided the trajectory triangulation work of the U.S. Forces in locating the German "Big Bertha" firing on Paris in 1918. Returning to Oxford after the Armistice in November, 1918, he completed his work for his M.A. degree there in 1919, and during the same period studied for, took entrance examinations upon, and was given credit for a substantial portion of the courses taught within the first two years of work at

Harvard Law School. Entering Harvard in the summer of 1919, he was graduated with an LL.B. from that Law School in the summer of 1920.

He came with our Firm immediately thereafter, was admitted into the partnership in 1929, and remained an able and true member of the Firm until his death. To his outside attainments he added membership in Who's Who in America, directorships on the boards of some of our most important clients, and a place of highest respect in the eyes of many outstanding lawyers and businessmen.

Bruce was survived by his wife, Dorothy Marie Blue Bruce, and two children from his marriage with Clara Chrisman, Homer Jr. and Caroline B. (Mrs. Vanderhoef). A third child, Robert, was reported missing in action in World War II.

99

BRADY COLE

Brady Cole and John Bullington by happenstance fell into an unusual grouping. They joined the Firm in the mid 1920s as associates when very few lawyers were being hired. They were younger than the strong senior group who arrived before 1920 and yet they were senior to the outstanding group in the class of 1929. This was in the days when someone had to give up some interest for a partner to acquire additional interest (or to become a partner in the first place), so advancing toward the senior level was a very slow process. It was as though a spotlight was thrown on these two men who were both extremely able and competitive by nature. Their methods of attaining success were so entirely different, as were their personalities, that their careers are a story within a story.

Brady Nixon Cole was born in Port Sullivan, Texas in 1901 and attended Hearne public schools and the University of Texas, graduating with highest honors from both schools. He grew up on a farm near Hearne and had to struggle financially all the way through school. Upon graduation with honors, he was not initially offered employment with the Firm but agreed to work without pay. He married a hometown girl, Ann Marshall, in 1934, and one obtains perspective on his early death 39 years ago by noting that all three of his wedding attendants, John Maginnis, John McCullough, and Albert Jones are still living. It also should be noted that Cole's dogged commitment to his profession led him to delay his marriage to his long-time fiancee until he had successfully negotiated the then tortuous twelve-year road to partnership in the Firm. He was short, inconspicuous in appearance, and gave the appearance of being quiet and shy. Serious health problems required him to use a cane the last several years of his life.

Rather than attempting to summarize his legal career, let us borrow from Mr. Andrews' tribute to him from the Oct. 29, 1953, *Office Review*:

Brady Cole, with the Firm 1923 - 1953.

It was a fortunate day for Brady Cole when he chanced to be assigned to work for Mr. Wharton, for out of that association came an affection of the older lawyer for the younger, and an interest in the latter, that gave Brady Cole his great opportunity. Mr. Wharton early perceived that ability and those traits of character which became conspicuous to the large number of able lawyers and business executives who came to know Brady in after years. He assumed almost a parental relationship to Brady. He took him to live in his home. About 5 years after meeting Brady, he suffered the devastating bereavement of losing his only son at the age of 17. Brady, thereafter, as much as it was humanly possible, came to take Frank's place in Mr. Wharton's affections.

He had Brady work with him in all his cases. The *Office Review*, Dec. 21, 1922 (Vol.2, p.400) records that Mr. Wharton had just been employed by The Texas Company "to cooperate with

Messrs. Gifford & Bull, special patent counsel for The Texas Company, and Mr. Dearborn of the staff of The Texas Company, in the appeal of the suit of Gray and The Texas Company vs. McAfee and The Gulf Oil Company." This suit is one into which the young man was brought. Mr. Wharton, in the summer of 1923, was engaged in defending the title of The Texas Company to 76-1/2 acres in the rich West Columbia field (The Texas Company vs. Davis, 113 Tex. 321. Decided June 30, 1923 and October 31, 1923). Brady assisted in this, also. It was through contacts such as these that Brady made his first acquaintance with officials of The Texas Company, an acquaintance which provided him, in the end, his greatest field of endeavor. Mr. Wharton was ever alert to see to it that Brady received the recognition and advancement in the Firm that his merits deserved, and it was he who, in 1934, proposed Brady for membership in the Firm to begin January 1, 1935.

The field of patent law seemed to call especially for the exercise of the talents he possessed. It called for almost endless technical research and investigation — research in widely separated domains of knowledge. The patent litigation for The Texas Company into which Mr. Wharton brought him was a challenge to him. Into it he threw himself with all of his tremendous energy, application, and ability. It is not surprising that, in the end, he came to be recognized as one of the few great patent lawyers of the country.

Much of his work was done away from Houston. He spent long stretches of time in New York and Chicago. The lawyers with whom he worked there were in a better position to speak of his true worth, ability, and accomplishments than his partners, even. One of these, with whom he was asso-

Texaco Building, Rusk at San Jacinto, Houston, circa 1965. A long-time client, The Texas Company moved its headquarters from Beaumont to Houston in 1908, establishing general offices in the Stewart Building. In 1914, construction was begun on this 13-story building, which is now used for storage.

ciated more than anyone else, was R. J. Dearborn, Chief Patent Counsel for The Texas Company. Mr. Dearborn speaks with first-hand knowledge and out of an abundance of opportunity to form a correct judgment. He made this statement:

Brady was the most careful and outstanding and effective lawyer I have ever worked with and while I worked in the role of supervisor for Texas in all these matters and while many eminent lawyers took part in this and that, Brady and I were together in all. We ate together, we slept in the same hotels, and we just were very close friends.

101

From George Haight, an eminent patent lawyer:

Brady was a great lawyer and a great all-around student; for instance, I never met one, even professors of history, who knew so thoroughly as did he, the history of Texas, of the Southwest, and of Mexico. Not only was he interested in history, but in many other fields of learning; and he had that facility which is said to be one that marks the educated - that is, he was always able to use his acquirements in a novel situation.

Among the warm friendships that resulted from The Texas Company association was the one between him and Capt. T. Rieber, then Chairman of the Board. If Brady had handled no other important matter than the controversy between Barber Asphalt Corporation and the Anglo-Saxon group of the Shell Oil interests, it alone would have been enough to entitle him to fame. A more complicated and confused situation than the one with which he was called on to deal could hardly be imagined. Barber, having obtained concessions in Venezuela for production of asphalt, extended its operations to include oil. Seeking to obtain assistance in the way of capital contributions, it entered into contracts with members of the Shell Group. Controversies subsequently arose. Vast amounts of money were involved. Litigation resulted. The suit filed by Barber in England and carried to the House of Lords ended in a defeat for Barber.

By this time (1945) the Guggenheims, the principal owners of Barber, prevailed on Capt. Rieber, former Chairman of the Board of The Texas Company, to take over the management. Capt. Rieber, having seen the work done by Mr. Cole, immediately sought his services. The story of all of this is recounted in Vol. 27, p. 88, of the *Office Review.* Two trips to Venezuela, one to the Island of Trinidad, and one to London, much conferring with learned Venezuelan lawyers, much research into the law of that country, much negotiating in London, ended in a settlement highly

satisfactory to Barber and in the payment to Mr. Cole, in the winter of 1946-47, of the largest fee the firm ever collected.

One other of such friendships must be mentioned, even at the expense of unduly protracting this narrative, for it, too, brings in review one of Brady's most notable achievements. When the Government, during World War II, decided to do the unheard-of thing of building a 24" pipeline from the Texas oil fields to the Atlantic seaboard to check the ravages of the German U-boats, there was organized the War Emergency Pipelines, Inc., made up of eleven major oil companies. For the unusual legal problems that would be encountered in such a novel undertaking, a lawyer of unusual capability was required. Col. Harry T. Klein, then General Counsel for The Texas Company, knew of such a lawyer in the person of Brady Cole. Brady was made Associate General Counsel of the Agency, having charge primarily of the legal matters relating to the construction and operation of the system. He was welcomed into this work by Burt L. Hull, then President of The Texas Pipeline Company, who was put in charge of the construction of the enterprise. Brady's contribution to the remarkable feat of building this pipeline as an instrumentality in aid of the successful waging of the war stands as a signal instance of patriotic service.

Brady had an abiding interest in Mexico and Mexican affairs. One of his last pieces of business was to negotiate an agreement for the purchase of one of the largest bakeries in Mexico City by his client, the National Biscuit Company, this being so recent that the work by him was completed just before he left on his vacation last August. But back of that lay many trips to Mexico in recent years, a wide circle of acquaintances and friends there, great interest in our Mexico City office and participation in its affairs. Indeed, it was he who selected the offices there and negotiated the lease for them — offices which we have always regarded as being quite attractive.

We now come to the sad chapter of our narrative. Brady fell a victim of a strange and extraordinarily virulent germ following a nervous breakdown in the fall and winter of 1947. In January he was taken to New York City to enter Harkness Pavilion of the Presbyterian Medical Center. His condition there became exceedingly grave. He rallied, however, and was able to leave the hospital in May. This illness may have been traceable to over-exertion on his part in the long trial of one of The Texas Company cracking cases in Chicago which lasted from mid-April to mid-October. From this illness he never entirely recovered and always thereafter carried a cane.

He kept up his furious drive, nevertheless, doing thereafter some of his most important work, the reorganization of the Matador eight-hundred-thousand-acre ranch being one of the most impor-

tant. His acquisition of the Famosa bakery in Mexico City, occurring during this period, has already been mentioned, and the very last was the settlement of an estate in Houston, the results achieved in which were such as to cause one of his partners to write, "The accomplishment of the foregoing results will in my opinion be a lasting tribute to Mr. Cole's genius and perseverance."

Cole was admitted to the firm of Baker, Botts, Andrews & Parish, January 1, 1935; died September 21, 1953, and was survived by his wife and three sons, Brady Marshall Cole, 17; Richard Rosser Cole, 14; Clarence Wharton Cole, 11; one sister, Mrs. Walton Carter, and one brother, Fred L. Cole.

In 1919, the National Biscuit Company took out a permit to do business in Texas. Baker Botts handled the general corporate work for Nabisco, including various filings with the Secretary of State of Texas. The Firm assisted in the acquisition of Block 113 of Houston in 1924 for the construction of a National Biscuit Company plant, and was involved in a similar acquisition for Nabisco in 1946. The plant shown in this 1921 photograph still stands at the corner of Ruiz and Crawford, Houston.

JOHN P. BULLINGTON

If Cole can be seen as the epitome of the bright young lawyer driven to become a success, John Perry Bullington can perhaps best be understood as "the natural," a man seemingly destined for greatness as a lawyer. He was born in 1899 in Palisade, Colorado, the son of Dr. Stephen Davis Bullington and Maude Gilliland Bullington. He attended Morgan Park Military Academy in Chicago, was graduated from the University of Texas in 1925, Yale Law School in 1927, and studied one year at the University of Paris. The word patrician had not been invented in Texas in that day, but compared to Cole's background, such an adjective might be appropriate. In addition, he was a giant of a man physically with a dominant personality and a very quick mind. There is almost a consensus among his contemporaries that if the word genius could be applied to any partner, it would be Bullington.

One of his partners described Bullington with these words, "His outstanding characteristic was determination to succeed in everything he undertook. This was aided by a fine intellect, a capacity for work, an eager curiosity concerning all fields and branches of law, the ability to read and comprehend with great rapidity, and the determination to solve a problem no matter how difficult." One of the Firm "briefers" of that day stated that he hated to brief for Bullington because if he told you to find a case, it was useless, because if there were such a case he would already know about it. At the time he became a partner, only Capt. Baker had spent fewer years as an associate before being admitted. Bullington, like Bruce, handled numerous cases before the U.S. Supreme Court. (One of the letters of condolence when he died was from the Clerk of the Supreme Court who knew him well.) He and Feagin testified extensively at U.S. Congressional hearings. In one brief, in refuting the idea that holding companies were of U.S. ori-

John P. Bullington, with the Firm 1927 - 1948.

gin, Bullington presented evidence that the first holding company was created by Cato, 100 years before Christ was born. His versatility also resulted in his heading two different sections of the American Bar Association. Bullington took an active part in community affairs. In addition to being extremely active in bar work, he served as President of both The Museum of Fine Arts and the Houston Country Club. He also participated in Firm management, especially recruiting. He originated the idea of employing at least two outstanding law graduates each year, and Parish stated that Bullington participated in the hiring of every lawyer from 1932 to 1948. (He did not become a partner until 1935.) He was instrumental in broadening the Firm recruiting program to the national level.

In those days, the Southern Pacific Railroad had its choice of Baker Botts partners to serve as its General Counsel. When Jules Tallichet died in

The Museum of Fine Arts, Main and Bissonet, Houston, 1924. John P. Bullington was later president of the Museum.

1937, Bullington was chosen, but he did not restrict himself to that work. He was the first partner to serve on the Board of Schlumberger. His ability to read and speak French fluently served him well in this respect. He contributed articles to many publications, especially in the field of international law, was the American representative to the Inter-American Bar Association, and was a member of the Council of Maritime Law Association of the U.S. As an indication of his tremendous energy and curiosity, it was said that he took up photography, bought all the equipment, and in a matter of weeks was at the professional level in ability.

Bullington had been blessed with ample gifts, and he was driven to make the best use of his talents. By all accounts, he worked and played hard. His partners assumed that he was the coming "star" of his generation. Then he died suddenly in New Orleans in 1948 at the age of 48 after trying a lawsuit in the Fifth Circuit. For decades after, his contemporaries recalled the powerful image of this giant bundle of energy and intelligence — often ending with a sad shake of the head while contemplating what Bullington might have done in the twenty or so years "stolen" from him by his early death.

He was survived by his wife, Frankie Maude Carroll Bullington (sister of Mrs. Dillon Anderson), a daughter, Kate, and a son, John.

If one looks for consolation in the deaths of these two brilliant men, Bullington at 48 and Cole at 52, it could be that they accomplished far more in their short life span than most people ever accomplish in a full career.

H. MALCOLM LOVETT

Henry Malcolm Lovett came to Baker Botts as a contemporary of Cole and Bullington. His years of association with the Firm now exceed those of Jesse Andrews (62 years) and even Capt. Baker (64 years), the previous record holders. He was employed July 11, 1924 and celebrated his 67th year on July 11, 1991. Lovett has met or served with every partner of the Firm except the first three.

Lovett was born January 8, 1902 in Princeton, New Jersey, the son of Edgar Odell Lovett, who later became the first president of Rice Institute. He moved to Houston at age seven and attended both public and private schools in Houston, graduating from Rice at the age of 19 in 1921 and Harvard Law School in 1924.

His first job between Rice and Harvard was with Texas Commercial National Bank. The President of the Bank told him that he hated to start him on the lowest rung since he was a college graduate and that he would put him on the second level. His salary was $40 a month.

Lovett's employment letter is so amusing that it has been read at Firm meetings. It is not generally known that it was also published in the July 15, 1924 issue of the *Office Review*. To understand how difficult it was to obtain employment with the Firm in those days, one must realize that Lovett had the inside track. Not only was he a Harvard Law graduate with excellent credentials, but his father was a close friend of Capt. Baker, and Rice Institute was a major client. The *Office Review* item written by the Managing Partner, Ralph Feagin, is quoted in its entirety:

The following letter from the Firm to Malcolm Lovett, who had just been graduated from the Harvard Law School, will be found self-explanatory. It embodies the arrangement made for the temporary employment of Mr. Lovett:

This confirms arrangements made by Mr. Feagin

H. Malcolm Lovett, with the Firm since 1924.

with you this forenoon, as follows:

1. We do not feel justified at this time in taking another lawyer into our Organization nor do we have any reason to contemplate the addition of another man at any time in the near future. Consequently, we cannot offer you permanent employment nor can we hold out any hope of permanent employment at a later date.

2. It so happens, however, that Miss Connerly, our Librarian, vacated her position a few weeks ago and the position is still vacant. It is our plan to fill the position at some time in the early future by the employment of another young lady law graduate. In the meantime and pending the employment of someone to fill the place permanently, you are to come into our office and discharge the duties of Librarian as outlined in our Plan of Organization. You will, of course, do such other and different work as may be assigned to you from time to time. The employment is temporary. You would not care to remain in the position indefinitely nor would we care to have you remain. When the place is filled permanently, unless our position has changed, we will have no other employment to offer you.

We welcome you into the Organization and are sorry that the arrangement cannot be more permanent and more attractive; however, it is our desire to be of assistance to you in beginning your career and we believe you will find this work interesting and profitable for a time.

It is expected that each member of the Organization will go out of his way to assist Mr. Lovett in getting started and in discharging the duties which he has assumed.

Lovett was a trial lawyer from 1924 to 1929 (as were practically all beginning lawyers in those days) and then became a corporate and wills, trusts, and estates lawyer. He worked on financings for Houston Lighting & Power and United Gas under Parish, among others. In the 1940s, Lovett was doing so much work on gas sales contracts for Pan American Production Co. that he became an expert. It was because of his experience in this field that he began doing work for Tennessee Gas Transmission (now Tenneco).

Tenneco became a client when it was spun off from Chicago Corp., and Stone & Webster was the underwriter. Not only was Stone & Webster a client of the Firm, but the man in charge in the home office was from Fort Worth and knew Frank Coates. Lovett, however, developed a close relationship with the company's former and long-time CEO, Gardiner Symonds. Lovett went on the Tenneco Board at age 57 and remained until he became director emeritus at age 70.

Among Lovett's other clients were Texas National Bank of Commerce (Director), Southwestern Drug Corp., Browning Ferris Machinery Co., and Karl Hasselman interests (we still represent the heirs in connection with a gas field in Germany).

Among Lovett's most active civic interests were Rice University where he served as Chairman of the Board of Governors, The DePelchin Faith Home (which he headed for many years), and the Children's Bureau Association of Houston.

Lovett played the part of his father in a recent theatre production, "The Trust," which is the story of the William Marsh Rice murder. He appeared by video to open the production.

Lovett's wife, Martha, died in 1991. He has four children: Eliza Randall, Mary Hale McLean, H. Malcolm Lovett, Jr., and Edgar Odell Lovett, II.

Long-time client Tenneco did not limit its efforts to gas transmission, but branched out into retail service stations, oil and gas exploration and production, real estate, and later shipbuilding, and farm machinery. Tenneco signed a regular retainer with the Firm in 1946. H.Malcolm Lovett was a member of the Board of Tenneco and is currently an emeritus director. This photograph of a Tenneco service station was taken during the early 1960s.

Houston struck the national consciousness in 1928 by hosting the Democratic National Convention in the Convention Hall, constructed entirely of wood on the site of the present-day Coliseum, Bagby at Walker.

Downtown Houston, circa 1928. In the foreground is Union Station. At the upper rear, the Convention Hall is under construction. The Esperson Building has been completed, but the Gulf Building has not yet risen.

CHAPTER

4

The Niels Esperson Building at the corner of Travis and Rusk dominated the Houston skyline for many years. Baker Botts moved into the building when it opened in 1927 and remained there until One Shell Plaza opened in 1971.

THE DEPRESSION AND THE WAR YEARS:
1929 - WORLD WAR II

THE CLASS OF 1929

The 1920s closed with a flurry of hiring at Baker Botts. In little more than a year in 1929-30, eight new lawyers entered the Firm. Two came as partners, the rest as associates. Four of this cluster – Gaius Gannon, Frank Coates, Tom Davis, and Tom Scurry — came to Houston as a result of a momentous recruiting spree into the Dallas-Fort Worth area by Walter Walne. Their arrival marked a departure in the Firm's traditional practice of staying close to home to recruit established lawyers. The remaining included three top graduates from the University of Texas and the second recruit from Yale University, Dillon Anderson, John Bullington being the first.

The class of 1929 ran head-on into the Great Crash of the same year. As the regional and national economies sputtered, Baker Botts found less need to hire new lawyers in the 1930s. Indeed, only six laywers who would become partners came to the Firm from 1931 to 1940.

Yet the Firm was hardly stagnant in the depression decade. Houston recovered more rapidly than most regions. In addition, the vast regulatory changes of the New Deal opened new opportunities for Baker Botts in utility law, oil and gas, labor, and a variety of other areas.

The Firm was very fortunate in having Ralph Feagin return from his Electric Bond & Share assignment on June 1, 1933. He had worked for a large public utility holding company and was an expert in this field of law when the breakup of the utility holding companies came. The legislation may not have been popular in Texas, but it gave the legal business a substantial boost. Ultimately, New Deal legislation provided the impetus for the reorganization of two long-term clients, HL&P and United Gas. Baker Botts took a leading role in these reorganizations and as a result became lead attorneys for two newly created independent companies instead of local counsel for the national holding companies that had owned these "local" concerns before the changes required by the new regulations of the 1930s.

Hiram Garwood died in May 1930, so in a period of four years, the Firm lost two of its most illustrious partners —Parker and Garwood. In 1931, the name was changed to Baker, Botts, Andrews & Wharton, a name it would carry for the next 15 years. Although these were trying years, not a single lawyer was terminated during the great depression.

The 1930 City Directory lists these addresses:

- Jesse Andrews - No. 6 Jansen Place - Kansas City, Mo.
- Homer L. Bruce - 5118 La Branch
- Clarence L. Carter - 1506 South Blvd.
- James A. Baker, Jr. - 1216 Bissonnet
- Francis G. Coates - 1205 Barkdull

- Gaius G. Gannon - 2151 Troon Road
- Palmer Hutcheson - 1405 North Blvd.
- H. Malcolm Lovett - 2022 Bissonnet
- W. Alvis Parish - 3918 Mt. Vernon
- John T. Maginnis - 1405 McGowen
- James L. Shepherd, Jr. - 2106 Brentwood
- Jules H. Tallichet - 25 Courtland Place
- Walter H. Walne - 1405 South Blvd.
- Brady Cole - 205 Webster
- John P. Bullington - 16 Courtland Place
- Miss Willie A. Rowell - name now in all caps like the lawyers and a new title - "Office Manager." Lives in Garden Villas.

It is obvious that two new real estate developments had been created in the previous decade. River Oaks was now open, and the Baker family group had developed Broadacres, the North and South Boulevard area.

One glimpse of life in Houston in these years is provided by the remembrances of John McCullough:

I arrived in Houston, as I remember, on October 29, 1929 which I think may have been the day called Black Friday on Wall Street. I remember that at that time several lawyers, all of whom were unmarried at that time, were living at a rooming house at an address of a large frame house called 500 Westmoreland Street, which is right at the south end of Louisiana Street. The place where that rooming house was located is now occupied by part of the right-of-way of the Southwest Freeway. Among the residents who were there at the time I arrived were Tom Davis and Bill Ryan. . . . Another Baker, Botts man who resided there and whom I met for the first time was Dillon Anderson. At that time, streetcars were still operating in Houston and the streetcars went around a loop from downtown, out beyond, farther south than our rooming house there, and came back right by the side of that rooming house so that we could just come out the front door and catch the streetcar and come right down Louisiana and Travis Street and go in front of the then-office of Baker, Botts firm on Travis, in the Niels Esperson Building. At that time we represented the streetcar company and got free passes on the streetcar, so we thought that transportation was fine. One of the gentlemen who later turned out to be one of the most wealthy in Houston. . . rode the streetcar and had an office in the Esperson Building. That is Mr. Bob Welch, who later formed the Welch Foundation.

In 1938, the firm occupied all of the 16th floor in the Niels Esperson Building and began to expand to the 17th. The two floors were connected by a spiral

Like other land developments, River Oaks had to be sold, so its developers maintained the Country Club Estates Building downtown on Fannin as a sales office.

NEW MEMBERS, 1929 - 1930

Name	Birth-Death	Law School	Years with Firm	Partner Date	Specialty
Gaius G. Gannon	1897-1957	U. Texas	1929-1944	1929	trial
Francis G. Coates	1893-1971	U. Texas	1929-1971	1929	utilities
Tom Martin Davis	1905-	U. Texas	1929-	1940	railroads
William M. Ryan	1905-1946	U. Texas	1929-1946	1940	trial
Dillon Anderson	1906-1974	Yale U.	1929-1974	1940	trial
John T. McCullough	1906-	U. Texas	1929-	1944	general
Tom Scurry	1898-1944	U. Texas	1930-1944	1933	trial, oil & gas
John T. Maginnis	1906-	U. Texas	1930-	1948	corporate, utilities

NEW MEMBERS, 1931 - 1939

Name	Birth-Death	Law School	Years with Firm	Partner Date	Specialty
Joseph C. Hutcheson, III	1907-	U. Texas	1931-	1945	trial
Denman Moody	1909-	U. Texas	1935-	1948	trial
William R. Brown	1915-1983	U. Texas	1937-1983	1950	trial, HL&P
Hugh M. Patterson	1909-1983	U. Texas	1938-1983	1950	labor, legislative
Garrett R. Tucker	1915-	Yale U.	1939-	1949	patent
Thomas M. Phillips	1916-1991	U. Texas	1939-1991	1950	trial

stairway. The large partner offices (sometimes known as "Battleship Row") were spread along the Travis Street side. Beginning with Capt. Baker's large corner office at Travis and Rusk and moving south, we find Parish, Feagin (with an adjoining office for Raymond Neilson, his assistant), and then a large lobby space which contained the glass enclosed office of Miss Rowell, the office manager, who had a view of the lobby, the receptionist, and the two telephone operators. Beyond the lobby were Baker, Jr. and Coates. The other wing of the office ran west from Capt. Baker's office down Rusk St. with the Library occupying much of the space at the end of the hall. Lawyer offices occupied only one side of the hall until one got past the File Room and Accounting, which occupied the interior space, but lawyer offices opened into the Library from both sides of the building. The Firm occupied this building for 44 years (1927-1971) and the connected companion building, Mellie Esperson, from its completion to 1971. The physical layout of the Niels Esperson Building remained the same even after the Mellie Esperson Building was finished.

C. H. Wilson was the Accounting Department and his assistant, Jessie Bridgwater, was the Billing Department. Next to Accounting was the File Room with a unique arrangement. A partition that separated the two did not go all the way to the ceiling so that Accounting and File personnel could yell back and forth without seeing one another or using the phone. This created some amusing situations when a lawyer entered the accounting section and heard Jessie Bridgwater talking in a very loud voice with no one else in the room.

A sense of life at the Firm in these years comes from an interview with an associate who was with the Firm during the 1940s:

Mr. Ralph Feagin was really a tough managing partner. I remember one morning, I was in the men's room about 7:00, and I was washing my hands. I wasn't making any money at the time and I had a tie on that was frazzled. He said, "Wait just a minute." So he goes in his office which is right across from the men's room comes back and he's got a straight razor. He lifts up my tie and cuts off that frazzled part. He wouldn't give me any raise to get me a new tie.

Interviewer: Or even give you a tie.

Associate: No, wouldn't give me a tie, but he very neatly cut it off with his straight razor as we were alone there at 7:00 in the morning. I'm glad that he didn't cut my throat.

The File Room was manned by attractive young ladies – some were Phi Beta Kappa graduates of Rice drawing $80 a month. One was a model, another married the President of Mission Mfg. Co., and the husband of a third later headed Champion Paper Co. in Houston.

There was no air conditioning at that time, but there were ceiling fans, and paperweights were essential for all desks. The preferred location was on the south or southeast side of the building for the prevailing breeze.

For any reader too young to know what the lifestyle was in those days, even for partners in the Firm, life was fairly simple. They owned nice homes and had hired help. In the 1920s, cooks were important. Bruce reported that when he made $200 a month, had two suits, and rode the street car to work, he had a cook. Many members of the Firm apparently observed the custom of Sunday afternoon "calls" at the homes of their colleagues, and the Firm held regular get-togethers, some for business and some for social reasons, with lawyers expected to attend. By the 1930s, everyone had a car, but there was no air conditioning, no television, and air travel was primitive. One went to the Bay, the Gulf, or rode around in a car. The wealthy had homes on the Bay, and the typical summer vacation for the well-to-do was to send the wife and children to the Hill Country in Texas or to Colorado for much of the summer and to join them for a few weeks. Going to Europe was almost unheard of because it involved a train ride to New York and a slow round trip by water to Europe. As far as we know, the only early partners to get to Europe other than Peter Gray were those who served in World War I. Capt. Baker did have a summer home at Bass Rocks, Massachusetts, which he used for both business and pleasure.

For the younger folks, this was the era of the big dance bands both before, during, and, briefly, after the war. Bandleaders were at least as well known then as major sports figures today. Galveston was "wide open," and the Balinese Room on the pier at Galveston was known to every Houstonian.

The interview of Thad T. Hutcheson, Sr. is of special interest for a number of reasons (he was interviewed in 1985 when he was terminally ill; he is no longer living). First, some information about Hutcheson:

1. He was the son of Palmer Hutcheson, one of our leading senior partners, and was born in 1916. He was aware of some of the Firm's activities in the 1920s and even visited in the Firm offices before they were moved in 1927.

2. He was one of the early victims of the Firm anti-nepotism rule, and, as a matter of fact, his father withdrew from the Firm in 1945 in order to practice with him and his brother in the firm of Hutcheson, Taliaferro & Hutcheson (later, Hutcheson & Grundy). He mixed with the partners socially and dated Capt. Baker's granddaughter, who lived with Capt. and Mrs. Baker.

3. He practiced law with the Fulbright firm at one time and came from a family of eminent lawyers.

4. His son, Thad T. Hutcheson, Jr., came to the firm in 1966 and is currently a senior partner.

His comments follow concerning Baker Botts and various lawyers in these years:

Well, quite a colony from Houston developed at Bass Rocks, Gloucester, Massachusetts. And of course, the man that I think of as one we might call the patron saint of Baker & Botts, Capt. James A. Baker, had a place up there, he and Mrs. Baker. I had the honor and pleasure of visiting them there many times with my father and mother and my brothers, Palmer Jr. and Edward. My family went up there each summer. I don't really know how it came about, but I'm sure one of the drawing cards was a man of the stature of Capt. Baker and the charm of Mrs. Baker and their beautiful home (called "Rockhaven") which I can still visualize. As I grew up—(I'm understanding what I should do is sort of narrate my own experiences or contacts as I can remember them with Baker & Botts)—I'm now talking about the period in largely the 1920s to the mid 1930s. I was very much aware of the role of the Firm in my family's life. I think the thing I remember most vividly was the extremely strong tradition of the lawyers attending Firm meetings, which, as I recall them, were weekly on a Thursday night or some specific night each week. I'm sure I saw in my household what was undoubtedly repeated in many lawyers' households for Baker & Botts; and it's typical of what goes on now, trying to adjust your home and social scene to the obligations that you feel and many times proudly feel to your firm. I remember my mother and father discussing when some event appeared to conflict with Firm meetings, that was one of the discussions that my father usually won because his trump card used to be to say, "But Eleanor, you know Capt. Baker expects us to turn out for regular Firm meetings unless we have a very important reason not to do so." I might digress to talk about Capt. Baker.

Well, as I've already indicated, he was one of my heroes for many reasons, and I know he was to many people. I was aware, though it's hard now to distinguish between how much of it I realized at the time and how much I've learned through the years, that my father enjoyed a particularly personal relationship with him. He handled some matters for Capt. Baker that were personal to him. And of course, he had the greatest respect and admiration for Capt. Baker, and all of the younger people were very fond of him. I might refer to a personal side, and I along with many other young men in Houston—(as we seemed to have dates more frequently than they do now)—many of us were in strong "pursuit" of his lovely granddaughter, Alice Baker Jones, who lived with him for a period of time. Mrs. Jones and Alice lived with Capt. Baker at "The Oaks." And it was a very strong tradition among the young men in my group that if we hoped to make any progress toward obtaining approval of that young lady, in fact if we wanted to be welcome to come by and take her out on a date, we had better be sure to comply with the "instructions" of Capt. Baker and Mrs. Baker in every way! But he was a gentle, cordial and friendly person, and it was always a pleasure to see him when we went by on social occasions there. And he was wonderful to talk to. He could talk to younger people very easily, but always with a grandiose manner that made you know you were talking to a most unusual leader and distinguished gentleman.

His home, "The Oaks," was an entire compound, really, beautiful trees and a beautiful home with a circular driveway. You drove up under the porte-cochere there and that was where you first came under the scrutiny of Capt. Baker. He would

often answer the door when you came by. Now I always understood, though of course I never attended them, that the Firm meetings were held in the basement of "The Oaks" in a room that he had arranged for that purpose. Incidentally, I understand that "The Oaks" was later given to Rice Institute, and then passed on to the M. D. Anderson Cancer project, being the site of some of the earliest cancer research efforts in Houston. The Firm meetings I'm referring to and know of as a youngster were generally held at Capt. Baker's house. Then too, I saw more of Capt. Baker when I had the privilege of working . . . doing what we call . . . it was a clerking job, for my father in Baker Botts in the two summers when I was in law school, in 1938 and 1939.

Of course, there are other members of the Firm, I might mention, that I remember both as a youngster and then a little bit through that work up here. A grand gentleman, Judge Jesse Andrews, he was just another noble character, a gentle, strong, wise person, and he, I'm sure, largely because of his deep friendship with my father, was always extremely gracious to me and always had time to visit with me and talk with me. He had a wonderful manner about him in addition to great ability. I knew Mr. Ralph Feagin very well and Mrs. Feagin again through my father and mother. He was about the same, maybe you'd call it vintage of my father, or position in the firm. I also recall Mr. Henri Tallichet, one of the most congenial and cheerful lawyers I ever knew. Then there was Mr. Walter Walne, Sr. His home was back of my parents' home, or ours was back of theirs over on North and South Boulevard. There was a very definite family quality about the firm. I suppose it might be appropriate to continue talking about other lawyers that I knew. I remember Mr. Clarence Wharton, a character in many ways, a brilliant lawyer with "bulldog tenacity" - also a writer and authority on Texas history. I do remember, I guess I remember it as a Baker & Botts "offspring," when there was a little bit of a what I'd call a flurry that I could sense around the home. My father didn't talk to me directly about firm business, but it was when as I remember the Dallas lawyers came in . . . I'm thinking of Mr. Frank Coates, Tom Scurry, and Mr. Gaius Gannon. The profession has gotten so ambulatory now that moving around doesn't create too much of a sensation, and it wasn't a sensation, but it was an interesting new thing that they brought in a definite group, as I later gathered, to fill a particular gap that they felt they had. I think Mr. Walne was very much involved in bringing them here. Of course, I knew Mr. Jim Baker, Jr. and knew him all of his life as a dear friend of my family. He was with the firm then and, of course, during all those periods of time that I had any contact with it, up to his death. And then John Bullington was a particularly strong character that I had contact with and I've sort of unintentionally passed by Mr. Jim Shepherd who, of course, we viewed as a strong business-getter, what they would call a "rainmaker," as I understand in the language of firms now. He enjoyed bar association activities and was quite a friend and companion of a lot of the younger lawyers when they'd go to social activities and things of that nature, particularly connected with the bar association. So I knew him quite well and all these men I've mentioned, when I later came to practice in Houston, were extremely gracious, and people with whom I occasionally had professional contact and certainly many personal contacts. John Bullington, I recognized in sort of historic perspective, as a symbol of a break from the older partners' group to the younger partners' age, as it seemed to me. He was quite a leader in that area. He was active as I saw it in their . . . we didn't call it recruiting then because most of us were looking for jobs when we got out . . . but he seemed to be instrumental in much of the hiring. At least he was when I got out of school. And he and his wife Maudie were people that sort of

"bridged the age gap."

I went to the University of Texas Law School. I loved it and the law and worked hard at it and came out reasonably successfully, having worked on the Law Review and so on. And one of the nicest things, and one of the things that helped sharpen my appetite for the law was the willingness of this Firm, Baker Botts, to let me work with my father in the summers as a clerk while I was in law school. And I had my first introduction there to the difference between the purely academic approach to law and what a law firm and the practice of law really involved. It added greatly to my enthusiasm, and I like to think it helped me do a little better. I did most of my work in the library. The other young men in Baker Botts, young lawyers, were very cordial to me and took me to lunch and talked to me about practical problems and so on.

Concerning the Anti-Nepotism Rule
My brother Palmer, who was always very close to me . . . he was just two years ahead of me . . . had gone on to law school; and I knew that my father, like I guess many fathers, particularly lawyer fathers, wanted one or more of his sons to practice law; and I know he hoped that some day he could practice with them. But while we were in college, as best as I know . . . I don't know anything strictly private . . . I think that was when Baker Botts crystallized its rule that is rather harshly referred to as the anti-nepotism rule; and at least it was an informal practice. And I pretty well felt that it would turn out as it did, that they could not consider sons after about 1936 or 1937 or thereabout.

I guess I'll step back a minute to carry on my career as you requested. When I got out of law school, well, this is the first time I've ever said it on the record . . . there was only one place, in my opinion, a lawyer wanted to go when he graduated from Texas Law School and that was to hope to get an invitation from Baker & Botts. I say there was only one place, it was the place they would generally prefer. It had the prestige and the general reputation of getting the best one or two men out of the senior law class at the University of Texas and seemed to make a point of doing it. And, I hope I'm not treading on any confidentialities, but that's when I learned exactly what was happening, because in spring of my senior year at law school, John Bullington called me and asked me to have lunch with him up in Austin. He said he was coming up to talk about hiring out of my class. Among other things, one of the great prides I had, and I'm sure it meant something to my father, I happened to win in my senior year the Baker Botts prize for the best law review comment . . . and I think that had come about the time of John Bullington's call to me. In any event, it was a check for $75, and I deeply appreciated it and the significance of it. He said that they had gone over my class and that I was the person they would normally pick out of the class, but he said "of course, we can't do that, because you're your father's son." And I said, "Well, John, you tell that to my Dad, instead of me." I also said, "Frankly I've known that's the way it was going to be." So he said, "Now we want to know who you'd recommend." So in a way that was a great compliment and I've tried to view it that way over the years. I've been kidded a little bit about it from time to time, but tried to think of it in proper perspective. But I think that of the large firms, for instance, Baker Botts has a tradition in a way that is recognized. I think they are envied and admired by many of their friendly competitors and should be, and I know I've always been proud to be related in any way.

Concerning the Firm
But I think, on differences between firms, I think that Baker Botts never had to grow in a great surge or by leaps or bounds, like some of the other firms that decided they wanted to become big firms. I

just never have felt Baker Botts ever suffered from that like some other firms because they started out about the biggest here. And it seems as if their growth has been more orderly. I'm sure there are times when it looks like the Firm jumps way ahead in numbers, but I think that's one of the great virtues. Of course, they have a history that goes even beyond Capt. Baker.

What I have been trying to say was it appears to me that Baker Botts has been most successful in allowing there to exist a well-rounded man or woman while at the same time being a successful professional and loyal Firm supporter. Now that's a priceless ingredient. I doubt that this admirable quality comes from any one person or committee

Willie A. Rowell became an employee of Baker Botts in 1908 and retired in 1955. This photograph was taken in 1911 during Miss Rowell's "famous" trip to the Rocky Mountains.

in this Firm. It comes in part from Capt. Baker who valued such qualities. Somehow it's been preserved well by the people who came after Capt. Baker.

Concerning Non-Lawyer Personnel
To cast back, if I may, when I was up here as a clerk, of course, and then in later years, two of the most impressive people, and I haven't mentioned them, were Miss Rowell and Miss Ruth, as they called Miss Ruth Andrews. They were the dominant force in the personnel department! And Miss Rowell sat there by the elevator, I remember, and she saw everything that went on and I think she read all the correspondence and so on, and they were two very domi-

Willie A. Rowell in her car, circa 1912.

Irma Harvin, pictured here in 1961, succeeded Willie A. Rowell in the early 1950s as office manager. Her son, William C. Harvin, was later managing partner of the Firm.

nant ladies. I think they lived out in Garden Villas and they had a dog kennel, as a hobby or something. I remember my father had a place at the Bay at La Porte, purchased from his partner at Baker Botts, Mr. C. L. Carter, and we used to drive out Telephone Road, which is the same way you go to Garden Villas. We would often pass Miss Rowell and Miss Ruth driving this little old Model A or T Ford or something - driving back and forth. All the secretaries were afraid of Miss Rowell. And she would go around all day to see what secretary wasn't working and then she'd go get some paper off another one's desk and put it on the idle secretary's desk and, like all secretaries today, they didn't like to do work for somebody else other than those they were assigned to. So she had to, as I saw it, suffer from some of the unpopularity of being a harsh taskmaster. This makes me think of Mrs. Harvin, a very wonderful lady. I'm sure you have a great deal on her. She succeeded to many of the responsibilities formerly handled by Miss Rowell. As Miss Rowell got very old and rather disabled, Mrs. Harvin, who was a younger and calmer, more organized person took over.

GAIUS G. GANNON

Gaius Goddard Gannon was born in Dallas on October 20, 1899 and lived there until he came to Houston to join the Firm. Gannon was one of the four outstanding lawyers recruited by Walter Walne from the Dallas-Fort Worth area in 1929.

It was almost by accident that Gannon became a lawyer. He never had a law degree, and yet became an outstanding trial lawyer and later served as Chief Justice of the First Court of Civil Appeals. Gannon was instrumental in having the First Court of Appeals moved from Galveston to Houston.

Gannon attended a Catholic elementary school in New Jersey, the Holy Trinity High School in Dallas, and then for four years studied poetry, prose, philosophy, and psychology at Georgetown University. While visiting in Austin, he learned that an examination was being given in torts. Being a free spirit, Gannon took the exam "for fun," and to his surprise, passed it. He attended the University of Texas for a semester and, with the aid of several weeks of tutoring, passed the Texas Bar examination in 1919. He then began his practice with the Dallas firm of Smith, Robertson and Robertson, which lasted until he received Walne's invitation ten years later.

Although he was with Baker Botts only 15 years (he left in 1944 to enter private practice on his own), Gannon made a reputation as an outstanding trial lawyer. Tom Phillips, himself an expert trial lawyer with the Firm, stated that Gannon probably had the greatest courtroom skills of anyone he had seen in the courthouse. Shirley Helm, an outstanding plaintiff's lawyer in Houston, was quoted as saying "without question he was one of the finest trial lawyers in the U.S. and the finest local lawyer Texas has ever known."

Gannon was a restless individual and became easily bored. In a *Houston Post* report in November 1955, less than two years before his death, he

Gaius G. Gannon, with the Firm 1929 - 1944.

made two interesting statements:

> "Even after I received my license I had no intentions of practicing law. I went to law school (one semester) not with the idea of becoming a lawyer but to receive more education. The thought of going to work seemed dull so I went to school."

In the same interview, after noting that Gannon was a voracious reader, the reporter quotes Gannon as saying:

> "I'm trying to find out what everything is all about and I'm trying to find the meaning of life."

Surviving Gannon on his death, September 17, 1957, were his wife, Mary Payne Gannon, four sons, Dr. John Payne Gannon, Gaius G. Gannon, Jr., George Robertson Gannon, and Robert Gibson Gannon, and a daughter, Anne Gannon.

FRANCIS G. COATES

John T. McCullough's tribute to Frank Coates, published in the January 27, 1972, *Office Review*, furnishes an excellent review of Mr. Coates' career:

Francis Graham Coates was born in Baltimore on October 31, 1893 and died at Santa Fe on November 16, 1971. His survivors included his wife, Mrs. Emily Davis Coates, three daughters, Mrs. Emily Fairfax Coates of Houston, Mrs. Cynthia Poppell Coates of Aspen, Colorado, and Mrs. Merrick Brants Coates of Sydney, Australia, a son, Francis G. Coates, Jr. of Aspen, a brother, George Hunter Coates of San Antonio, and six grandchildren.

Mr. Coates spent his early years on a ranch near Albany, Texas, and Shackelford County continued to be one of his favorite places and ranching one of his favorite interests throughout his lifetime. He received his B.A. from Yale in 1916. When the United States entered World War I, he attended the First Officers Training Camp at Leon Springs; he received his commission there and later served in Europe in the Field Artillery, attaining the rank of Capt.

Mr. Coates received his LL.B. from the University of Texas Law School in 1920. He was a member of Chancellors and of Phi Delta Phi. He became a Life Trustee of the University of Texas Law School Foundation and was honored as Outstanding Alumnus of the Law School at the 1962 Law Day Ceremonies.

Mr. Coates started practicing law in Fort Worth and served as Assistant District Attorney of Tarrant County from 1922-24. He formed the firm of Coates & Mastin in 1924 and continued with that firm until he came to Houston to become a member of Baker, Botts, Parker & Garwood on July 1, 1929. He served as Special Counsel to the City of Ft. Worth 1925-29. Tom M.

Francis G. Coates, with the Firm 1929 - 1971.

Davis started practicing law in 1928 with Coates & Mastin and moved to Houston in 1929 a few months before Mr. Coates moved here.

Mr. Coates was active in the affairs of the Museum of Fine Arts of Houston and served as its President. He was one of the organizers of Hedgecroft Clinic, which was created shortly after World War II to treat and furnish therapy for polio patients. He was greatly interested in fine horses and served as a director of the American Horse Show Association. He was on the Board of Visitors and Governors of St. John's College of Annapolis, which also has a school at Santa Fe.

In his position as Special Counsel for the City of Ft. Worth, Mr. Coates had become expert in the field of public utility law. This field was his first assignment with our Firm, and he devoted substantial time to our representation of the Distribution Division of United Gas Corporation.

Prior to the erection of One Shell Plaza, Tenneco built its headquarters on Milam at Lamar, Houston. This photograph is from the late 1960s. The Memorial Professional Building can be seen just to the left of the Tenneco Building. The drugstore in that building was a popular lunch spot for Firm employees until the building was demolished for the construction of Allied (First Interstate) Bank Tower.

Frank, with the assistance of others in the office, handled for United a proceeding involving the City gate gas rate at Laredo. *United Gas Public Service Co. vs. State et al.*, 89 S.W. 2d 1094 (Tex. Civ. App. 1094, e.ref.); 303 U.S. 123 (1938). In the rather early years of Tennessee Gas Transmission Company, Mr. Coates was active in our representation of that Company. He served on the Board of Directors of Texas Gulf Sulphur Company and was instrumental in having Tom Phillips selected to succeed him on that Board.

A number of the lawyers and others now with the Firm did not know Mr. Coates well because in recent years, with declining health, he had spent substantial time at Santa Fe. Those who did know him well will remember Frank as a generous and kindly person, a man of warm personality, and particularly as a partner who was highly interested in the welfare of our younger associates and who extended himself to hasten their progress in the Firm and to promote them in the community.

It is interesting to note that for a boy who grew up on a ranch in West Texas, Coates became one of the most polished, sophisticated lawyers in the Firm. He was not as well known throughout the office as Parish, Shepherd, and some of his contemporaries, but those who knew him had a high regard for him.

Tom Davis recalls that Walter Walne originally came to Fort Worth to interview Davis, but Davis was out, and he talked to Frank Coates. Walne was so impressed with Coates, according to Davis, that he hired him as a partner and brought Davis along as "water boy."

Coates had contacts on the East Coast through his public utility work. He was responsible for the Tennessee Gas work coming to our office and served on that Board at one time.

Although Coates was never Managing Partner, his influence was felt before the Firm had an Executive Committee. He was well acquainted with New York firms and their management techniques. For years, he was Chairman of what was then the Salary Committee, and he took a broad view of that assignment. He constantly asked for more information on the associates in order to help the Committee make its decisions, and he was thus indirectly responsible for much of our statistical data now on computer. Coates was also the prime mover when the Firm decentralized and created departments of practice.

122

TOM MARTIN DAVIS

Tom Martin Davis has always been considered one of the strong leaders of the Firm in a general way, but because the Railroad Department operated as a separate entity, his talents were not as widely known throughout the Firm as some of the other partners. Davis is a modest man and would never brag, but he was forced to answer questions from our Firm history writers. An attempt will be made to summarize his career from that interview.

He grew up in Austin, Texas. His parents were Louis Davis and Caroline Kone. His grandfather, Judge Kone, was from Hays County and the first Commissioner of Agriculture for the State of Texas. At a Texas A&M football rally Davis attended in 1920, the speaker referred to a fine team from VMI that had beaten Penn State. He had never heard of VMI but told his father that he wanted to go to college there. The father investigated, found that it was a good school, and agreed. Davis enrolled in the fall of 1921. He was Captain in the Corps (the highest rank awarded) and won the Stonewall Jackson award for the highest four-year scholastic record.

He enrolled at the University of Texas Law School. Dean Hildebrand told him, "Now young man, if you will study hard and won't go to those dances, won't smoke cigarettes, will exercise every day, and make good grades, Baker, Botts, Parker & Garwood will offer you a job." Davis states he followed only part of this advice, but even so was editor-in-chief in his senior year. Still, Baker Botts did not offer him employment. One day he was called in to interview with a Mr. Frank Coates, a Fort Worth lawyer who did offer him a job. He later came with Coates to Baker Botts when Walter Walne came calling.

At Baker Botts, Davis immediately began assisting Walne in trying lawsuits. When Walne finally allowed Davis to make an argument in a case, Walne was at first so nervous he left the

Tom Martin Davis, with the Firm since 1929.

courtroom. Davis told Walne in 1932, three years after he came to the Firm, that he was tired of carrying books and wanted to try some lawsuits. He was given a list of railroad county court cases and thus began his trial career and railroad association. He later started working with John Bullington on more important cases. A bit later, John Torian of Southern Pacific asked Davis to spend every day with him for a year and a half working on cases before the National Railroad Adjustment Board. Bullington shortly thereafter gave Davis a case before the National Labor Relations Board and Davis became a "labor lawyer," the only one in the Firm. When Bullington died in 1948, Davis succeeded him as head of the Southern Pacific work and continued to be in charge of the Firm's labor work. In addition, he did general trial work. He was given the title "General Counsel of Southern Pacific in Texas and Louisiana" and carried that title until he retired. He had become a part-

The *Sunbeam*, Southern Pacific's answer to its competitor's *Sam Houston Zephyr*, ran out of the Dallas Union Terminal to Houston's Union Station. Southern Pacific passenger service between Dallas and Houston, however, ended in 1958. Tom Martin Davis was general counsel of the Southern Pacific for Texas and Louisiana.

ner in 1940. Davis recites that Capt. Baker gave up his full senior interest so Davis, Dillon Anderson, and Bill Ryan could become partners. Capt. Baker went on a salary of $600 a month.

Davis produced minutes of the Houston Texas Central Railroad of 1870 and 1873 naming the then Baker Botts Firm as general attorneys. William Marsh Rice attended the meetings as a Board member.

Davis considered the Rice University "will contest" in the 1960s as one of his most exciting cases. The indenture had provided that the Institute was to be free and for whites only. George Brown was chairman of the board and asked the Firm to file a suit to set aside this provision. Dillon Anderson filed the suit and when he became ill, Davis tried the case (successfully of course). There were two interesting aspects to the case. Davis had attempted to keep Rice graduates off the jury. One juror after the case told him "Mr. Davis, there was one question you didn't ask. I never attended Rice because I was turned down when I applied." The presiding judge told Davis that during the entire trial he lis-

tened to his wife at breakfast arguing the other side of the case.

Davis has been active in the community for many years, especially in the United Fund where he served as President and Chairman of the Board. He also served on the Board of the Museum of Natural Science and was President of Neighborhood Centers, Inc., the second largest recipient of United Fund grants.

Davis is married to Dorothy Dunn and has two children: Tom, Jr. and Joan (Mrs. O'Leary).

The Museum of Natural Science, at the northern end of Herman Park, Houston, circa 1969. Tom Martin Davis has been one of the leaders of this Museum.

WILLIAM M. RYAN

Much has been made of all the young promising partners the Firm lost during and just after World War II. Bill Ryan was the youngest of them all, and although it is difficult to judge one so young, he was regarded by his peers as being second only to Bullington in intellect, legal skills, and potential.

William Morris Ryan was born on December 31, 1905 in St. Louis, attended public schools in Abilene, Texas, attended St. John's University at Collegeville, Minnesota, and graduated from St. Edward's University in Austin in 1925. He was then principal of Laredo Junior High School in 1925-26 and for five months attended the National University in Mexico. He obtained his law degree from the University of Texas in 1929 and joined the Firm with that talented class of recruits.

Although an accomplished trial lawyer, Ryan's interests ranged widely as his early education indicates. During World War II when so many trial lawyers were in the service, Ryan was described as rushing from court to court with little time to prepare for trial. Some of his contemporaries remembered his ability to look at a jury list of 25 or 30 names, put the list in his pocket, and thereafter call every juror by name.

Ryan died in his home on June 28, 1946 at the age of 40. He was survived by his wife Rosalie, two sons, two daughters, mother, and five brothers and a sister. Perhaps Dillon Anderson knew him best, and his tribute in the July 26, 1946 *Office Review* gives one an indication of Ryan's wide range of talent and interests:

> Bill Ryan, Tom Davis, John McCullough and I all came to the office the same year - 1929. We all moved into Miss Mary Masterson's old home at 500 Westmoreland Street where we had rooms. Though Bill endeared himself to everyone who knew him in the office and out of the office, I feel

William M. Ryan, with the Firm 1929-1946.

> that none knew him better or loved him more than we who were his contemporaries. It seems entirely fitting therefore, that one of us should write this tribute to his memory.
>
> We have seen the elements of greatness in one of us who has gone. The chapter was all too short, but in many ways complete, for he so lived that at any point his living had to be broken off, completeness was a part of the story.
>
> It is not often that the privilege comes to know people like Bill Ryan. His was truly an electric personality. Here was a man of action, daring in his concepts, indefatigable in his devotion to what he believed was right; yet, there was not a ruthless bone in his body. Strong in spirit as a lion, he was as tender in his feelings as a lamb. He loved his fellow men and in his great love for all about him, he wielded a great influence for good. There ought to be more people like Bill Ryan.
>
> Bill gave of himself, his energies, his affection,

and his sympathetic understanding to all about him. He did more good things in his time than many people - nay, most people - who live to be twice the age at which he passed on. No cause, however small, was beneath his dignity; no cause, however large, was beyond his effort. Literally thousands of people in all walks of life felt and saw the light of his good works. Just how he managed to do all the outstanding things he did - many of which came to light only after his death - was a source of wonderment to his many friends. In all his accomplishments he moved and acted with simplicity of purpose and almost Christ-like humility.

As a lawyer he possessed unique talents and gave of them generously for his clients. This was true as to his paying clients and to his non-paying clients alike. Though he was perhaps best known throughout the State for his trial work, he did not thus limit his practice. He added dignity and prestige to the task of dealing with the State Legislature in Austin. He was recognized widely as the most effective man in Texas in that field. The state officials were proud to be friends of Bill Ryan and they always welcomed his opinion on legislation and other state affairs.

As a counselor and adviser he was equally outstanding. His patience and painstaking attention to matters of small dollar and cent import were as great as he gave to large affairs with which his clients entrusted him. His clients loved and honored him to a rare degree.

As a partner in our Firm his work was in the true spirit of team play. Exemplar of fair play, he never failed to give due weight to the other fellow's viewpoint. He carried on in the tradition of those who have gone before and added in full measure to the tradition of the Firm. His memory is a vital living part of our heritage in the Firm.

As a citizen in the community he was a leader. He was perhaps the best known and most active Catholic layman in the State. Deeply religious and devoted to the tenets of his chosen faith, he was without bigotry and intolerance. For the model his life was, we who knew him best and many who knew him but slightly will always cherish the memory of Bill Ryan. To those who knew of his professional attainment as well as those who knew him only as a man and citizen, he can always be remembered in the terms of one of the beatitudes:

"Blessed are the pure in heart, for they shall see God."

DILLON ANDERSON

Dillon Anderson was born July 14, 1906 in Prosper, Collins County, Texas, the son of Joseph and Elizabeth Dillon Anderson. He attended public schools in McKinney, Texas and then attended Texas Christian University but graduated from the University of Oklahoma in 1928 and Yale Law School in 1929. He became associated with the Firm in 1929, was admitted as a partner in 1940, and served as Managing Partner from 1947 until 1952.

Anderson was a man of many talents, but it was his experience in World War II and immediately thereafter that gave him national prominence. He was exposed to the group of Eisenhower admirers who later talked the General into offering himself for office, and Dillon became an active member of this group. Perhaps one of these gentlemen, Justice Ammi Cutter of the Supreme Judicial Court of Massachusetts, can best summarize Dillon's career. The report was adopted by the Council of the American Law Institute where Dillon was active for many years·

Dillon Anderson, a member of the Council of the American Law Institute since 1948, was born in McKinney, Texas, on July 14, 1906. He died on January 28, 1974.

No one could have been a more devoted son of Texas than he was. Nevertheless, his education, activity, interests and influence went far beyond that State's borders. He took his bachelor's degree at the University of Oklahoma in 1928, and his LL.B. at Yale in 1929, after study at Texas Christian University. Both in war and in peace he served the nation. He was a director or fiduciary of many corporations and institutions, with far more than regional significance.

After his admission to the Texas bar in 1929,

Dillon Anderson, with the Firm 1929-1974.

he became an associate of the Houston firm, now known as Baker & Botts. There he engaged in a general practice, at first with a considerable emphasis on litigation. As time went on, his practice became much more general, with increasing participation in business, financial, and public legal problems. He became a partner of the Firm in 1940 and remained a member until his death, except for certain periods of Federal service.

In October 1942, Dillon joined the Army Specialist Corps as a major. He was assigned to duty with General Albert C. Wedemeyer, then Chief of the Strategy and Policy Group, Operations Division, War Department General Staff, for work on staff operations analysis during critical stages of the North African invasion. He was then the only non-West Pointer in the group.[5] In December he transferred to the Army of the

---

[5] For Anderson's typically colorful account of his war experiences, see *Baker, Botts in World War II*, pp. 1 to 57.

United States and was assigned to the Legal Branch of the Office of the Director of Material, Army Service Forces (then General Lucius D. Clay), headed by William L. Marbury of Baltimore, a member of this Council. There he joined others who subsequently had close affiliations with the Institute.[6] For a year he engaged in a great variety of efforts to expedite the procurement and distribution of munitions and supplies.

One with Anderson's knowledge of the petroleum industry gained from his Texas practice was not long to be left in Washington. In September 1943, as a lieutenant colonel, he was assigned to Cairo for about two years of work on oil and other problems in many parts of Asia Minor and the Arabian peninsula. He visited areas then far from the beaten track. As a colonel, he concluded his work in Cairo as Assistant Chief of Staff, G-5, of the United States Armed Forces in the Middle East. For his services in the region, he was awarded the Legion of Merit. He returned for a year of liaison work with Congress, in the War Department Special Staff.

After leaving the army in August 1945, he returned to practice in Texas. Rapidly, he became engaged in a vast variety of banking, business, public, and charitable enterprises, in addition to his highly successful professional activities. Among companies of which he was long a director were Westinghouse Electric Corporation, U.S. Plywood-Champion Papers, Inc., Federated Department Stores, and Monsanto Company. He was a trustee of two major foundations and also of the Carnegie Foundation for International Peace

and the Brookings Institution. He was active in associations, both national and regional, with interests in foreign policy matters.[7]

Dillon had been active in efforts to elect President Eisenhower in 1952, and kept closely in touch with foreign and defense affairs during the next decade. From 1955 to 1956, he served as Special Assistant to the President for National Security Affairs, with major responsibility for the operations of the National Security Council. This was an exacting duty in the periods following two instances of serious presidential ill health. In 1955, he attended the Big Four "summit meeting" in Geneva as a member of the United States delegation.

Dillon himself was hospitalized in 1956. This led, shortly thereafter, to his return to Houston. He remained, however, a consultant to the National Security Council until 1960.

With all his many interests, he still found time for writing short stories which first appeared in the *Atlantic Monthly* and *Colliers,* and later were collected in three volumes, *I and Claudie* (1951), *Claudie's Kinfolks* (1954), and *The Billingsley Papers* (1961). The first two books, with a distinctly Texas regional atmosphere, dealt with two engaging and ingenious, but slightly disreputable, minor entrepreneurs. They, as Dillon described them (*Claudie's Kinfolks,* p. 1), spent their time "chowsing around from pillar to post, never latching on to a real good thing." Billingsley, the somewhat more sophisticated subject of the final collection, was a 1920 ex-All-American football player (see *Billingsley Papers,* pp. 14-15), a successful lawyer of sorts despite a flair for poker, dogs,

---

[6] The Legal Branch, in addition to Mr. Marbury, its chief, included then or later: Ammi Cutter, his deputy; Arthur Dixon, Joseph F. Johnson, H. Chapman Rose, Charles Willard, and John Minor Wisdom, all members of the Council; and Robert R. Bowie and Benjamin Kaplan, each of whom became an advisor or reporter on Institute projects.

[7] Among these were the Council on Foreign Relations, Inc., The Foreign Policy Association, The World Affairs Council of Houston, and the Houston Committee on Foreign Relations of which Dillon was president in 1950-51. He received honorary degrees from Texas Christian University in 1954 and Allegheny College in 1956. He was a fellow of the American Academy of Arts and Sciences and was active in various bar association matters.

The adventures of Clint and Claudie are represented in this picture from the dust jacket of Dillon Anderson's first book, "I and Claudie" (Little, Brown and Company, 1951). The dust jacket also presented the following biographical summary of Dillon Anderson:

A Houston lawyer, Dillon Anderson is a hard-working civic leader, well-known in Texas and beyond. He is a director of the Houston Fat Stock Show and Livestock Association, Houston Transit Company, Galveston Electric Company, Houston Chamber of Commerce, Union National Bank of Houston, Houston Symphony Society, and Texas Fund Research and Management Associates. He is a trustee and president of Foley Brothers Store Foundation, a member of the American Law Institute, American Bar Association, Houston Country Club, Ramada Club, Bayou Club, Eagle Lake Rod & Gun Club, Texas Club, and the Metropolitan Club of Washington, D.C.

sports, and hunting.

No quick summary can give the flavor of Anderson's short stories. His fiction certainly was not autobiographical, for he bore no resemblance to any of his characters. The literary activity, however, gave Dillon relaxation and escape from professional and other pressures in some way, which not even he clearly understood. His gently humorous writing was one significant manifestation of an amazing versatility.

With all his many activities, interests, and writing, Dillon had a full and happy family life. In 1931, he married Lena Carroll, one of three talented sisters, the oldest of whom had married one of his partners. In Lena, he found devoted support, understanding, and encouragement. Her calm help to him during his final illness was superb. They had three daughters and numerous grandchildren, all living sufficiently near the Houston area to keep the family closely united. Only a month before his death, Dillon was to see a granddaughter happily married.

In early years, he and Lena spent much of their spare time at the Carroll family place in Camden, Texas, about ninety miles north of Houston. After World War II, the Andersons established for themselves a farm, known as Bug Hill, at Independence, Texas. There they raised cattle and engaged in light agricultural pursuits. It provided a center for their children and grandchildren. Various members of this Council have enjoyed the Anderson's hospitality in this pleasant countryside, particularly beautiful in the spring bluebonnet-paintbrush season.

Dillon was as diligent as his health and public responsibility permitted in attendance at Council and Institute meetings. It rapidly became recognized, even in his early days on the Council, that he spoke only when he had something worthwhile to say. He often had and expressed an instinctive feeling that some proposal or comment was unsound or inconsistent with common sense. He was politely but colorfully insistent in pressing the reporter, or a non-concurring Council colleague, on such occasions. Particularly was this true when he felt that Texas views and legal practices would not be reasonably reflected in the proposed action.

He was, on one occasion, the principal speaker at the dinner at the annual meeting. His usual wit made this a memorable event. Many Council members and their wives will long recall the amusing, complicated stories, which he told us with dramatic effect, deadpan countenance, and perfect timing, at several agreeable Council dinners.

He will be greatly missed in this Council, particularly by those of us who also served with him during World War II, in a closely-knit group of hardworking, congenial lawyers. Seeing the Andersons on these Institute occasions, was for us one of the great rewards of our labors here.

Anderson also wrote a book entitled *My Years With Eisenhower,* but copies were distributed only to family and a few very close friends.

Among his many talents, Anderson was a golfer (he shot in the 70s), a hunter (Eagle Lake Rod and Gun Club), and a poker player. As a matter of fact, it is said that some of his poker cronies appeared in his short stories, disguised, of course.

Brady Cole and Bill Ryan, among others, had a part in planning for the Mexico City office, but it was Anderson and Henry Holland who put forth the final effort from the Houston office. Anderson and Fausto Miranda, the senior partner there, formed a friendship that lasted a lifetime.

Anderson was drafted to be Managing Partner of the Firm. He was not a volunteer. Although he was able in any field he chose, he was anything but a hands-on manager in the day-to-day operations of the office. He allowed administration personnel substantial leeway in the routine of running the office. It should be noted that in those days the Managing Partner was expected to carry a regular workload in addition to being Managing Partner. With his outside commitments, it was obvious that he had little time remaining for daily management functions.

Anderson was the most visible national symbol of the Firm in the years after World War II. History books will duly note his service under Eisenhower. Firm lore will continue to offer stories about "the D.A." for as long as those who knew him remain. But for anyone wanting to get to know this man on a more personal level, his works of fiction are the best introduction to the lively mind of Dillon Anderson.

Anderson died January 28, 1974, at the age of 67. His children are Susan (Mrs. Charles Whiteford, Jr.), Lena (Mrs. Jerry Van Kyle), and Elizabeth (Mrs. Ronald E. Martin).

JOHN T. McCULLOUGH

John Temple McCullough became an associate in October 1929 and became a partner in 1944. He was from Mooreville, Texas, and his father was later Mayor of Waco. He attended the University of Texas where he was a 165-pound all-conference center on the football team. He obtained his law degree in 1929 and was recruited by Managing Partner Walter Walne. In 1938, he married Jewel Butler. They have two daughters: Nelda (Mrs. David Hirsh) and Judith (Mrs. Brandon Reilly).

Both McCullough's tone and the extraordinary changes he lived through after coming to Baker Botts are evident in a speech he made at a Firm dinner held in his honor in November 1979:

> In recent weeks I have considered various subjects that I might talk about briefly tonight. I concluded that you might be interested in hearing some things about the Firm's clientele when I came with the Firm in 1929, and some of the similarities and some of the differences between our practice then and now. Perhaps you would be interested also in such explanations as I may have to offer on the reasons for some substantial changes that occurred during that period of fifty years.
>
> When I arrived in 1929 the Firm had substantial clients in numerous industries, including
> 1. Banking
> 2. Public Utility
> 3. Railroad
> 4. Oil and Gas
> 5. Insurance
> 6. Lumber and Timber
> 7. Chemical
> 8. Food Product
> 9. Automobile
> Among our important clients were, in the banking industry,
> 1. South Texas Commercial National Bank,
> 2. Guardian Trust Company, and

John T. McCullough, with the Firm since 1929.

> 3. Second National Bank.
> South Texas was located in its own building on lower Main Street in what was then the "Financial District" of Houston. First National Bank was then located at the corner of Main and Franklin in what is now called the Lomas Nettleton Building. Four other banks were located nearby.
>
> Guardian Trust Company was located in the Niels Esperson Building, in the space presently occupied by Allied Bank, and Second National Bank was located in the building which then carried its name, situated on the southwest corner of the intersection of Main and Rusk.
>
> Capt. Baker was Chairman of the Boards of both South Texas and Guardian. The name of South Texas was changed to Texas National Bank at about the time it moved to the newly constructed Texas National Bank Building at Main and Polk. In 1964 it merged with National Bank of

Commerce to become Texas Commerce Bank with its principal office in the Gulf Building.

Guardian Trust Company merged with Second National Bank in 1945, and the name was later changed to Bank of the Southwest.

Among the public utilities we represented were

1. Houston Lighting & Power Company
2. Houston Gas and Fuel
3. Houston Street Railway Company
4. Stone & Webster
5. Western Union Telegraph Company

United Gas Corporation was organized in the early 1930s and included Houston Gas & Fuel Company and many other gas distribution and gas pipe line companies.

We were general counsel in Texas for the Southern Pacific Lines, and we also handled some work for the MK&T and other railroads and for Railway Express Agency.

In the oil and gas industry we represented

1. Atlantic Oil Producing Company
2. Sinclair
3. Standard Oil Company of Texas
4. Continental Oil Company

and we handled important litigation for Texaco.

Atlantic and Sinclair are both now parts of Atlantic Richfield, for which we still do substantial work. Standard Oil Company of Texas was a wholly-owned subsidiary of Standard Oil Company of California, and the operations formerly handled by Standard of Texas are now conducted under the name of Chevron, USA, Inc. We still handle matters from time to time for Chevron.

In the 1930s, Pan American Production Company and Salt Dome Oil Corporation were organized and they became very active oil and gas clients.

In the 1940s and 1950s, we had a substantial number of lawyers who were active in the day-to-day handling of oil and gas work, such as the preparation of oil and gas leases, drilling contracts, farmout agreements, joint operating agreements,

division orders, title opinions and opinions on various oil and gas questions.

In the insurance industry, our clients included

1. Travelers
2. Hartford Accident & Indemnity Company
3. Ocean Accident and Guarantee Corporation

and a number of others.

We had a substantial number of lawyers who handled large dockets of damage suits for insurance companies, the local transportation company (the streetcar company and later the bus company), railroads and our public utility clients. From time to time we handled substantial loan transactions for the Equitable Life Assurance Society and for Prudential Insurance Company and occasionally for other large insurance companies such as Connecticut Mutual.

The Firm was quite active in the lumber and timber industry; our clients included

1. W. T. Carter & Bro.
2. Long Bell Lumber Company
3. Pickering Lumber Company

The client first named, which was a partnership comprised of the descendants of W.T. Carter, owned a large lumber mill and large acreage of timber centered in Polk County. It sold the surface of the land and its facilities several years ago to Champion International Corporation, subject to the reservation of certain mineral interests. . . .

In the food product industry, the Firm represented

1. Borden
2. National Biscuit Company
3. Swift and Company
4. Armour
5. Wesson Oil & Snowdrift Company
6. Imperial Sugar Company
7. Sugarland Industries

In the automobile industry the Firm represented Ford Motor Company and Firestone Tire

Armour & Co. wharf at the Port of Houston, 1917. Baker Botts began representing Armour & Co. in 1898, principally in litigation matters ranging from personal injury to antitrust suits involving its operation of cottonseed oil mills in Texas. According to an early edition of the *Office Review*, when a representative of the central law office of Armour & Co. at Chicago came to Houston in 1922 to observe and assist in litigation involving Armour & Co., he remarked that most of the law firms in the South handled his company's business in a very slipshod and unsatisfactory manner, but that he could truthfully state that Baker Botts handled and disposed of business as efficiently as any firm in the United States.

and Rubber Company and also handled work for other tire companies.

In the chemical industry, Union Carbide and Carbon Company and a number of its subsidiaries were clients of the firm, and we handled substantial work for DuPont and Texas Gulf Sulphur Company.

Capt. Baker was chairman of the Board of Trustees of Rice Institute. In those years and probably into the late 1950s, Rice was active in mortgage lending and we handled substantial volumes of that work for Rice.

Other good clients included Southwestern Drug Corporation, F. W. Heitmann Company (hardware), Lone Star Cement Company, and Ernst & Ernst. Our first representation of some important clients stems from recommendations of the Firm by Ernst & Ernst.

In describing the Firm's practice as it existed when I came to the Firm in 1929 and for some years after that, I have referred to nine industries and to some of our clients in those industries. The Firm was not departmentalized in those years to the extent it is now. In fact the only very noticeable departmentalization was office practice on the one hand and trial work on the other, although certain lawyers were recognized as experts on particular subjects.

We had no tax department, no will, trust and estate department, antitrust department, labor department, patent department or department on international and foreign law. Tax matters were far less important than now. In 1930 Houston had a population of 292,000 and the demand for estate planning was not great. The principal concern with antitrust laws was with those of Texas rather than federal laws. Tom Davis has told me that he handled his first labor law matter in 1934, for the railroad, and that the National Labor Relations Act was not passed until 1935 and held constitutional in 1937.

. . . There is no doubt in my mind that the

F. W. Heitmann & Co., near Main and Commerce, Houston, circa 1900. F. A. Heitmann, president of F. W. Heitmann & Co., was president of the National Hardware Association. The Heitmann company prided itself in being "the first exclusive iron dealer in Texas." The Firm's association with F. W. Heitmann & Co. dated from July 24, 1918. Baine P. Kerr's involvement in the consolidation of F. W. Heitmann & Co. with Bering-Cortes Hardware Company was reported in a 1959 issue of the *Office Review*.

greatest changes in the Firm's practice and business over the years since I came to work in 1929 resulted from the "New Deal" legislation which I have mentioned. Of course lawyers were as vociferous as their clients in complaining about the New Deal legislation, but in retrospect one may wonder how lawyers would have survived without the legislation.

. . . If tonight marked the end of my association with the Firm, it would indeed be a sad occasion for me. I have never regretted my decision in 1929 to come to Baker & Botts. It has always been a challenging place to work, and when I have had occasion to identify myself I have had pride in saying "I am with Baker & Botts". My wife and I have established long-lasting friendships as a result of

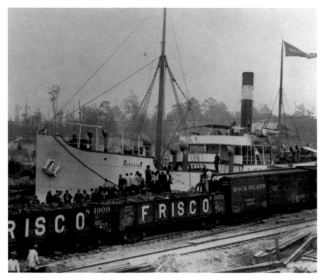

International & Great Northern R.R. Co. wharf, Houston, circa 1914. Baker Botts represented I.&G.N. as part of the Missouri Pacific Railway Company, the "Gould System," until 1895. When I.&G.N. went into receivership in 1914, Capt. James A. Baker was appointed sole receiver for the railway. The Firm received fees for its services to the receiver until 1924. This photograph shows the unloading of anthracite coal at the Houston Ship Channel.

Houston Post Building, Houston, 1911.
Capt. James A. Baker wrote in 1923 as follows:
"The Post is our esteemed client, and occupies a business of commanding influence in this community. The Post should continue to grow and its influence correspondingly increase. Its business is in our office. We need not expect any business from its competitors.'"

associations which originated in the Firm. I hope to remain able to come to the office regularly for the foreseeable future, and with this expectation there is no sadness for me tonight.

There were no departments at the time of his employment. McCullough engaged in a wide assortment of office practice, especially oil and gas and corporate work. He was the Firm's leading expert on "doing business in Texas" questions. He was drafted to become Managing Partner to succeed Dillon Anderson in 1953 and remained in that position for 19 years, longer than any who have held that title. McCullough was a thorough lawyer and a wise counsellor. Many lawyers testified that no matter how long they worked on a paper, McCullough would always make a constructive suggestion which had not occurred to them. He was a lawyer's lawyer and even those much senior to him sought his counsel.

He served in a period when there were strong aggressive partners, many senior to him, but he had such a strong reputation for being fair and impartial that he was able to function under all circumstances.

Conscientious would be another way to describe McCullough. He made it a point to pass out "the word" to each lawyer personally after the annual salary review. He, of course, notified associates when they were to be admitted. McCullough had an agenda and was very precise. He talked to each person in order on his list. One associate who realized he was likely to be admitted as a partner at year end reported that he hung around outside McCullough's office most of the afternoon on the appointed date, "drinking water in the hall, talking loud and kicking waste baskets." He gave up at 5:30 and went home. His name appeared at 6:30 and McCullough tracked him down in a cafeteria to tell him he was to be a partner.

McCullough never wasted words and collected his thoughts before be spoke. When associates went in to discuss a topic, there would be long pauses in the conversation while McCullough looked out the window. Many associates reported that they volunteered comments on any number of subjects just to fill the void in the conversation and later felt foolish when they reflected on the conversation.

As the Firm grew and decisions became more complex, McCullough relied on some of his contemporaries for advice. With the counsel of Frank Coates, he inaugurated a formal departmental system, and finally in 1969 an Executive Committee was created with the young partners being represented, including the next Managing Partner.

Sinclair Gas station in the Houston Heights, circa 1940. One of the Firm's first oil and gas company clients, Sinclair Oil Company placed Baker Botts on retainer in 1918. The Firm handled Sinclair's purchase of American Republics Corporation of Houston in 1955. To record legal documents timely, Baker Botts coordinated their dispatch via five airplanes and two cars from Houston on one pivotal Saturday in March 1955. After stops in 63 counties in Texas, 14 parishes in Louisiana, and a handful of counties in Arkansas, Alabama, and New Mexico, the ground work had been laid to complete the deal in New York. Printing bills alone for the work ran in excess of $250,000. *The Wall Street Journal* reported that the $75 million production payment was then the largest production payment ever carved out in connection with the purchase of an oil property.

Galveston-Houston Electric Railway Company, circa 1911. The days of the Galveston-Houston interurban ended in 1937 when, with the assistance of Baker Botts, Galveston-Houston Electric Railway Company abandoned the interurban line and reorganized its Houston to Galveston bus service into the Texas Bus Lines.

TOM SCURRY

When Walter Walne decided to broaden the base of the Firm and made a search of Texas for lawyers, Tom Scurry was one of the four attorneys he selected.

Scurry was born in 1898 and served as an ensign in the Naval Air Corps in World War I. He obtained his law degree at the University of Texas in 1919 and had a very successful practice in Dallas with the firm of Phillips, Townsend & Phillips, the older Phillips being a former Chief Justice of the Texas Supreme Court. Walne enticed him to come to Houston on January 1, 1930. He was made a partner three years later.

Gannon reported that, on the day Scurry arrived, he was greeted warmly by Walter Walne and escorted to his office where he found folders on some 80 cases waiting to be tried. After a few years of trying lawsuits, Scurry was assigned to share with Shepherd the responsibility for the work of our oil and gas clients. He was engaged in this work when he died two days after his 46th birthday on April 10, 1944, in a hospital in Dobbs Ferry, New York.

Scurry left three children, Tom, Murphy, and Nancy and a charming widow, Sarah Chambers Scurry (Sally). Tom was very popular with his partners, and Mrs. Scurry maintained this warm

Tom Scurry, with the Firm 1930-1944.

relationship for the next forty years, often attending Firm gatherings until her death in the 1980s.

An interesting historical note is the fact that, like Capt. Baker, Scurry's father once commanded the Houston Light Guard and attained the rank of Captain. An article from the *Houston Post* appears below:

January 28, 1896

Capt. and Mrs. Thomas Scurry of Dallas arrived in the city yesterday morning in route from New Orleans to their home in North Texas. The gallant captain and his accomplished bride were overwhelmed with congratulations by Houston well-wishers. During the day many of the old members of the Houston Light Guard paid their respects to their old commander. Capt. and Mrs. Scurry departed for Dallas last night.

The River Oaks home of Tom Scurry. Many Firm functions were held here. The home was designed by John Staub and has long been a favorite on the River Oaks Garden Club Azalea Trail.

JOHN T. MAGINNIS

John Temple Maginnis was born in 1906 in Alexandria, Louisiana but moved to Houston when he was eight. He attended elementary school where the Convention Center is now located and lived at 1400 McKinney in the area later owned by Texas Eastern. He attended Central High School across the street from the old post office at 700 San Jacinto. As an interesting historical note, he saw the first full-size ship come down the ship channel in 1914. He graduated from Rice Institute in 1927. While attending high school, he worked for the *Daily Court Review*, met lawyers and judges, and developed an intense interest in law as a profession. Tom Maes, manager of the *Daily Court Review*, took an interest in Maginnis and allowed him to work his way through Rice. Through Tom Maes' influence, when Maginnis attended the University of Texas Law School, Governor Hobby arranged for Maginnis to be employed in the State Treasurer's Office after classes. During the summers, he continued to work at the *Daily Court Review*. He was second in his class at U.T. and was one of two graduates selected by the Firm. Albert Jones was the other lawyer employed from his class. According to his interview with historians, he considered Baker Botts the leading law firm in the state and interviewed with no one else. His was the class of 1930.

Maginnis knew Capt. Baker well and was often invited to The Oaks. He particularly remembers lunches on the lawn and Firm meetings in the basement.

His first assignment was to assist Jules Tallichet in Southern Pacific work. He did considerable railroad work but after doing some admiralty work became a corporate lawyer and finally headed the Firm's public utility section.

Like so many others, Maginnis served in World War II and had attained the rank of Lieutenant in the Navy. After he returned from the

John T. Maginnis, with the Firm since 1930.

service, Maginnis became active in the public utility field and was the first head of that department when it was created. He served on the Board of Directors of Entex, Inc. and acted as its general counsel.

Maginnis was active in community affairs and twice served on the Board of the Houston Chamber of Commerce. He was also extremely active in Bar Association work. He was Chairman of the Section of Corporation, Banking and Business Law of the State Bar of Texas and later served as Chairman of this Section of the American Bar Association, the largest section of the American Bar. It was partially through this work that he came to represent a number of large insurance companies in substantial Texas loans. He headed the financing for what were then the Bank of the Southwest and First City National Bank buildings. He represented Equitable in the sale of the downtown Foley properties to Foley Brothers

The Shamrock Hilton, at Holcombe and Main, Houston, circa 1956. Firm client The Equitable Life Assurance Society loaned the money to flamboyant Houston oilman Glenn McCarthy to build the hotel (then a good distance away from downtown) and foreclosed on the loan when McCarthy's operations defaulted. Firm client Hilton Hotels later acquired and managed the property until it was demolished in the 1980s.

Store Foundation. Possibly his proudest achievement was the workout of the Equitable loan to Glenn McCarthy when McCarthy defaulted on his loans for the Shamrock Hotel and McCarthy Oil & Gas. Equitable took over these properties and Maginnis worked five years with Warner Mendel, General Counsel of Equitable. Maginnis was pleased to report that after five years, Equitable recovered all of its money and "never lost a nickel."

Maginnis also did substantial work for the American Bar Foundation and was elected a Fellow for life.

Maginnis was known as a "work horse" even by Baker Botts standards. Numerous young corporate partners have reported sending him a forty or fifty page instrument assuming that he would OK it after possibly glancing at it. Instead it would come back two or three days later with numerous corrections indicating that he had studied it in great detail and had made corrections that hadn't occurred to the lawyer preparing the instrument.

He is just as tenacious in his personal life. In July 1990, on being congratulated on his physical and mental condition despite earlier health problems, he replied that five miles on the treadmill every morning helped. At that time he was 84 years of age.

He and his wife Jayne (Miller) live in Houston.

JOSEPH C. HUTCHESON, III

Joseph Chappell Hutcheson, III is one of those rare people of his generation who was born in Houston (on January 5, 1907), as was his father before him. His grandfather, after the War Between the States, obtained his law degree from the University of Virginia and came to Texas to practice law. He served in the Legislature and was Chairman of the House side of the Joint Committee that established the University of Texas. His father was a lawyer, served as Mayor of Houston in 1917, resigned to accept an appointment as a Federal District Judge, and later served on the Fifth Circuit Court of Appeals.

Hutcheson himself attended prep school at Andover, and graduated from the University of Virginia in 1928. He graduated from the University of Texas Law School in 1931 and came to Baker Botts the same year. The only other firm he considered was the leading firm in Brownsville.

Hutcheson became a trial lawyer because it was the general understanding then that to become partner one must become a good trial lawyer. He worked closely with Clarence Wharton, who Hutcheson thought was the outstanding trial lawyer in Texas. He gradually picked up a docket of damage suits for the Transit Co. and Light Co. For the first two years, he "officed" in the Library. Before he entered the Army in World War II, Hutcheson did some work for Schlumberger under Bullington, not knowing that this would help shape his career.

Hutcheson would never volunteer this, but even though he could have entered the Navy in World War II as an officer, he chose to enter the Army as an enlisted man. After six months, he attended OCS at Fort Sill, Oklahoma (Field Artillery). He was retained as an instructor there for fifteen months before he could break away and go to Europe. (Freeman advises that when he himself graduated at Fort Sill, Lt. Hutcheson

Joseph C. Hutcheson, III, with the Firm since 1931.

was the first to congratulate him.)

While he was home on leave during the war, Ralph Feagin, the Managing Partner, advised Hutcheson that the Firm would make a commitment to admit him after the war if he would in turn agree to come back to the Firm. As far as our records reflect, this was the only commitment ever made in this manner. In his interview, Hutcheson emphasized several times how close he was to Ryan, Bullington, Davis, Anderson, and McCullough and how that added to his pleasure in practicing law at Baker Botts.

In a discussion of how to be a successful trial lawyer, Hutcheson modestly stated that while Gannon and Ryan could win cases on charm and personality, he had to win by knowing more law and facts than the opposition.

After returning from the service, Hutcheson inherited the Houston Transit Co. docket but very shortly thereafter began handling litigation

Schlumberger Building, Leeland Street, Houston, circa 1935. John P. Bullington was the first of several
Firm members, including Joseph C. Hutcheson, III, to serve on the Board of this long-time client.

for what is now Chevron and spent much of the
remainder of his career handling substantial litigation matters for major oil companies, including
cases before the Texas Railroad Commission.
After Bullington's death in 1948, Hutcheson succeeded him on the Board of Schlumberger and
worked closely with the top Schlumberger officers
until he retired.

Schlumberger was a private company until the
early 1960s, and while Hutcheson was on the
Board, it elected to go public by buying a pub-
licly-held company. Baine Kerr worked on the
security aspects of that transaction.

The starting salary was $100 a month in
1931, and it was generally understood that there
would be a $50 raise after six months. The depres-
sion was coming on, however, and there was no
raise at the end of 1931. At the end of 1932,
Hutcheson finally received a $25 raise. This was

good news because on Janmuary 1, 1932, the Firm
had notified all lawyers that it might not be able
to keep them that year and that they would be
given 30-day termination notices if necessary.

Hutcheson never participated in the active
management of the Firm and had no desire to do
so, but his wise counsel was often sought, and he
was part of McCullough's "kitchen cabinet" long
before the Firm had an executive committee.

In 1933, he married Mary Catherine Jacobs;
Mary passed away in 1980. Hutcheson later married Virginia McLeod Brelsford.

141

Capt. James A. Baker on the front page of the *Sunday Houston Post*
magazine section on October 3, 1937.

DENMAN MOODY

Leroy Denman Moody is the son of the late Dr. George Harrison Moody and Bebe Denman Moody of San Antonio. His mother was the daughter of Texas Supreme Court Justice Judge Leroy Denman. He was born in San Antonio on January 11, 1909.

Moody and Ted Lewis were married in 1930 but both continued in school at the University of Texas until 1933 when Denman received his law degree and Ted her B.A.

Moody practiced alone in San Antonio until February 1, 1935 when he was employed by the Firm. He immediately plunged into an active trial docket until World War II arrived, when he served as a Major in the Judge Advocate General's Department.

Moody headed up both the trial and admiralty sections after the war and became active in Bar activities. He was a member of the American College of Trial Lawyers, President of the Houston Bar Association (1956-57), and President of the International Association of Insurance Counsel (1960-61). He was also a member of the Antitrust Section of the American Bar Association.

In later years, Moody handled a variety of substantial cases, some in the antitrust field with Brien Dillon and for more than ten years, assisted by Bob Jewett, was involved in the litigation involving the Estate of Sarita Kenedy East and the Catholic Church in South Texas. A book on this litigation was published in 1990 with the provocative title, *If You Love Me, You Will Do My Will.*

Moody's father and uncle accumulated several large properties in Edwards County, Texas over a 19-year period, now known as the Denman Moody Ranch. It has long been a popular place for hunts and long weekends of recreation for Baker Botts lawyers.

Denman Moody, with the Firm since 1935.

Denman and Ted Moody have a son, Denman, Jr., and two daughters, Bebe Denman and Rhetta Allen. Another daughter, Ted, died in 1974.

WILLIAM R. BROWN

William Russell Brown was one of those rare individuals who became a partner in one area of practice and spent the remainder of his career in another field of law.

Brown was born in Holly Springs, Mississippi on July 5, 1915 and earned both his BBA and LLB degrees at the University of Texas, graduating from the law school with honors in 1937. His entire legal career was spent with the Firm. Like so many others, he served his country in World War II and attained the rank of lieutenant in the Navy. He was devoted to his wife, son, and daughters, Ruth Cunningham Brown, William Russell Brown, Jr., Mrs. Thomas M. Smith (Betsy), and Virginia Lee Brown.

A State Senate resolution (SR No. 777) adopted in memory of Brown described him accurately as "this kind, quiet, gentle-natured man." This does not sound like the description of a trial lawyer; nevertheless, until after he became a partner in 1949, Brown spent his career trying lawsuits for numerous clients of the Firm. One of the senior state district judges named Brown as the best trial lawyer to ever appear before him.

Onc of Brown's primary trial clients was Houston Lighting & Power Co. He worked well with the then President, S.R. Bertron, who was also from Mississippi. When Bertron died suddenly in 1952 and Al Parish left the Firm to become President of the Light Company in 1953, Brown was elected to the Board of Directors and spent the remainder of his career performing various services for HL&P. He was not only General Counsel, but handled or supervised rate hearings and was involved in major management decisions.

An article appearing in a publication of Houston Lighting & Power Co. on July 29, 1974 is of interest because the Light Company has long been a major client of the Firm and because it features Brown and clearly reveals the close relationship

William R. Brown, with the Firm 1937 - 1983.

between the two institutions:

William R. Brown is the current member of the company's Board of Directors with the longest tenure of service, having been elected to the Board in 1953.

Brown is a partner in the Houston law firm of Baker & Botts and is the Light Company's General Counsel. Two cases which stand out in his memory are his work in representing HL&P in its first request for a rate increase in 1960, and more recently handling the litigation surrounding the Cedar Bayou plant.

To the Board he brings more than 36 years' experience in the vital area of public utility law which is becoming more complex and more involved in decision-making.

Brown grew up in Holly Springs, Miss., a small town steeped in Civil War history. As a high school student there, he became interested in law

144

and frequently sat in on trials at the courthouse to satisfy his craving for information about the subject. "I had a job jerking sodas at the drugstore where all the lawyers would meet. They were there so much that I surmised being a lawyer had to be an easy job," joked Brown.

On to UT

When Brown graduated from high school, Mississippi was mired in the Depression. "I heard conditions were better in Texas and so I packed my bags, bought a train ticket and enrolled in the University of Texas at Austin," said Brown. At UT, Brown compressed seven years of study into five by going to summer classes and in 1937 he received a business degree with high honors and a law degree with highest honors.

During his senior year, Brown interviewed with Baker & Botts and was hired as a staff lawyer following graduation at a salary of $100 a month.

Soon after joining Baker & Botts, Brown was assigned to handle some of the Light Company's local legal matters. "The president of the company in 1937 was S. R. Bertron, a native of Port Gibson, Miss. Because we were both Mississippians, we got along well," Brown recalls.

Bertron dies

In 1953, President Bertron died unexpectedly and the company chose W. A. Parish, then a partner at Baker & Botts, to succeed him as president. That same year, Brown was elected to the Board of Directors at the age of 39.

In his 20 years on the Board, Brown has witnessed two decades of dramatic growth by the company. In 1953, HL&P's total plant investment was $206.4 million and its system generating capacity 815,000 kilowatts. In 1973, total plant investment was $1.6 billion and system capacity 8.45 million KW.

Dedicated effort

"The Light Company is a strong and successful company today because of good management and dedicated effort," said Brown. "This company has been run efficiently, by people who have had the foresight to plan ahead," said Brown.

Brown feels the greatest challenge the company will face in the future will be in the area of financing. "The company will need tremendous amounts of capital to finance the construction programs necessary to keep pace with this area's increasing needs for electricity. But money will be increasingly difficult to obtain, and certainly more costly at today's unprecedented interest rates. In addition, other costs are rising and this too will put added pressure on rates," said Brown.

Organizations

In addition to his positions at Baker & Botts and on the Board of Directors, Brown is also chairman of the Standing Committee of the Public Utilities Section of the American Bar Association. He is also a member of the Texas and Houston Bar Associations. Brown still finds time to golf and occasionally he returns to his native Mississippi to hunt.

Brown died of a heart attack on April 8, 1983 in Pebble Beach, California.

HUGH M. PATTERSON

Hugh Morris Patterson was one of the more colorful partners at Baker Botts. He was tall and distinguished in appearance. He had strong opinions on most subjects and did not hesitate to express them, often in a very earthy way. He may have been the nearest thing to a modern equivalent of Tallichet as to language but not temperament. Patterson usually had a smile on his face.

Patterson was born in Monticello, Arkansas on December 16, 1909. He graduated from Arkansas College and was a high school football coach for several years before he entered the University of Texas Law School. He graduated in 1937 but came to Baker Botts in 1938 from the firm of Phillips, Trammel, Estes, Edwards & Orn in Fort Worth.

Patterson had almost parallel careers in law and in the community. He was best known in the Firm as a labor law specialist, but he also handled oil and gas matters before the Railroad Commission and was active in the environmental and Constitutional law areas of practice. He represented Firm clients in Austin during the legislative sessions. He was especially active with chemical clients and developed a close relationship with the top executives of DuPont and Union Carbide. He was Co-General Counsel for the Texas Chemical Council for years. Patterson was a regular at a roundtable at the Houston Club and is so well remembered that a Hugh Patterson story can be heard there occasionally nine years later.

Patterson was married to Mildred McDavid, a native of Fort Worth and a Rice University graduate. He died in Houston November 28, 1983 at the age of 74.

A November 30, 1983 *Houston Post* article, reproduced here, furnishes an excellent summary of his civic activities:

Hugh M. Patterson, with the Firm 1938 - 1983.

November 30, 1983

Longtime Houston civic leader Hugh M. Patterson has died after a short illness. He was 74.

Patterson, a senior partner in Baker & Botts law firm, spearheaded efforts to beautify downtown Houston, support the 9-5 district-citywide City Council makeup, study state court operations and improve the Texas Medical Center.

He was president of the Houston Chamber of Commerce in 1971, served as chamber director from 1966 to 1979 and helped found the chamber's Greater Houston Community Foundation.

Active in the state Democratic Party, Patterson in 1972 helped organize Texas Democrats for Nixon.

A memorial service for Patterson, who died Monday, will be at 10 a.m. Thursday at First Presbyterian Church, 10 Oakdale.

"I have a deep sense of personal loss," said Louie Welch, chamber of commerce president.

"He was an outstanding lawyer who had a real love for this city," said William Harvin, managing partner of Baker & Botts. "He had a talent for applying the Constitution in a traditional way."

"Patterson 'invented' the Greater Houston Community Foundation and was president of it for 10 years," Welch said.

The foundation was formed as a tax-exempt organization to receive gifts for development of Tranquility Park and beautification of the banks of Allen's Landing and Buffalo Bayou.

Patterson was a member of the Texas Judicial Council. He worked on the drafting of many state legislative bills, including those setting up the Gulf Coast Waste Disposal Authority and the Harris-Galveston Coastal Subsidence District.

He was a member of the Houston City Charter Commission in 1972. In 1979, as a member of the Greater Houston Commission, he supported election of nine City Council members by district and five at large.

Patterson was a member of the board of directors of the Texas Medical Center at the time of his death. He was a director of a non-profit corporation formed to acquire and improve Center Pavilion Hospital to house the medical examiner's facilities and other agencies.

He was a delegate to the Democratic National Convention in 1968, but he bolted the national ticket in 1972 to serve on the steering committee of Texas Democrats for Nixon.

Patterson was born in Monticello, Ark., graduated from Arkansas College and received his law degree from the University of Texas School of Law. He was a trustee of Arkansas College, from which he received its Distinguished Alumnus Award in 1974.

He served as lieutenant commander in the Navy during World War II.

Survivors include his wife, Mildred, his brother, Sam C. Patterson of French Camp, Mississippi, and his sister, Mrs. O. L. Graham of Nashville, Tennessee.

A bird's-eye view of the Texas Medical Center, Houston, circa 1965. Hugh M. Patterson served on the Board of the Texas Medical Center; William C. Harvin is now chairman of that Board.

GARRETT R. TUCKER

Garrett Rezeau Tucker, Jr. was the first graduate of an Ivy League School with no Texas connection to practice with the Firm. He was born in New York City, attended Amherst College, and then graduated from Yale Law School in 1939. Although he had considered getting away from New York, it was an interview with John Bullington which made his decision firm. In 1985, Tucker described Bullington as "the most impressive man I ever met."

The hiring of Tucker indicates both the impression he made on Bullington and Bullington's influence in the Firm. The only other lawyer employed that year was Tom Phillips, who was No. 1 in his class at the University of Texas. Judge Joe Greenhill, former Chief Justice of the Texas Supreme Court and now Of Counsel in the Austin office, tells the story that although he (Greenhill) was No. 2 in that class he was not hired by Baker Botts. The indications are that Tucker, backed by Bullington, was selected over Greenhill for one of the scarce job offers made in those Depression-era times.

Tucker's career began in the usual way. He shared a table in the library with Phillips for two years and then shared an office and one dictating machine with Phillips. He enlisted in the Navy in World War II and was one of those rare people whose military experience affected his career. He was a lieutenant in the Navy and heavily involved in communications. He learned to his surprise that, even with his classical education, he could easily grasp the technical and engineering aspects of this program and even become a teacher before he served in the Pacific.

When he returned from the service, he was ushered into Frank Coates' office and told that he was a corporate lawyer and would work on Tenneco financings. He became a partner in 1950.

A dramatic change in his career took place

Garrett R. Tucker, with the Firm since 1939.

when Brady Cole died suddenly in 1953 and there was no one to take his place in the patent litigation field. Tucker had briefed for Cole for a short period before the war. This and his World War II experiences were factors in his willingness to make a sudden career change and take on Cole's substantial docket.

The same year he became partner (1950), someone convinced him he should run for the Houston Independent School District school board. He did and, surprisingly, won. He was appalled by the conditions in the black schools and made an effort to do something about it. To understand the reception he got in the corporate world one would have to realize how much attitudes in Houston have changed in 40 years. He did not run for a second term.

"Rez" Tucker remained in the patent litigation field the remainder of his career and learned, like Brady Cole, that it meant many lonely days,

148

From its rudimentary well logging in the 1920s in France, Schlumberger has grown to be one of the largest well surveying companies in the world. This picture shows one of Schlumberger's electrical well logging trucks in the 1950s.

weeks, and even months, often out of town, working on matters that not even his law partners understood. He lured Frank Pugsley away from General Electric to take charge of the day-to-day operation of the Patent Department. Among his clients were Schlumberger, Humble (the Standard Companies), Texaco Development, and especially Texas Instruments, which under his direction became a very substantial client.

In 1936, Tucker married Phyllis Burnell. They have three children: Garrett, III, Judith (Mrs. Earle), and Jeffrey J.

THOMAS M. PHILLIPS

Thomas Marion Phillips was a trial lawyer first, last, and always. He liked people, was very active in bar activities, and was a strong advocate at all times for whatever position he chose.

Phillips always detested cold figures and biographical data but some of this is essential. Phillips was born in Greenville, Texas in 1916 and grew up in Marlin in very modest circumstances. It is not known whether it was a friend or a rival in later years who referred to him as "the barefoot boy from Marlin."

Even though he admitted skipping half of his classes in high school, he graduated from the University of Texas first in his class scholastically. Even the very formal *Office Review* item which recorded his employment, admitted that he was president of his Senior Law Class in 1939 and "had made an excellent record." He was employed by the Firm in February 1939 to report when he graduated in June. If Phillips ever did anything after that other than brief or try lawsuits, he wouldn't have wanted it known. During World War II, he served in Military Intelligence from 1941-45.

He returned to the Firm after the war, made rapid strides in the litigation field, and was made a partner in 1950. There were 16 partners in the Firm until he, Holland, and Patterson brought the total to 19.

Phillips spent so much time at the courthouse with a heavy trial docket that it was no surprise that he knew most of the trial lawyers in Houston and formed friendships with both state and federal district judges that lasted a lifetime. Even being elected President of the Houston Bar Association was no surprise, but serving as President of the State Bar of Texas (1967) required a bit more effort. He also was a member of the House of Delegates of the American Bar Association and a Fellow in the American College of Trial Lawyers. In 1973, he was elected as the Outstanding Alumnus

Thomas M. Phillips, with the Firm 1939 - 1991.

of the University of Texas Law School.

One interesting incident occurred when an account executive for one of the brokerage firms came by Phillips' office and recommended a stock. Phillips relentlessly cross-examined the broker as to reasons for the recommendation until his secretary came to the broker's rescue by reminding Phillips that this was not a courthouse and there was no jury.

For years, Phillips was head of the Trial Department and watched the practice slowly change. As he began, the Firm was handling thousands of cases for numerous insurance clients, and Travelers Insurance Co. was the leading fee-paying client of the Firm for a number of years. It was not unusual for a lawyer to carry a docket of 200-300 cases.

As the emphasis shifted from volume to fewer but more substantial cases, he made the adjustment.

According to Phillips, some of his more interesting cases were

1. Representing the State of Alaska in the tidelands litigation with the federal government. He won the case in the Federal District Court and the Court of Appeals for Alaska, but lost it in the U.S. Supreme Court.

2. *Ginther-Warren vs. Taub.* This involved over twelve years of time and was a successful attempt to regain an oil and gas lease for two elderly gentlemen who were without funds and had no files. Very substantial sums were involved.

3. *Ceco vs. Zachry.* His client was a subcontractor in the construction of an Atlas missile base near Abilene in which the jury awarded the client more than it sought. Again large amounts were involved.

During his tenure as President of the Houston Bar Association, Phillips initiated a program to provide free legal services for indigents. With the assistance of Gordon Gooch (also of Baker Botts), he activated the Houston Legal Foundation and devised a system whereby every lawyer in Houston was required to represent an indigent without charge when his turn came on the docket. The purpose of the Foundation was to provide a core of legal experts to assist the indigent. The federal government eventually assumed this project.

One glimpse into the character of Tom Phillips is provided by Ralph Carrigan in his eulogy of Phillips in the Fall 1991 issue of the *Office Review*:

One lasting memory—the second case I followed [Tom] through was a Travelers insurance case in a then very rural Matagorda County. A farm hand leaving a small service station-grocery in an insured farm truck crossed the on-coming lane of traffic into his own lane of traffic only to be met head-on by an automobile which had swerved to miss what its driver thought was a potential head-on collision in his own lane. Severe injuries resulted. In preparing the farm hand, an amiable man of very limited education, Tom was puzzled by his earlier statement on deposition that he had left the service station and pulled into the highway at a 45 degree angle. "Joe," Tom asked, "How in the hell do you know what a 45 degree angle is?" "Mr. Phillips," came the reply, "When I was in the Army they taught us to stand at attention with our feet at a 45 degree angle." Paraphrasing Tom – "Joe, I tell you what I want you to do at the time of the trial. You go ahead and tell the jury just as you have already that you pulled out on to the highway at a 45 degree angle. Then I'm going to ask you how do you know what a 45 degree angle is. At that point, Joe, I want you to stand up from the witness chair, snap to attention, and tell the jury that the Army taught you to stand at attention with your feet at a 45 degree angle." Tom did and Joe did and the jury loved it. Tom and Joe could do no wrong after that. Tom, of course, won the case. The story that came back, which I could never verify, was that the Travelers Insurance agent in Bay City placed a large sign in his office stating: "Insure with Travelers and let Tom Phillips try your case."

Phillips passed away in Galveston on August 8, 1991. He was survived by his wife, Edna, and a daughter, Jane Hobson.

Texas Gulf Sulphur Company facility at New Gulf, Texas, circa 1915. For many years, the Firm represented the Texas Gulf Sulphur Company. Francis G. Coates and, later, Thomas M. Phillips served on its Board of Directors.

HENRY F. HOLLAND

Henry Finch Holland had only a brief career with the Firm. He was employed on September 1, 1945, became a partner in 1950, but withdrew to serve in the State Department under Eisenhower in March 1954.

From 1936 to June 1942, Holland was in private law practice at San Antonio. He was a native of Brownsville and was graduated from the University of Texas Law School with an LL.B. degree in 1936. He held a B.A. degree from the University of the South in Sewanee, Tennessee.

During the period from June 1942 to September 1945, Holland, as a member of the Foreign Service Auxiliary, was assigned to the American Embassy at Mexico City where he served variously as special assistant, assistant to the counselor of Embassy for Economic Affairs, and as Labor Attache.

Holland is best remembered for his work in planning the Mexico City office in 1947. He came directly to Baker Botts after several years of service in the American Embassy in Mexico. He was fluent in Spanish, had a broad acquaintance with economic conditions in Mexico, and, most important of all, knew Fausto Miranda well. He worked closely with Dillon Anderson and Miranda in establishing the Mexico City office.

The Managing Partner stated in the *Office Review* when Holland was employed that he would work with Davis in labor matters and would work with Firm clients in Central and South American matters. Instead, Holland became an expert in Federal Power Commission matters for Tennessee Gas Transmission, and a substantial amount of his time was devoted to this work when he left for his Washington assignment.

Holland served as Assistant Secretary of State for Inter-American Affairs, 1954-56, and elected to open an office in New York when he returned to civilian life. He was still with the firm of

Henry F. Holland, with the Firm 1945 - 1954.

Roberts & Holland when he died of cancer at his home in Greenwich, Connecticut in 1962. He was only 49 at the time of his death.

Holland came to the Firm almost as a lateral partner (he had been out of law school nine years and served only four years as an associate), but he was so closely associated with opening the Mexico City Office that the decision caused no problem. If there were any doubts, Holland's energy, ability, and his engaging sense of humor quickly won him a place in the Firm. As a matter of fact, when he left, there was no one in the Firm to immediately replace him on the important FPC docket.

Holland was survived by his wife, Betty Adams of San Antonio, and three children, Ann, Henry, and William.

The Mexico City offices of Baker, Botts, Miranda, Santamarina y Steta were at No. 1 Paseo de la Reforma and later at No. 76 Paseo de la Reforma. No. 1, the first location of the Baker Botts Mexico City office, was destroyed by an earthquake in the 1950s. In 1973, the Mexico City office became the independent firm of Santamarina y Steta, and the two firms signed an agreement of association which remains in effect. Close ties exist between the two firms—many lawyers from each have enjoyed tours of duty in the other; annual events such as the Houston office "Prom" and the Mexico City office Christmas party are attended by lawyers from the other. The highlight for many was undoubtedly the lavish celebration of the 100th anniversary of the partnership of Peter W. Gray and W. B. Botts hosted by the Mexico City lawyers in 1966 and featuring baby bullfights, an epic soccer match, and much goodwill.

Some of the young men whose careers were delayed by World War II, but who returned to or joined the Firm after V-J Day:
Top row, l. to r., B. John Mackin, John F. Heard, James K. Nance; *bottom row, l. to r.,* A. B. White and Baine P. Kerr,
all of whom were later partners, and author J. H. Freeman who retired as Assistant to the Managing Partner in 1984
but even now reports to the office almost daily. His photograph here will be a surprise to him.

CHAPTER

5

Downtown Houston in 1940. The City Hall had recently been completed.

THE POST-WAR FIRM: 1945-1971

The Depression had not ended for the Firm when World War II began. As a matter of fact, only five lawyers were hired from 1932 through 1940. The Firm was devastated by the War. Not only did a number of the older associates leave for the military, but many who were employed just as the War began only signed the roster before leaving. A commitment was made to every person who entered the military that a position would be waiting when he returned. The war experiences of twenty-three men who returned from the military are included in *Baker, Botts in World War II.* This book was well received and has gone into a second printing. Considering the fact that the Firm had fewer than 40 lawyers at this time, a remarkable assimilation project was accomplished.

One of the more memorable Firm parties was a welcome home dinner party for World War II veterans given at the old Houston Country Club on Lawndale. It was a joyous, emotional occasion with wives attending, of course. Some of these folks hadn't seen one another since before the War, and all formality went out of the window. The dinner bell rang at 8:00 p.m., and, according to one eyewitness, the first people were not at their seats until 9:15. Some claim the aftermath of the Parish farewell party exceeded this one in exuberance, but it was a stag affair and there were not nearly as many who would admit to being witnesses.

Houston Country Club, 1930s. Edwin B. Parker was instrumental in the organization of the club in 1904 and was its second president. Several other Firm partners have also been president of the Houston Country Club. Initially, the Club leased land from Rice Institute and constructed a nine-hole golf course and a small clubhouse on land that is now the site of the abandoned Jefferson Davis Hospital. In 1909, the club purchased grounds near Harrisburg on Bray's Bayou and built the clubhouse pictured here. After HCC moved to new facilities on the west side of town in 1957, the old property became Gus Wortham Park. Many Firm events have been held at the various HCC locations.

157

For the period immediately before World War II, as well as afterward, we have numerous eyewitnesses. There are common themes in the interviews of lawyers of this generation:

- Financial hardship (beginning salaries were very low and those who served in the military had to take pay reductions when they returned).
- A very rigid discipline.
- The favorable treatment of the World War II veterans was viewed very positively. The Firm commitment that all veterans had a place when they returned and long-time associate Al Fulbright's cheerful letters keeping them posted on Firm news during the war made very favorable impressions.

Alfred H. Fulbright, a long-time Firm lawyer who retired as an associate in 1966. He was the principal editor (he called himself "Pusher") of *Baker, Botts in World War II*.

- They were also pleased that the partners and their wives took enough interest in them to invite them to dinners in their homes and to social events. They made a point of saying this was not done because of obligation or for recruiting purposes, but because it gave both parties pleasure.
- It was all worth it to work for what they considered the best firm available, they were awed by the intellect and ability of the partners, and especially enjoyed the close relationships developed with their contemporaries over the years. One gets the impression that money was not even a consideration in making their decision. Indeed, in the "buyers' market" for young lawyers in the post-war decades, not even honor graduates from leading law schools had much bargaining power with the major corporate law firms, including Baker Botts.

Another common theme among lawyers who served during this period was the people who made an impression on them. They may not have remembered all of the partners, but there were three nonlawyer people they all remembered, and no history would be complete without their mention. They were "Rowell," "Miss Ruth," and "Chester," as some referred to them.

Miss Willie A. Rowell, the office manager, is discussed in a lawyer interview elsewhere.

Two of Miss Rowell's enforcers were Ruth Andrews and Chester Woodard, both very unlikely selections. "Miss Ruth" was a sister of Jesse Andrews, but no one ever talked about that (and some didn't know it). She was a maiden lady who lived with Miss Rowell and who was totally looked after by Miss Rowell. She was a slight grandmotherly looking lady and not a person one would expect to see employed in a large law office. She was in charge of supplies, stationery, and equipment, and it was she who decided whether a lawyer was using too many pencils or was wasting stationery. Miss Ruth also

"Miss Ruth" Andrews, sister of name partner Jesse Andrews, makes her rounds in the office, 1952.

was in charge of "the table." This was a creation of Miss Rowell's. Any secretary who had an overload put the excess on "the table," and no secretary could be caught loafing while there was work on the table. Miss Rowell took pride in the fact that the Firm had the lowest secretary to lawyer ratio of all the major firms in Houston, and yet the secretarial work was promptly performed.

There are many stories concerning Miss Rowell and Miss Ruth. Recently one of the senior partners recalled that he had been with the Firm about a year and was feeling pleased that employees were calling him "Mister" and that he was respected as a professional. One day he was reading in the Library with his feet propped on a table. Miss Ruth spotted him and her only statement was, "Boy, get your feet off that table."

On another occasion one of the senior partners dictated a number of letters before lunch and asked that they be put on personal stationery. When he came back from lunch and asked if the letters were ready, the secretary told him she could not get any stationery. Miss Ruth had told her "_____ (using his first name) is using too much stationery. He can't have any more." There was no exception. The partner smiled and said "Miss Ruth shouldn't talk like that."

Chester Woodard's title was Porter. He may as well have had only one name because he was known in the office and all over town as "Chester." He was in charge of the Firm's banking run and mail delivery to clients' offices. It was said that Chester could gain admittance to the offices of more C.E.O.s in town than some of the partners. Chester's salary was extremely modest but all five of his children received college degrees. He moonlighted for the partners in various capacities.

One of Chester's assignments was training the mailroom personnel, especially summer messengers. Again, there was a system, and it was the Baker Botts system, and there was no other way to handle the mail. Chester could be heard rushing

down the hall telling some son of a prominent Houstonian all that was wrong with the way he was doing the job. In a recent interview, James A. Baker, III said that Chester was the toughest boss he ever had. Working for Ronald Reagan was a picnic by comparison.

J. H. Freeman recalls that after he succeeded Raymond Neilson as the head of the Accounting Department, and finally had his own office and secretary, Miss Rowell stopped him as he was about to catch an elevator and said, "J. H., would you carry those two heavy briefcases downstairs for Chester. He has a bad back."

Chester A. Woodard, pictured in this photograph from 1961, served as Firm porter and messenger for many years.

When Chester retired as Porter in 1966, the Firm gave him a very liberal retirement benefit, and he lived well until he was 93, going to spas twice a year to take "the baths." When Chester's wife died (she predeceased him), a number of partners went to the funeral, and one was called on to eulogize her. Although he had never met Mrs. Woodard, he was a trial lawyer and performed well. Even though Chester was 93 when he died, his funeral filled the church, and Baker Botts was well represented.

Some have asked how Miss Rowell got such authority. The Firm had a tradition of making maximum use of nonlawyer personnel even before the turn of the century, and by 1912, when Parker prepared his first Plan of Organization, he devoted one-half page to Capt. Baker's duties and one and one-half pages to those of Mr. Stephens, the Administrator at that time. In addition, Miss Rowell had been Capt. Baker's secretary and had his confidence. Also, she cared for the sister of Mr. Andrews, the second senior partner, and had his support. In truth, however, Miss Rowell probably didn't need this backing. She ruled by force of personality.

When Miss Rowell retired in 1955 after 47⅓ years, she was pleased with the fact that she had never had a full vacation in any year. The Firm was her life. Miss Rowell was not forgotten when she retired. When she had to sell her home in a suburb, one of the partners, Jim Lee, helped her to obtain a premium price, and the Firm arranged for her to move to a retirement home represented by the Firm. Maude Tomlinson, who succeeded to her position at a later date, looked after her on a day-to-day basis and got her money out of the

Sharpstown Bank a day before it collapsed. The Firm, again by special influence, arranged for her to stay in a full nursing unit during her terminal illness. Because of this assistance, Miss Rowell was able to leave a fairly substantial sum to Rice University, and to this day several scholarships are granted at Rice each year through the "Willie Rowell and Ruth Andrews Scholarship Fund for Needy Women."

The loss of numerous key partners was mentioned in the formal history. When Parish left the Firm on December 31, 1953, the Firm had over the past ten years already lost Tom Scurry, Gaius Gannon (withdrawal), Bill Ryan, Brady Cole, John Bullington, Palmer Hutcheson (withdrawal), Ralph Feagin, and Walter Walne. Fortunately, the

---

JOHN McCULLOUGH'S ANNOUNCEMENT OF WILLIE ROWELL'S RETIREMENT

July 5, 1955

To all in the office:

On March 1, 1908, Miss W. A. Rowell became an employee of Baker, Botts, Parker & Garwood. The Firm had its offices in what was then known as the Commercial National Bank Building (now the Western Union Building), on Franklin Avenue immediately East of the Southern Pacific Building. The lawyers in the office at that time were Capt. James A. Baker, Edwin B. Parker, Jesse Andrews, Clarence R. Wharton, H. M. Garwood, Thomas H. Botts and Clarence L. Carter. Miss Rowell was secretary for Mr. Andrews for awhile and then served as secretary for Capt. Baker for approximately ten years. In 1919 she became office manager, having under her supervision officially all office personnel except lawyers and the Accounting Department and unofficially most of the lawyers. She continued in this capacity until a number of years ago when the Firm had grown to such size that supervision of the stenographic force and the file room was shifted to Mrs. Harvin.

Effective July 1, 1955, after completing 47-1/3 years of service with the Firm, Miss Rowell retired. She will be in the office a week or so longer, however, primarily to handle the purchase of furniture and equipment for the new offices we are acquiring in the Mellie Esperson Building and problems incident to the removal of the wall which will bring all the hall in the Mellie Esperson Building except the elevator lobby within our doors. I am sure that Baker Botts has never had in its service a person who was more faithful or more devoted to the Firm than Miss Rowell. The sadness occasioned by her retirement is tempered only by the hope that she will enjoy some well-earned leisure.

The functions heretofore performed by Miss Rowell will be performed by Mrs. Harvin, who has herself been with the Firm more than 28 years. Mrs. Anderson will be in charge of the File Room, and Miss Tomlinson will handle the assignment and distribution of work among stenographers. Any stenographers who are in a position to take on additional work from time to time should in the future check with Miss Tomlinson instead of Mrs. Harvin.

– John T. McCullough

Downtown Houston in the late 1940's. The Mellie Esperson Building had been completed, adjacent to the Niels Esperson Building, and the Firm's offices soon expanded to include space on the 15th and 16th floors of the newer building.

Firm had young partners waiting in the wings, and they simply moved up to take over. Financially the Firm continued to grow at a steady pace after the war, but the gross reached $1,000,000 for the first time only in 1946. Al Parish was so pleased that he circulated a list of all fees collected that year to all partners.

Feagin, Parker's protégé, died in 1946, and Parish was instrumental in selecting Dillon Anderson to become Managing Partner in 1947.

John McCullough was the next Managing Partner, and he served for 19 years. McCullough, to an outsider, would not have been a likely candidate for the post. There were many partners senior to him and others better known both in the Firm and in the city. He claimed he was drafted because no one else wanted the assignment. The Firm was not looking for a rainmaker or a public relations representative, but one who could act as a conciliator, who was an excellent lawyer, highly respected, unbiased, and who had the confidence of his contemporaries. McCullough was that man.

The Firm had a tradition in the post-war period of having a New Year's Day party at the home of one of the senior partners. A buffet meal was served, and broadcast football bowl games furnished the entertainment. Some of the associates in the late 1940s developed the idea of

161

presenting skits at these functions, lampooning the partners. The program consisted of skits and songs with original words sung to popular tunes of the day. These were cleverly done and hilariously received. The Firm eventually outgrew this presentation, but the songs were compiled and printed in a booklet labelled "The Lowly Molies," copies of which are still available. In 1990, Jim Shepherd's widow sent to the Firm one of the New Year's song sheets which was in his billfold when he died. It is reproduced here to give the reader a flavor of these young associate productions:

(TUNE - JINGLE BELLS)

Baker, Botts,
Baker, Botts,
All work and no play,
Oh what fun it is to ride,
An ediphone all day.

Baker, Botts,
Baker, Botts,
All work and no play,
Oh what fun it is to file,
A work report each day.

Dashing through the Digest,
Searching for the law,
Turning through Advance Sheets,
Working fingers raw.

We start each morn at eight,
We stay till rather late,
But oh what fun to work and write,
Those long damn briefs at night.

Baker, Botts,
Baker, Botts,
Hard work is the way,
Oh what fun it is to hide,
In the men's room all the day.

The layout of the offices in the Niels Esperson Building was mentioned earlier, including the fact that numerous lawyer offices opened into the Library. Homer Bruce was the partner in charge of the Library, and he took any violation of Library rules as a personal affront. He was a very volatile person and minced no words when he spoke or wrote. Some of Mr. Bruce's memos were collector's items. Here are only a few:

TO ALL LAWYERS:

Library or Boiler House?

Last Friday, June 27, 1952, the incessant noise and confusion in the library became so unbearable that lawyers working therein were forced to suspend and temporarily go elsewhere. It has been suggested by the firm that I call this to the attention of those naturally interested in the matter. I therefore suggest the following points:

1.   The library is the office of certain lawyers. How would those of you with private offices like for several others to plant themselves in your office and carry on extended conversations about nothing in particular?

2.   We have nearly the whole floor of the building and a special conference room. There is no necessity for holding noisy or other conferences in the center aisle even though the center book shelves afford a comfortable place to rest an elbow.

3.   Walking around among the tables—by men and witnesses, should be done only when absolutely necessary.

4.   Trial lawyers, interviewing a number of witnesses, should not park the excess in the library.

5.   Doors have been placed on the offices surrounding the library for the purpose of confining the noise generated therein. When closed they perform this function fairly well.

Actually no part of this memorandum need be read except the heading.

– Homer L. Bruce

Montage of photographs of attorneys taken in the lobby of the Firm's offices on the 16th floor of the Esperson Building. These photographs were taken by Firm receptionist Betty Moore with a movie camera in October 1952. Pictured are, *top row, l. to r.*, Alvin M. Owsley, Jr., John T. Maginnis, Frank M. Wozencraft; *2nd row*, Homer L. Bruce, Thomas E. Berry; *bottom row*, Harold Young and Jean Dalby.

TO ALL LAWYERS:

Commerce Clearing House
Tax Court Report
No. 783, June 8, 1962

This number is missing. It and similar Tax Court Reports are circulated to Messrs. Bruce, Jewett, McCullough, Maginnis, Jewell, Croom, Piro and Berry. Each of them say they do not have it. I do not know. It is extremely important that this be located today. If any of you have it, please return it today to Mrs. Forrest.

– Homer L. Bruce

TO ALL LAWYERS:

Library Protocol

This memorandum is simply to reiterate some observations that have been made so many times in the past.

The best way to ruin a book is to open it, glance at a page and walk off leaving it lying wide open. An even better way is to pile up a number of open books on top of each other. *A record is being kept – not by Mrs. Forrest – of those who enjoy this practice. One young lawyer recently left and went back home to another state because he was not allowed to continue this practice.*

Replacing books is not the chore so many think. We now have five libraries and soon will have a sixth. It is not the function of Mrs. Forrest to replace books. When a lawyer reads something in a book and is through with it, it takes no time to replace it—not one tenth of the time he spends on coffee breaks. The messengers cannot do this work all day long, with the result that books pile up and others have difficulty locating the ones desired. Try putting a book back and see how easy it is.

– Homer L. Bruce

The next day a response appeared in the in-baskets of all the attorneys. The author was anonymous:

There are strange things done in the
midnight sun
By the men who toil for gold.
The Esperson Trails have their secret tales
That would make your blood run cold.
The Niels lights have seen queer sights
But the queerest they ever did see
Was the race of the moles, putting books back
in their holes
On the shelves of the sacred library.

– Robert W. Service
(Ex Mole 03)
Fairbanks, Alaska

Mr. Bruce was known to have confronted a young associate on one occasion. He walked up to the associate who had several books stacked in the disapproved manner and said, "How would you like to have your pay docked for the cost of repairing those books?" The immediate reply was "Mr. Bruce, it wouldn't be possible. My salary check isn't big enough to cover it."

Two other memos, one written by and one inspired by Mr. Bruce, are worth repeating:

TO ALL LAWYERS:

As you know, Mr. McCullough requested me to act for him as Managing Partner during his absence. From the facts set out below I believe you can realize how forcibly there has been brought home to me the problem Mr. McCullough has so often mentioned.

I have before me a statement of the delinquencies in the daily records of work for this year up to June 30. For those six months there are 311 lawyer-days for which no daily records have been turned in. There were 140 normal working days during this six months. These 311 days were the equivalent of 2 1/6 lawyers' time.

This might be compared to Sakowitz having two high powered salesmen selling goods actively all day long and turning in no sales slips during the six months.

– Homer L. Bruce

TO ALL IN THE OFFICE:

Christmas Cards

Today, Mr. Bruce brought to the attention of other partners an item which appeared in the Wall Street Journal of September 18, 1958, reading as follows:

BUSINESS REBELLION mounts against Christmas cards.

The First National City Bank of New York informs its friends it won't mail out any holiday greetings this Christmas. The custom has lost its personal character and has "become a matter of routine," says Bank Chairman Howard C. Shepherd. Two other major New York banks and the Prudential Insurance Co. speedily announced they were following suit.

The Greeting Card Association is miffed.

In Europe, 100 banks stopped the annual card mailing spree last Christmas.

He stated he knew from first-hand experience what a task it is for wives to address Christmas cards, *because* Mrs. Bruce had drafted him to assist in addressing theirs. *He suggested that we discontinue the practice of sending cards to others in the office and thus reduce the tasks of our wives and others preliminary to Christmas.* His suggestion met with unanimous approval from the partners present, and, while it is recognized that this is a matter of the individual's choice, I am confident that

none in the office would feel slighted if he or she did not receive a Christmas card from others here.

– John T. McCullough

To this day, many long-time Firm lawyers still do not send Christmas cards to others at the Firm.

Yet another example of Mr. Bruce's innovative thinking involved an antique Buick he owned, which was his pride and joy. (This was after he retired.) Once he needed a part that was not available in Houston. General Motors was on strike, so no order could be filled. After exhausting all other possibilities, Bruce started bombarding the home of the Chairman of the Board with telegrams. Shortly thereafter, he got a call telling him to meet a certain plane and his part would be on it.

The Firm name changes became more rapid after World War II:

1946	BAKER, BOTTS, ANDREWS & WALNE
1948	BAKER, BOTTS, ANDREWS & PARISH
1951	BAKER, BOTTS, ANDREWS & SHEPHERD
1962	BAKER, BOTTS, SHEPHERD & COATES
1971	BAKER & BOTTS

Jesse Andrews died on December 29, 1961, at the age of 87, still holding a senior interest and working full-time.

Even in the early post-war period, the way law was practiced had not changed substantially for years from the standpoint of technology and available equipment. There were probably more advances in the twenty years after 1954 than in the previous sixty years. One of the background interviews was with a lawyer who was employed in 1954 and addresses the subject in his 1985 interview:

When I arrived in 1954, I found that there was an organization that provided virtually all services for lawyers. It was designed to leave us free to practice law, 100% of our time. I further found especially in talking with people in other firms, my contemporaries that had gone elsewhere, that this arrangement in Baker & Botts was quite unusual, if not unique. For example, we had an accounting and a billing department, we had a file department that handled all of our filing, we had messengers, and we had other service people. We did not have to worry about hiring secretaries. We didn't have to worry about office furniture; all of these things were provided by the organizational side of the Firm, so that we were supposed to practice law 100% of our time and not worry about these things.

Next, I would like to comment about the technology that we had. I think it is accurate to say that we have always had the latest and the best, but the technology that was available in 1954 was remarkably primitive by today's standards. For example, if we wanted something copied, there were only three ways of having that done. The first was to hand it to a secretary and say copy this, which meant that she typed the document out on a sheet of paper and if you wanted more than one copy, she used carbon paper. Another way, relatively expensive and hard to get done by Miss Rowell was photostating, and the third way was what we called the purple ditto machine. That was about it.

Dictating equipment, we had the latest. The records were some sort of a bake-a-lite material in the form of thick cylinders. When you wanted to do some dictating, and you didn't have a record available, you called the mailroom and you asked for some dictating records. They brought you down a container, that's very much like a six-pack with a handle. It had six cardboard cylinders and in each cardboard container was the dictating cylinder. You put it in the machine and you

couldn't get a lot of dictation on it before you had used it all up and you could go through a six-pack in a hurry. And you would send your six-pack on to a secretary then. After she had transcribed what you had dictated she would send the used cylinders back to the mailroom where they would be put in a machine and the inscribed portion would be shaved off. As you can imagine, each cylinder got thinner and thinner, as it was repeatedly shaved off and finally the ends started cracking off and it got quite thin. The mailroom people, however, would preserve those and you could use them on the center half. If you got one set that was partially broken cylinders, you got very little dictating time in before that was gone and it was a mark of whether Miss Andrews liked you as to whether you got new cylinders or broken cylinders. By the early 1960s the technology had started changing very dramatically. By then all the dictating equipment had been changed and newer models had disks rather than cylinders and very thin discs that were not reused.

I can remember one time, Pat Murphy, John Kirkland and I noted that there were certain services that we needed that we didn't have. And we said it would be very helpful if the Firm would get a postage meter, a relatively new thing so that we didn't have to fight battles over stamps when we were trying to get things mailed at the last minute. We wanted some professional proofreaders and some other things and within a very short period of time all of these new services were provided. About 1960, I was visiting in San Francisco at the firm of Pillsbury, Madison & Sutro and the lawyer there wanted me to see their Flex-a-Writers. I had no idea what a Flex-a-Writer was and I inspected them and became intensely interested in them. They were automatic typewriters driven by paper tape made by Frieden. They were at the time the best automatic typewriters available if not the only ones. But, they were using these on long documents such as wills and trust agreements and I was very interested in them. I came back and talked with our Managing Partner, John McCullough, and explained to him what they were and how they would work and he suggested I take two of our ladies who were experts on office equipment out to the Frieden office and have a demonstration. I called out there and asked if they had a Flex-a-Writer and they said yes, they did and they could demonstrate it. We got out there and they started demonstrating it and they were set up to do it on repetitive form letters, that were to be used over and over as to which they wanted original typing. I was showing our ladies how they could be used for legal documents here in the office. Finally the Frieden man interrupted me, and he said, didn't you say you're with a law firm. And I said, yes. And he said something remarkable. He said, "How in the world are you going to use this machine in your law office?" Well, he never did understand that. That's when Frieden dropped out of the business. They didn't see their opportunities, but we bought one. I was the primary if not the sole user at the beginning. It was so noisy, we had to put it in a special room, we had to bring in some acoustical tiles and everything else. Finally, we got another and many other lawyers started using them. And we started really for the first time standardizing our forms in order to utilize these things. Keep in mind now, at this point, IBM had no product that would correspond at all with this. Sometime, I am going to guess in the mid-60's, IBM did come out with its first product along these lines. It was a magnetic tape machine rather than a paper tape machine. It was called a MTST. Some of us spent a great deal of time together trying to determine the merits of the products available at that time. There were a number, some paper tape, some magnetic and we opted in favor of the IBM product and have been with IBM products ever since. Of course, we have gone from MTST, to Mag Card to System 6 to Displaywriter and PC and there was running

through all of these times an explosion of technology available to lawyers as well as to others that was revolutionizing the law practice. I can remember when I was first up here the nearest thing we had to a calculator was an old Monroe calculator. We had an electric one and a mechanical one.

In the same interview, the partner discusses Miss Rowell.

Now one of the remarkable things about the system then was that we lawyers did not sign any letters. We prepared our letters, in the plural form, using "we" and "us," relating to the Firm, never the first person or the singular "I" or "me" and our letters were prepared and if they were to go out that day, the rule was they were supposed to be on Miss Rowell's desk by 4:00 o'clock. Miss Rowell then reviewed the letters from the viewpoint of the secretarial work. She was very strict on that, and she bounced a lot of letters back for that problem. She also read them with some other things in mind, particularly she kept an eye on what the young lawyers were doing and if she didn't like a letter as a practical matter, you redid it, or it didn't go out. And of course, she signed it with the name of the Firm at that time, which was Baker, Botts, Andrews & Shepherd, so a letter would conclude, "Very truly yours," and then signed in ink in her unique handwriting Baker, Botts, Andrews and Shepherd. That was the only way the recipient had of knowing who had written the letter. He wasn't supposed to know. It wasn't a secret, but when he wrote back he wrote to the Firm, Messrs. Baker, Botts, Andrews and Shepherd. I believe the institutional aspect of this ought to be obvious at this point. It was the Firm practicing law and the clients were clients of the Firm and not with any one of us. We were working as part of the Firm and not as individual lawyers. These were very important attributes, I thought.

Miss Rowell ran a very tight ship. When I

LAWYERS, 1868-1992

Year		Lawyers	Partners	Associates	Associates/ Partner Ratio
1868		2	2	—	—
1878		2	2	—	—
1888		3	3	—	—
1898		3	2	1	.5
1908		7	6	1	.16
1918		16	12	4	.33
1928		25	10	15	1.50
1938		39	16	23	1.44
1948		47	14	33	2.36
1958		76	25	51	2.04
1968		132	41	91	2.22
1978	(1/1/78)	199	79	120	1.52
	(12/31/78)	221	79	142	1.80
1988	(1/1/88)	329	121	208	1.72
1992	(1/1/92)	420	146	274	1.88

BAKER, BOTTS, ANDREWS & WHARTON

ESPERSON BUILDING

HOUSTON

BAKER, BOTTS, ANDREWS & WALNE

ESPERSON BUILDING

HOUSTON 2

BAKER, BOTTS, ANDREWS & PARISH

ESPERSON BUILDING

HOUSTON 2

BAKER, BOTTS, ANDREWS & SHEPHERD

ESPERSON BUILDING

BAKER, BOTTS, SHEPHERD & COATES

ESPERSON BUILDING

HOUSTON, TEXAS 77002

Telephone CA 4-9441

BAKER & BOTTS

ONE SHELL PLAZA

910 LOUISIANA

HOUSTON, TEXAS 77002-4995

These six samples of the Firm's letterhead represent all the names the Houston office of the Firm has known since the end of World War II.

168

DECADE GROWTH RATES TOTAL LAWYERS	
Year	% Increase
1918-28	56
1928-38	36
1938-48	21
1948-58	62
1958-68	119
1968-78	51
1978-88	65
1988-92 (4 years)	28

arrived, she gave me my office key and looked me in the eyes and said if you lose it, it will be $1 for another one. One time when I was in her office not long after that, Baker, Jr. came in and said, "Miss Willie, I lost my office key, I need another." She looked up at him and said, "Jim, that's the third one you lost recently and you don't get another one." Now keep in mind that Baker at that time was a Senior Partner in the Firm. Another time, I recall, I was in her office and a partner of some years was walking down the hall. "Hey boy, come in here," she said; "Do you think I am going to let this letter go out? Take it back and try again." That's the way she was. She was a very capable woman.

Now addressing the effect that working for Baker Botts had on his practice of law:

I want to talk, to add a few comments here, about excellence in the practice of law. I feel that each of us, including myself, was a better lawyer with the Firm than we would have been otherwise. Much better. We were acquainted with the history of the Firm, the reputation that it had and were constantly exposed to the work that had gone on

before since the briefs and the legal memoranda were collected together in the library and in the process and in the case of briefing, we would see briefing that had been done in the past. We would see the excellence of it. Opinion letters were collected there and we realized that it was a Baker Botts standard, the highest standard around. We all realized we had to meet that standard. It wasn't a personal standard necessarily that we were meeting. It was the Firm's standard which, in the case of most of us, was higher than our personal standard would have been had we not been with the Firm. I can recall, on many instances, that I'd be preparing a document or a letter and I'd be ready to sign off on it and then I would say to myself, can I improve it? Is it really up to the standard expected and often the answer was no and I would go through another draft. Indeed, sometimes, I would go through 2 or 3 more drafts before I turned it loose. This was a great thing for me and I think for virtually everyone because it induced us to reach heights of excellence in the practice of law I don't think that we would have reached on our own. Much of the tradition that I have heard of goes back to Mr. Parker. For a long time the Baker Botts Firm was Baker, Botts, Parker and Garwood and Mr. Parker was the Managing Partner of the Firm, perhaps the first one the Firm had. Through the years, I have had discussions about our Firm with lawyers throughout the country and when I note that we had a Managing Partner before the time of the first World War, I am uniformly met with amazement because the development of Managing Partners in law firms is generally considered to have occurred after that. We had Mr. Parker back then. One of the things that Mr. Parker got everyone to do was answer mail promptly. Indeed, I have heard it said that perhaps that practice, more than anything else, was responsible for the new business and the growth of the Firm in those days. Lawyers in this part of the world were notoriously dilatory but there was an inflexible rule around here that your mail had to be answered promptly. If the letter that came in by mail required a great deal of work, that might be deferred in order to do the work, but it was required that you send back by return mail at least a short, one sentence letter acknowledging receipt. Indeed, I can remember when I came with the Firm, many of my new assignments came from the office of the Managing Partner. The final sentence of the memorandum would be "Receipt has not been acknowledged." That was a signal that instantly I was to prepare a letter acknowledging receipt and saying that a reply to the letter would be coming in due course. I have heard it said that back in Mr. Parker's day, the answering of mail was even carried out on Sunday. Houston was a small town then. Lawyers came downtown to church and sometimes during the day on Sunday many would come by the office and tend to their mail that had been received.

The rapid growth in the size of law firms had not yet begun. The Firm had only 125 lawyers in late 1970. In the early 1960s at a meeting of large law firm leaders in New York City, the Managing Partner of one of the largest firms in New York presented a paper, the thrust of which was that after a detailed study it was determined that the maximum size to which a firm could grow would be 160. Beyond that, the firm would be unmanageable. It is not surprising that Managing Partners in those days were expected to carry on their law practice and manage on the side.

The preceding tables show how much of the Firm's growth has taken place in recent years. Except during World War II, this growth has been astonishingly steady since World War I.

Houston by 1960 was feeling a new pride as the city neared the 1,000,000 level. (The actual population figure was 938,000.) In 1962, NASA was completed. In 1963 there were ten new buildings downtown, including the two we know as

Tenneco and Exxon, and the total rental space downtown increased by more than 40%. The One Shell Plaza building (completed in 1970) was the beginning of an even bigger downtown building boom. The Hyatt Regency Hotel and Pennzoil Place were completed in the seventies, to be followed later by Texas Commerce Tower, RepublicBank Center and Allied Bank Plaza.

In the late 1960s, discussions were begun as to whether it was time once more to move "to the newest and finest building in town." Many possibilities were discussed (primarily buildings controlled by clients), but finally Gerald Hines announced plans for One Shell Plaza, and the Firm made arrangements for a participating interest and leased 3½ floors. By summer 1969, The Houston Intercontinental Airport was completed and Houston's population had reached 1,233,000. The move was made in January 1971, and one year later William C. Harvin assumed the duties of Managing Partner.

Among the many companies to turn to Baker Botts in the 1950s and 1960s were Gerald D. Hines Interests and Pennzoil Company. The Houston Galleria, shown here in 1987, catapulted Gerald D. Hines to the top ranks of the nation's developers. The acquisitions, divestitures, and public offerings of Pennzoil Company gave Baker Botts the opportunity to develop further its expertise in corporate matters. This photograph of Keith Funston, president of the New York Stock Exchange, and J. Hugh Liedtke, Chief Executive Officer of Pennzoil Company, was taken on July 8, 1963, the day Pennzoil Company's common stock was admitted to trading on the New York Stock Exchange.

Downtown Houston in the early 1970s. One Shell Plaza was the tallest building in Houston.

CHAPTER

6

The reception areas of the 29th and 30th floors of One Shell Plaza, Houston, respectively, 1971. Pictured are receptionists Kay Thompson, Betty Moore, and Natalie Taylor. The contemporary design of the new primavera-clad Houston offices was revolutionary and somewhat controversial in 1971. Many of the design ideas have now been widely copied by others for professional office space, and the Firm's offices in Austin, Dallas, New York, and Washington have deliberately incorporated features reminiscent of the Houston space.

One Shell Plaza, bounded by Louisiana, Walker, Smith, and McKinney, in downtown Houston, 1989. The Firm's offices were moved to this Gerald D. Hines building in 1971, and originally occupied the 29th, 30th, 31st, and half of the 28th floors. Currently, the Firm's Houston office occupies floors 29-39 and substantial space on the mall and basement levels, plus the top two floors of a nearby smaller Hines building at Rusk and Louisiana.

SINCE 1971

Even early after World War II, the Firm had developed fairly sophisticated management reports, but the information had to be compiled manually. For example, to complete a unit inventory, lawyer hours were first posted to a client card by item, the hours were multiplied by each lawyer's billing rate to convert to units, and then all units were added to obtain an inventory figure. This process required one month of time so that the information was always one month late.

In the 1960s, as computer capability developed, outside experts were consulted to assist in developing a computer system for the Firm. The problem was that the outside experts wished to develop a generic system which all law firms could use while Baker Botts insisted on obtaining the management information it was already using, but on a much speedier basis.

The problem was solved when D. Thomas Moody was employed as an associate in the corporate department. Moody had worked his way through school as a computer programmer and agreed to develop a personalized firm program in addition to practicing law. This was a very successful endeavor, and in 1973 the first computer was acquired. Moody became a partner in 1977, but resigned in 1982 to become president of Charter Oil Company.

Richard Berry, who assisted Moody and is now in charge of Data Processing, prepared the following history of Data Processing/Word Processing in April 1990:

Data Processing/Word Processing
History at Baker Botts

1967: MTST machines in Word Processing.
1972: Converted word processing centers from MTSTs to Mag Cards. Some secretaries' typewriters replaced with Mag Cards.
1973: Acquired first computer, an IBM S/3 Model 10, primarily for Work Records and Management Reports.
1976: Computer upgraded to an IBM S/370 Model 115, primarily to support text search database for Tenneco case.
1978: Word processing centers converted to IBM System 6. IBM Dictabelt (used "mylar-like" belts) dictating equipment replaced with Dictaphone Desktop Standard Cassette machines.
1981: Computer upgraded to an IBM 4341.
1982: Leased three IBM 8100 word processing systems; used by small group of word processing centers and secretaries. IBM first announced the Personal Computer with "open architecture."
1983: On-line accounting system; began major word processing conversion of all secretaries and word processing centers to IBM Displaywriters connected to multiple IBM 8100 systems.
1984: Computer upgraded to an IBM 4381; word processing conversion complete.
1985: On-line Work Records; began attaching IBM PC-XTs with Displaywrite 3 for

The Executive Committee of the Firm in 1972, at the time the decision was made to open the Washington office, was composed of, from left, William C. Harvin, Hugh M. Patterson, B. John Mackin, George H. Jewell, and Thomas Marion Phillips.

additional growth in word processing. Dictaphone Desktop Standard Cassette Dictating equipment replaced with Dictaphone Micro Cassette portable models.

1987: On-line billing system, on-line telephone bills for secretaries; upgraded telephone system to Rolm, which allowed lawyers access to Lexis and Westlaw via Cypress telephone workstations in their offices (firm-wide); implemented DISOSS on the host computer to connect all 8100 systems in all offices for word processing; Litigation Support Department started with own staff and multiple PC databases.

1988: Conflict of Interest system (BIS), computer upgraded to an IBM 3081.

1989: Firm-wide word processing conversion from IBM Displaywriters, PCs, and 8100 systems to Compaq PCs directly attached to the host computer, using WordPerfect 5.0 and DISOSS.

Currently use wide range of latest office systems equipment in the areas of

Telex/Facsimile, Duplicating, Dictation, Document Scanning, and Desktop Publishing (typesetting and graphics). Currently using optical disk ("WORM") technology to convert 8100 archive diskettes.

One's first tendency would be to be amused by the statement of the New York law firm managing partner made in 1961 that a law firm could not grow beyond 160 lawyers because it would not be possible to manage a firm of that size. He was probably correct — with the management tools then available. As the technology report just quoted indicates, very substantial strides have been made in the last twenty years. Certainly, this could not have been anticipated thirty years ago.

As of January 1992, the Firm has over 400 attorneys in four offices as follows:

	Partners	Associates	Total
Austin	5	19	24
Dallas	23	53	76
Houston	102	164	266
Washington	16	38	54
Total:	146	274	420

[As this is a history and is a book about people, the period from 1971 to date cannot be reported with historical perspective and since there are entirely too many partners to treat individually, only the Managing Partners will be mentioned briefly. William C. Harvin served from 1972 until 1984, and E. William Barnett has been Managing Partner since. (See their biographies at the end of this chapter.) Other items of interest will be discussed. A list of all partners of the Firm and the date admitted is included in the appendix.]

There are interesting family relationships in the long history of the Firm. The most obvious, of course, are the Bakers in the Firm, Capt. Baker, his father, his son, and his great-grandson, as well as

The Washington office of the Firm moved to this Hines building at 555 13th Street, NW in 1987. The Firm currently occupies space on the 5th and 6th floors and part of the 13th floor of this centrally located atrium building. The building conveniently sits atop the Metro Central Station of Washington Metro. Previously, the Firm occupied space on the 2nd and 3rd floors, and at various times part of the 4th floor, of the Olmstead Building at 1701 Pennsylvania Avenue, across from the Executive Office Building and the old Renwick Gallery. That location was first occupied in 1973.

The Dallas office of the Firm opened in 1985 on the 20th floor of what was then called LTV Center at 2001 Ross Avenue, across from the Dallas Museum of Art. Later, the Firm moved within the building to occupy all of the 7th through 10th floors. After The LTV Corporation (an occasional client) filed for bankruptcy, the building was renamed Trammell Crow Center after its developer, another Firm client. The Firm also occupies a suite of offices at 6510 NCNB Plaza, within the offices of client NCNB Texas. The Firm also briefly had an outpost in Pacific Place when increases in the number of lawyers outstripped the available office space. Two of the Dallas office intellectual property lawyers currently occupy temporary space in San Antonio.

The Austin office of the Firm moved to San Jacinto Center on Town Lake at the foot of San Jacinto Boulevard in 1987. Baker Botts lawyers occupy the 16th and part of the 15th floors. Before the move, the Firm had space on the 14th floor in the United Bank Tower at the corner of 14th Street and Lavaca. At various times, the Firm also had space on the 4th and 10th floors of that tower. In earlier years, the Firm leased temporary quarters during Legislative Sessions at various locations in downtown Austin.

the original Botts (Walter Browne) and his son (Thomas H.). Hiram Garwood had two sons practice with the Firm, Calvin and St. John. Clarence Carter's son, Winston, was an associate in the Firm. Thad Hutcheson's grandfather was Palmer Hutcheson, a senior partner, and David Kirkland's father practiced with the Firm. Former associate Carol Noel King was the first lawyer whose *mother,* Virginia Noel, was associated with the Firm.

As to the current status of the Firm for future historical reference purposes, the first pages of a client brochure currently in use accurately summarize the Firm's present position:

The founding partner of Baker & Botts began practicing law in Texas in 1840. Baker & Botts now serves clients across the country from offices in Houston, Washington, Dallas, and Austin. Our 400 lawyers represent both large and small public and private corporations, government agencies, commercial banks, insurance companies, investment banking firms, partnerships, non-profit organizations, estates, trusts, and individuals. Our clients include 48 of the 100 largest companies on the Fortune 500 list and 21 of the 60 largest companies based in Houston.

We practice in almost all areas of civil law. About half our lawyers work on business and financial transactions and half are involved in various types of litigation. The transactional side of the practice includes corporate, securities, mergers and acquisitions, banking, oil and gas, real estate, international, government contracts, intellectual property, business restructuring, tax, and wills, trusts, and estates work. Our trial lawyers handle a wide variety of civil litigation including cases arising out of business and commercial disputes, products liability and personal injury cases, and cases involving antitrust, admiralty, creditors' rights, energy, employment rights, environmental, intellectual property, and securities matters. In addition to transactions and litigation, our Washington and Austin offices represent clients before government agencies and have growing appellate and legislative practices.

In all areas of practice, we provide assistance to clients who challenge us with a wide variety of goals and needs. We endeavor to find the most appropriate and cost-effective response or strategy. We try to identify the most appropriate lawyer for the job, matching the complexity and risks of the transaction or litigation with the specialty and experience of the lawyer. In addition, where suitable we use a team approach, calling on both generalists and specialists, as well as lawyers from our four offices where needed.

Baker & Botts is organized and managed so that it can respond to clients in an informed and cohesive manner. The firm is led by the managing partner, located in the Houston office, and each of the other offices is supervised by a partner-in-charge. Each week partners meet to discuss and act upon matters of firm business and policy, based upon recommendations of an executive committee.

The firm is organized into departments, whose organizational lines have evolved from our clients' needs. Although the nature of our practice requires some degree of specialization, our lawyers often practice in more than one area. In addition, we believe that our lawyers should be able to shift the emphasis of their practices to meet changes in the law, the needs of our clients, and new professional interests. For these reasons, our departmental structure has been reorganized from time to time, and the lines between departments are not rigidly drawn.

Baker Botts lawyers follow many professional and civic interests. They have served on the governing boards of the American Bar Association and the Texas Bar Association. A number of partners have previously served in federal and state government positions, and several former Baker Botts lawyers now serve in the current national administration. Our lawyers often play significant roles in local, state, and national political campaigns in both major political parties and serve on the governing boards of many civic, cultural, and educational organizations.

We recruit the highest ranking students from the best law schools in the country. Thus, our lawyers come from virtually every state. Once they begin their practice at Baker & Botts they receive extensive supervised training. Each department conducts seminars concerning current issues in its areas of practice, and we often invite clients to these seminars as well. Our lawyers also participate in training programs offered by bar associations and other professional groups, so that their knowledge remains current.

OTHER PEOPLE OF NOTE

The people discussed in this book have been partners for the most part because there are better records available on the partners who spent their entire careers with the Firm, but the success of the Firm depended on two other groups—the associates and the nonlawyer personnel. There have really been three groups of associates other than those who became partners. One group served only a few years and moved on to other careers. Among these would be such people as Frank Andrews,[8] who left to found the Andrews & Kurth firm; John Charles Townes, who later became General Attorney for Humble Oil & Refining Co.; St. John Garwood, who served with distinction on the Texas Supreme Court; and George Barrow, who headed his own law firm for years, and served as President of the Houston Bar Association and Director of the State Bar. Another group would be those who served temporarily at a time of crisis such as in World War II and then departed. A number of women lawyers filled this role long before women became a routine part of the employment practice. As reported ear-

lier, Edwin B. Parker first employed women lawyers in the 1920s, but their roles were more limited than were those of the women employed during World War II. Finally, there were some lawyers who spent most or all their careers with the Firm and served not only during the war but for many years thereafter. Among such men were A. H. Fulbright, Paul Langford, Edwin Ellinghausen, and Theodore Morton. The first three retired at the same time and Morton a bit later. Morton's opinions were so highly regarded that Jim Shepherd regarded him as his deputy in the operation of the Oil and Gas Department. Fulbright was the man responsible for publishing *Baker, Botts in World War II.*

Finally, able, loyal employees and supervisory staff are essential to any law firm, and the Firm has been especially fortunate in this regard. The great pride in the Firm shown by the early partners was fully reflected in the admiration and dedication shown by many lifetime employees. They are too numerous to attempt to name, but some representative supervisory employees in addition to Miss Willie A. Rowell must be mentioned. Raymond Neilson served as Administrative Assistant to several managing partners, and C. H. (Charlie) Wilson served under him. Mrs. Irma Harvin served as a secretary, file room supervisor, and finally as a successor to Miss Rowell. Maude Tomlinson was Dillon Anderson's secretary in the Middle East in World War II, came to Houston after the war as his secretary again, and then succeeded Mrs. Harvin as office administrator. Ruth Ware headed Accounting after Charlie Wilson retired and ruled with an iron hand. Ruth Warren, who supervised the File Room for many years, was the last of these to retire. The most obvious explanation for the deep affection toward the Firm shown by all these people was that the Firm gave them substantial responsibility, and they responded in kind.

---

[8] Andrews officed with Baker Botts, and when a conflict developed within the Firm concerning the representation of two major railroad groups, Andrews was asked to take over the representation of one of these groups. The separation was by mutual consent.

PUBLIC SERVICE BY PARTNERS

Edwin B. Parker set a good example for Baker Botts lawyers by offering himself for public service at a financial sacrifice. First, it should be noted that he was recruited by a former Baker Botts partner, Robert S. Lovett, who was himself serving in Washington. Even before Parker, Peter Gray served as a District Judge, Texas Supreme Court Justice, and member of the Confederate Congress, and Judge James A. Baker served as District Judge. Listed here are some current and former Firm lawyers who followed these examples during or after their work at Baker Botts:

Dillon Anderson, *National Security Advisor to the President.*
Perry O. Barber, *White House Counsel*
*Richard Breeden, *White House Counsel and now serving as Chairman of the Securities and Exchange Commission.*
*J. Curtiss Brown, *Chief Justice, Texas 14th Court of Appeals.*
O. Don Chapoton, *Assistant Secretary for Tax Policy of the Department of the Treasury.*
Finis E. Cowan, *Judge of the United States District Court in Texas.*
*James R. Doty, *General Counsel of the Securities and Exchange Commission.*
R. Gordon Gooch, *General Counsel of the Federal Power Commission.*
Wyatt Heard, *State District Court Judge.*
Henry F. Holland, *Assistant Secretary of the Department of State for Latin American Affairs.*
Joe Ingraham, *Judge of the United States District Court in Texas and later Judge of the United States Fifth Circuit Court of Appeals.*
*Robert E. Keeton, *Judge of United States District Court in Massachusetts.*
*Bob Lanier, *Mayor of Houston*
Ray Mabus, *Governor of Mississippi.*
*Thomas R. Phillips, *State District Court Judge*

and now serving as Chief Justice of the Texas Supreme Court.
*Lee Rosenthal, *Judge of the United States District Court for the Southern District of Texas.*
Stephen A. Wakefield, *Assistant Secretary of the Department of the Interior and the Department of Energy, and later General Counsel of the Department of Energy.*
Frank M. Wozencraft, *Assistant Attorney General of the Office of Legal Counsel of the Department of Justice.*
Larry F. York, *First Assistant Attorney General of Texas.*

**Now serving (1992)*

Baker Botts lawyers have been very active in bar association work at the city, state, and national level. Peter Gray was first President of the Houston Bar, Capt. Baker was present when the state bar was founded, and James L. Shepherd, Jr. was Chairman of the House of Delegates of the American Bar Association. Shepherd also served as president of the State Bar of Texas, as did Thomas M. Phillips, both after WWII. The following lawyers have served as Chairmen of Sections of the American Bar Association since World War II:

E. William Barnett, *Section of Antitrust Law*
C. Brien Dillon, *Section of Antitrust Law*
J. Thomas Eubank, *Section of Real Property, Probate and Trust Law*
Mont Hoyt, *Section of International Law and Practice*
John T. Maginnis, *Section of Corporation, Banking and Business Law*
Ewell E. Murphy, *Section of International Law and Practice*
Frank B. Pugsley, *Section of Patent, Trademark and Copyright Law*
Frank M. Wozencraft, *Section of Administrative Law*

WILLIAM C. HARVIN

William Charles Harvin, James A. Baker, III, and William R. Choate have one thing in common. Each began his "legal" career as a summer messenger for Baker Botts. Clarence Wharton, a senior partner in the Firm, took an interest in Harvin and encouraged him.

Harvin graduated from San Jacinto High School in Houston and enrolled at the University of Texas in 1936, but withdrew in 1940 for service in the U.S. Navy. During World War II, Harvin served first on a battleship and then as a combat pilot. He then re-entered law school at the University of Texas.

Harvin began his employment with the Firm on March 1, 1947, and became a partner in 1956, the minimum time possible at that time. His specialty was litigation, and he eventually became head of the trial section. He advocated multi-staffing of substantial litigation matters, both as a training tool and as a service to the client on the assumption that the youngest lawyer would do all he was capable of doing at a lower billing rate than his senior.

When a five-man Executive Committee was created in 1969, Harvin was placed on it, and on January 1, 1972, he became Managing Partner. He was the first attorney employed after World War II to become Managing Partner. Some of the accomplishments under his tenure were:

- A formal retirement plan was created for senior partners making it obligatory to retire, but at the same time making it financially worthwhile.
- Whereas partner interests had previously been stated in percentages and someone had to give up a percentage to make room for a partner, a profit share system was adopted so that there were no restrictions on admitting new partners.

- The importance of quality in employing associates received even greater emphasis, but all associates who it was felt qualified continued to be admitted as partners. This did lower the associate-to-partner ratio.
- He especially emphasized being more selective in accepting employment and not taking all business that was tendered.
- He determined that our fees were lower than comparable fees charged by other firms and that associate compensation was on the low side. Appropriate action was taken.
- Possibly most important of all, a review system was set up for partners as well as associates. No longer was it possible to advance to the senior level lock step after becoming a partner (some referred to it as the civil service system), but partners were graded on performance. This resulted in a fairly dramatic increase in production.
- Since it was not possible for all to advance to the maximum interest level, the definition of senior partner was modified to include those with 80% or more of the maximum interest.
- The policy was maintained to be generous in compensation to employees, but conservative on other spending.
- Harvin set an example by taking leadership positions in the community. Some of his titles have been:
  - President of Houston Country Club
  - Chairman of the Board of Directors, Texas Medical Center
  - Chairman of the Board of Directors, Houston Chamber of Commerce
  - Senior Warden, Palmer Memorial and St. Martin's Episcopal Churches
- He created the position of Administrative Partner through whom all administrative offices would report and who would then report to the Managing Partner. Harold Metts was appointed the first Administrative Partner

in 1974. He was succeeded by Stanley Beyer, and then Scott Rozzell.

Harvin retired on December 31, 1983 and was succeeded as Managing Partner by E. W. Barnett.

E. WILLIAM BARNETT

Edward William Barnett was born in New Orleans on January 2, 1933, and grew up in Shreveport, finishing high school in 1951. He graduated from Rice University in 1955, and then attended the University of Texas Law School where he was a member of Order of the Coif and Chancellors and was Comment Editor of the *Texas Law Review*. He was employed by the Firm on March 17, 1958.

His primary assignment was in the antitrust area, and he handled a number of major antitrust cases. He also served as chairman of the Section of Antitrust Law of the American Bar Association where he had been active for many years. He was recognized early as a leader in the Firm and was asked to head the Firm Employment Committee and to serve on the Executive Committee when Harvin was Managing Partner. Bill Barnett also has been recognized as a Houston civic leader and has been selected Chairman of the Greater Houston Partnership (the parent organization of the Houston Chamber of Commerce).

Among the accomplishments in Barnett's tenure are the following:

1. The Dallas office was opened not as an outpost, but with a strong initial staff. It has been the fastest growing of all the offices, increasing from 8 lawyers in 1985 to over 80 in 1990. This growth reflects a plan for the Dallas office to become much larger and to achieve a position in Dallas comparable to the Firm's position in Houston. Essentially this plan contemplates a national practice centered in the Southwest, which provides the basis for future expansion.

2. In Austin, there was a small office used primarily as a convenience for clients and Houston lawyers. That office now has 23 lawyers plus a large staff of legal assistants.

3. The Washington practice had been limited to energy matters and related government agency work. Under Barnett's tenure, that office now has more than 50 lawyers and has broadened its practice to include corporate and SEC work, tax, real estate, government contracts, environmental, international trade, and trial.

4. The opening (re-opening) of a New York office was announced in early 1992.

5. He has emphasized community relations and participation in the general business community. The Firm is very active in pro bono work, civic and volunteer work in the community, and in support of the arts in the city.

6. Barnett has an open management style. Meetings of all lawyers are held several times each year, and associates are advised of client developments and the financial progress of the Firm.

7. Somewhat related to the above, the Executive Committee is larger and younger and invites every partner to meet with it during year-end planning. Partner retreats have also been initiated. Younger partners have a larger voice in Firm affairs.

8. Under his leadership, growth has required some departures from recent traditions. Not only are new law graduates actively pursued but also associates who have practiced several years, and lateral partners have been added. A number of Houston lawyers have moved to other offices. It is interesting to note that for the first 60 years all of the partners except Capt. Baker were lateral hires; but none were added since the 1930s until 1985. Laterals are now a key element of growth.

In this photograph, the Firm's three most recent Managing Partners, John T. McCullough, E. William Barnett, and William C. Harvin, were persuaded to stand together in the actual order their names appear below the photograph. McCullough was Managing Partner from 1953 to 1972, Harvin from 1972 to 1984, and Barnett since 1984.

The purpose of this book has been only to supplement the formal Firm history, to furnish more background on some of the partners who created and built the Firm, and to record in one location an index of the speeches and papers delivered at various times concerning the Firm history. It should be emphatically noted that the Firm is not so absorbed with the past that it is ignoring its future. If there is a common theme in the historical presentations, it is that these writers and speakers were looking to the future and could hardly wait for the Firm to mark its next milestone. The younger readers, who may be bored with the slow pace of the early days and not amused by the Firm lore which old timers enjoy, should nevertheless be inspired by the character, the intellect, and the vision of the early Firm leaders.

How then could one summarize the 150-year history of Baker Botts, and what lessons could one learn from the manner in which the Firm has carried on its practice?

It all began with Peter Gray who was clearly the outstanding lawyer in Houston (and perhaps in Texas) from the time he began his practice. He in turn was able to invite the very best lawyers to join him. He chose Walter Browne Botts in 1865 and an outstanding Huntsville railroad lawyer, James A. Baker, as a third member of the Firm in 1872. All was logical and planned to this point.

Then fate took a hand. Judge Baker had a son who graduated from college and signed a contract to teach at that college for two years. Judge Gray was in ill health and died shortly after Judge Baker arrived on the scene. By the time of the deaths of the two older partners, Capt. Baker had the help of only two young lawyers (Lovett and Parker, both destined for greatness), but for the most part young Baker had total responsibility for the future of the Firm. We do not know why Capt. Baker decided to read law rather than teach or who made the decision that he would practice with the Firm, but one could conclude that had he elected to become a professor, there would be no Baker Botts today.

Resuming this summary of history, Capt. Baker began to build the Firm after the death of his father and Col. Botts. As Jesse Andrews pointed out, possibly the greatest of his many talents was his ability to pick people. The Firm had a very lucrative railroad practice, and, again, it selected only the best lawyers available.

In the early days of the University of Texas Law School, the Firm's supremacy was unquestioned, and it could pick and choose among the top graduates. There was no such thing as recruiting since the professors simply pointed out the best students to the Baker Botts partners.

As law schools grew larger and more outstanding graduates were available in the 1950s and 60s, the competition increased, and the Firm was no longer able to maintain its huge lead in the quality of lawyers, but it had something else going for it.

Edwin B. Parker was one of Capt. Baker's first selections, and he was the organization man personified. Whereas most firms before his time were made up of a number of individuals practicing law out of the same office, he visualized the Firm as an institution, and he was certain that the whole was greater than all its parts. We are amused when we read that after Parker took charge, lawyers were not allowed to sign their own letters. They were writing not for themselves but for the Firm. This was Parker's way of emphasizing that the Firm was more important than the individual. He was a driver of men, and some of his contemporaries resented him, but he and Capt. Baker should be credited with creating the Firm as we know it.

Most successful institutions have what some would call mystique and others esprit. They transform individuals and inspire them to heights they could never attain on their own. The New York Yankees had it at one time, as did the Boston Celtics and the Notre Dame football team. In the military, one thinks of the Marine Corps. This brings us to a key man in Baker Botts' history.

While Parker created the "institution" and delivered rather severe lectures on the subject, Hiram Garwood was one who could inspire devotion rather than command it. He is also a good example of the Firm's inspiring a man to rise above himself. He was a politician and a good trial lawyer when he was recruited by the Firm at age 40. But, he caught the spirit and not only rose to incredible heights professionally but also had the gift to put into words a message that has inspired generations of Baker Botts lawyers.

One small excerpt from a speech by Judge Garwood, a partner from 1904 to 1930, has been repeated in every Plan of Organization prepared by the Firm. As long as Baker Botts lawyers read these words and believe, the future of the Firm will never be in doubt. He said of the Firm:

> I have always thought of it, not as a mere temporary association of individuals, however pleasant or however profitable, but as a permanent INSTITUTION, just as Harvard or the Bank of England is an institution, with a strength, a life and individuality made up from, yet greater than, all or any of its members, in that the accumulated knowledge and achievements of its members, past and present, become the common capital of all to preserve, increase and transmit to those who shall come after us.

APPENDIX I

BAKER BOTTS PARTNER ADMISSIONS
1840 - January 1, 1992

1840
Peter W. Gray

1865
Walter Browne Botts

1872
Judge James A. Baker

1887
Capt. James A. Baker

1892
Robert S. Lovett

1900
Edwin B. Parker

1904
Hiram M. Garwood

1906
Jesse Andrews
Clarence R. Wharton

1909
Clarence L. Carter

1915
Thomas H. Botts
Jules H. Tallichet

1917
Walter H. Walne

1921
Ralph B. Feagin
Palmer Hutcheson

1923
W. Alvis Parish

1927
James A. Baker, Jr.

1929
Homer L. Bruce
Francis G. Coates
Gaius G. Gannon
James L. Shepherd, Jr.

1933
Tom Scurry

1935
John P. Bullington
Brady Cole

1938
H. Malcolm Lovett

1940
Dillon Anderson
Tom Martin Davis
William M. Ryan

1944
John T. McCullough

1945
Joseph C. Hutcheson, III

1948
John T. Maginnis
Denman Moody

1949
William R. Brown
Garrett R. Tucker

1950
Henry F. Holland
Hugh M. Patterson
Thomas M. Phillips

1953
John F. Heard
B. John Mackin

1955
Robert K. Jewett
Baine P. Kerr
James K. Nance
Andrew Ben White

1956
William C. Harvin

1958
William Rufus Choate
C. Brien Dillon

1960
Frank G. Harmon
George H. Jewell
Frank Burruss Pugsley
John S. Sellingsloh

1961
Frank M. Wozencraft

1962
Ross Staine
James G. Ulmer

1963
John B. Abercrombie
Ralph Stephen Carrigan
James P. Lee
Richard B. Miller

1964
Wiley N. Anderson, Jr.
Thomas E. Berry
Ewell E. Murphy, Jr.
Alvin Owsley

1966
Finis E. Cowan
J. Thomas Eubank
Charles G. Thrash, Jr.

1967
R. D. Richards, Jr.

1969
E. William Barnett
Reagan Burch
Moulton A. Goodrum, Jr.
B. D. McKinney

1970
Sam G. Croom, Jr.
Richard B. Dewey
William C. Griffith
Robert J. Piro
Robert L. Stillwell
Walter E. Workman

1971
O. Don Chapoton
John C. Held
James C. Johnson
Robert J. Malinak
James D. Randall

1972
Perry O. Barber
R. Gordon Gooch
Richard C. Johnson
William G. Woodford

1973
Daryl Bristow
Joseph D. Cheavens
John M. Huggins
Thad T. Hutcheson, Jr.
Harold Metts

1974
F. Walter Conrad, Jr.
Michael Scott Moehlman
Stephen A. Wakefield
Larry F. York

1975
Stanley C. Beyer
Larry B. Feldcamp
Mont P. Hoyt
Frank W. R. Hubert, Jr.
John L. Jeffers
Philip James John
Ronald L. Palmer
Jeron L. Stevens
Lewis Proctor Thomas, III
Wade Hoyt Whilden
Mark E. Winslow

1976
Richard R. Brann
William R. Burke, Jr.
James L. Leader
John P. Mathis
Roy Nolen
James Michael Turley

1977
John P. Cogan, Jr.
James R. Doty
J. Patrick Garrett
D. Thomas Moody
L. Chapman Smith

1978
Bruce F. Kiely
Robert A. Webb
Theodore F. Weiss, Jr.

1979
David A. Burns
David P. Cotellesse
Fred H. Dunlop
I. Jay Golub
Hugh Rice Kelly
William C. Slusser
Benjamin Gladney Wells

1980
Joseph A. Cialone, II
John B. Connally, III
J. Gregory Copeland
Charles M. Darling, IV
Michael L. Graham
Stephen M. Hackerman
Richard L. Josephson
John E. Neslage
Rufus W. Oliver, III
R. Joel Swanson
Geo. Irvin Terrell

1981
Justin M. Campbell
Carol C. Clark
Rufus P. Cormier, Jr.
Alan Shore Gover
Michael Paul Graham
Ross Harrison
Diana E. Marshall

1982
Louis L. Bagwell
Stacy Eastland
Roderick A. Goyne
Randall A. Hopkins
James R. Raborn
Alan D. Rosenthal
Walter J. Smith
James A. Taylor
Stephen G. Tipps
C. Michael Watson

1983
James Edward Maloney
Stephen A. Massad
Randy J. McClanahan
Randolph Q. McManus
Scott E. Rozzell
Charles Szalkowski

1984
J. Patrick Berry
George F. Goolsby
James A. Hime
Gray Jennings
Allister M. Waldrop, Jr.
Karen L. Wolf
Robert P. Wright

1985
J. Michael Baldwin
Thomas J. Eastment
W. John Glancy
Robert W. Jordan
Lee L. Kaplan
Marley Lott
B. Donovan Picard

1986
Richard C. Breeden
Keith P. Ellison
Steven R. Hunsicker
Kerry C. L. North
Tony P. Rosenstein
Lee H. Rosenthal
James C. Treadway, Jr.

1987
Neil Kenton Alexander, Jr.
Andrew M. Baker
Linda Broocks
Larry D. Carlson
Rod Phelan
Joe S. Poff
Phillip N. Smith, Jr.
William F. Stutts
Kirk K. Van Tine

1988
Bryant C. Boren, Jr.
Ronald W. Kesterson
Jack L. Kinzie
George C. Lamb, III
Gregory V. Nelson
Robert W. Strauser

1989
Thomas H. Adolph
Pamela B. Ewen
Ronald K. Henry
Robert W. Kantner
Jay T. Kolb
Stephen L. Teichler
Robb L. Voyles
David E. Warden

1990
Earl B. Austin
Jonathan W. Dunlay
Claudia Wilson Frost
Michael S. Goldberg
J. David Kirkland, Jr.
Jerry W. Mills
Holly A. Nielsen
David R. Poage
David N. Powers
Stuart F. Schaffer
Louise A. Shearer
George T. Shipley
Hugh Tucker
Robert M. Weylandt
R. Paul Yetter
Patrick Zummo

1991
James A. Baker, IV
Paul B. Landen
Ronald C. Lewis
Gene J. Oshman
Margo S. Scholin
Bobbie T. Shell
James E. Smith
Patricia M. Stanton
Gail W. Stewart
David Tannenbaum
James M. Wallace, Jr.
Stephen Wallace

1992
Shelley W. Austin
Kenneth M. Bialo
Robert M. Chiaviello, Jr.
Robert I. Howell
William D. Kramer
Mitchell D. Lukin
John W. Martin
Scott F. Partridge
Jefferson Perkins
Andrew C. Schirrmeister, III
David Sterling
Rodger Tate
John B. Veach, III

"THE PATRICK CASE"
by Capt. James A. Baker[9]

The litigation known as the Rice Litigation extended over such a long period of time, both in Texas and New York, stretching from May, 1896, to about 1906, and there was such an accumulation of records during that time, enough to fill a room ten feet square, it goes without saying that about all I can do tonight is to give you the outline of a picture and let you fill in the shades and colors—give you a crayon, so to speak.

The history of the litigation readily divides itself into two phases: The one with which the firm was primarily connected and, the second, the testimony leading up to the conviction of Patrick and the probate of the 1896 will. As the purpose of this recitation tonight primarily is to preserve a record for the information of the firm, I will consider first the part that the firm played in this litigation.

William M. Rice was born in Springfield, Massachusetts, in 1816, and was educated in the common schools of that village, for a village it was at that time. He was about fourteen years of age when he hired himself as a clerk in a country store for a very nominal salary, but, coming from New England parents, as he did, and being imbued with habits of economy and thrift, he worked incessantly from the time he went into that store until he was twenty-three or twenty-four years old, when, by his thrift, he had saved enough to buy out his employer and became proprietor of this country store, making a small cash payment and agreeing to pay the balance on time. It consisted of an assorted stock of goods, wares and merchandise. He ran the business some years. Then he

The *Patrick* case was a sensation all across America. The headlines shown here are from New York, Chicago, Albany, Rochester, Denver, Philadelphia, and Houston newspapers of the day. The work of Capt. James A. Baker in saving the estate for Rice Institute enhanced the reputation of the Firm throughout the country. A report of one aspect of the case may be found in *People v. Patrick*, 74 N.E. 843 (N.Y. 1905)

[9] This summary of the Patrick case is a reconstruction of a speech given by Capt. Baker at a Firm meeting, the name of the firm then being Baker, Botts, Parker & Garwood. As seen in this summary, Capt. Baker's speech modestly downplays his role in the investigation and trials.

heard and read of the Battle of San Jacinto, and the achievements of Houston, and all the great pioneers of that day. He heard the call of the wild, so to speak, and he made up his mind that he was going to cast his fortune in Texas. So he had all of his goods, wares, and merchandise packed and shipped them on a boat—a sail boat—consigned to himself at Galveston and he came to Galveston overland, passing down the Ohio and the Mississippi to New Orleans and from there by boat to Galveston. There he awaited patiently the coming of the ship which never came. He told me it went down at sea with all of his treasured wealth and he had no insurance.

He came from Galveston to Houston and started clerking again in a store here. By his thrift and economy, he saved enough to start a little store of his own—perhaps on Market Square. His business continued to grow and after a while he established the firm of William M. Rice & Company, wholesale grocers and dry goods, and sold goods all over Texas, as far North as the Red River. In those days supplies for the people of Texas came to Texas in boats and were landed, for the most part, at Galveston and Houston. A great many also came from New Orleans, going up the Mississippi, and up the Red River to Jefferson, Texas, where they were distributed.

Mr. Rice came to Texas about 1839. He resided in Houston continuously until 1865. Some time in the '40s he married Paul Bremond's daughter. Paul Bremond was one of the pioneers of Houston, who came here with W. R. Baker, and with Abraham Groesbeck, for whom the town of Groesbeck is named, and with W. J. Hutchins, for whom the town

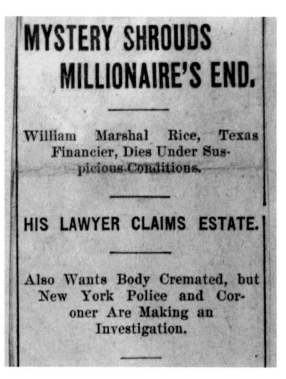

MYSTERY SHROUDS MILLIONAIRE'S END.

William Marshal Rice, Texas Financier, Dies Under Suspicious Conditions.

HIS LAWYER CLAIMS ESTATE.

Also Wants Body Cremated, but New York Police and Coroner Are Making an Investigation.

of Hutchins is named. There were no children born to his marriage with Miss Bremond. She died some time during the war and in 1865, just after the close of the war, he was married to his second wife, a Mrs. Brown, who was a sister of Mrs. Fred Rice, who was the mother of Joe and Will Rice. In other words, the two Mrs. Rices were sisters.

The war broke up Mr. Rice's business. All of his money went into goods and the goods went into the country and the people were unable to pay and so on the day he was married he left with his wife for New York. From 1865 until 1872 he lived at different places in New York, in boarding houses and apartments and rent houses, never acquiring a home in that city. In 1872, he moved to Dunellen, New Jersey, and there built a very handsome home. He told me it cost about $75,000 in that day, a very handsome home. He lived there until 1882, going to and from New York and doing some business there, probably as the eastern representative of the Houston & Texas Central Railroad Company—its financial representative. In Dunellen, New Jersey, he met Judge Bartine, a lawyer, who was on the bench there for a number of years. He was named as one of the executors in the will of 1896.

While Mr. Rice was living in New York, he frequently came to Texas. His interests in this state were very large because of the indebtedness to him of a great number of people all over Texas—indebtedness contracted before and during the war. Because of this indebtedness he acquired a great many lands all over the state which grew in value. He had large interests in Houston and came back quite often and lived in hotels here. After he sold his Dunellen home in New Jersey he never acquired another home. He had no children by his second wife.

He intended for many years—way back as far as 1872—to leave the bulk of his fortune to some educational institution. In 1872 he prepared a will in which he provided, in substance, that his beautiful home in Dunellen should be used as the site of a great institution of learning, and afterwards, before 1891, he prepared another will in which provision was made for this school to be located somewhere else.

In 1891, after spending some six months in Texas, he decided that inasmuch as he had made his fortune in Texas he would dedicate it to the youth of Texas and that the school which he had in mind should be located in Houston. In that year he had a charter prepared in the name of William M. Rice Institute for the Advancement of Literature, Science and Art. The charter provided that the trustees should be seven in number and should be self-perpetuating. He was always very prudent and he made himself Treasurer of the institution and said very frankly he expected to serve as Treasurer as long as he lived, and he did. The trustees were himself, his brother, F. A. Rice, A. S. Richardson, who was at that time Secretary of the Houston & Texas Central Railroad Company, Caesar Lombardi, the father of the Lombardi who is now associated with us in the Northwest in some matters, and E. Raphael, a brother-in-law of Mr. A. B. Cohn, who is now connected with the Rice Institute, and myself. At the time the trustees were elected in 1891, he said: "Well, I am going to start off that institute by giving them my note for $200,000, bearing interest at the rate of 2 1/2% per annum, payable annually, and payable at my death," and he said: "If it is just the same, I will take care of the note," and he took care of it very faithfully and he paid the interest on it every twelve months, provided there were any applications pending for loans. He paid the interest pretty regularly, and that was the beginning of the Rice Institute.

Shortly after that he gave it a note for $17,000, executed by G. L. Porter, who had married his niece. Mr. Porter had failed, in the meantime. He had been a wholesale grocer. Mr. Porter was a fine man and a good business man and he paid that note afterwards, both principal and interest. Mr. Rice gave the Institute 10,000 acres of land in Jones County. He and his wife made a deed to it and the deed was delivered and the Rice Institute went into possession. Afterwards it sold it for a good price.

Later on, his wife and he frequently talked about

POLICE THINK RICE WAS MURDERED

Dr. Curry Says Millionaire Had Been Dead an Hour Before Jones Summoned Medical Help.

CHECK FORGERIES WERE CLUMSY

NEW YORK, Oct. 6.
Frederick B. House, attorney for Albert T. Patrick and Charles M. Jones, who are in the Tombs accused of forging the name

the Institute. She was a very ambitious woman, but she was fond of society, and she was fond of being in the public eye, and she was anxious, very naturally, to see the Institute develop during the lifetime of Mr. Rice. Time and again she would get on this subject and urge Mr. Rice to build this institute now. In the meantime he had donated to the Institute the tract of land on Louisiana Street—about six acres—which he intended for the site of the Institute and she said: "Let

Journal,
Albany, N. Y.
Oct. 27-1900.

MILLIONAIRE RICE WAS POISONED.

Prof. Witthaus Found Mercury and Arsenic in the Stomach.

New York, Oct. 27.—Prof. Witthaus, in his chemical anlysis of the stomach of William Marsh Rice, reports that he

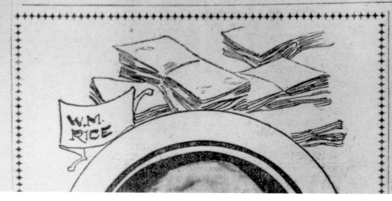

4

Oct. 6th 1900.
Chicago, Ill, American.

W. M. RICE MURDERED TO LOOT MILLIONS.

Police Admit He Was Poisoned and Evidence Indicates the Motive Was to Pilfer His Wealth.

Special to the Chicago American.
New York, Oct. 6.—An estate of $15,000,-000 is the stake that was sought by the murderers of William M. Rice.

That the aged millionaire was put to death by the use of poison, and with the us put a little cottage there for ourselves and put up the buildings and see it grow and develop under our eyes," but he said, "No, I am not in a humor to build. I am going to leave it to the younger men—these trustees—to do the building and, besides, I know more about making money than I do about building school houses and I am going to devote the balance of my life to piling this estate for this institution." Afterwards, he and his wife executed and delivered two deeds to the Rice Institute, one conveying 10,000 acres of land in Louisiana, very fine timber lands which at that time were supposed to be worth $3 an acre but which the trustees afterwards sold for about $85 an acre; that is, they sold the timber and still hold the fee to the lands. At the same time, Mr. Rice and his wife executed and delivered to the trustees a deed to the old Capitol Hotel, but both papers were delivered with the agreement that they would not be recorded until after his death, and they were not, and in delivering the deed to the Rice Hotel he stated, in the presence of his wife, that after it was filed for record, the Hotel should forever thereafter be known as the Rice Hotel. So upon his death the name was changed. The Institute had at the time of Mr. Rice's death in 1900 in money and securities and this land in Jones County about $50,000 available to the trustees in the litigation that was to follow his death. Of course, the income was supplemented then by the rent of the Rice Hotel, which the trustees got.

In 1896 Mrs. Rice died in Waukesha. Mr. Rice was with her. After her death he went on to New York. Her remains were interred in Waukesha in September, 1896. Mr. O. T. Holt, a prominent attorney of Houston at that time, filed for probate the last will and testament of Mrs. Rice. As soon as it was filed, my firm wired Mr. Rice. My firm, and its predecessors, had been the counsel of Mr. Rice ever since about 1840. Peter W. Gray was his first counsel, and then Col. W. B. Botts, then Gray, Botts & Baker, and then the successive firms represented him continuously for forty years or more. He was shocked and surprised at the will that his wife left and immediately wrote us to pre-pare his will and outlined in great deal how he wanted it prepared. The letters were written in his own handwriting and he suggested that the will be not typewritten. I prepared his will and returned it to him with instructions as to how it should be executed and filed away in the vault a copy of the will with all his letters on the subject and copies of my replies. He directed us to contest his wife's will, because he thought it was executed under circumstances that would justify him in setting it aside if he could.

Mrs. Rice and her attorney, who wrote the will, no doubt thought that she had a half interest in her husband's estate, which was supposed to be about four million dollars, and she made a great many bequests, aggregating, I suppose, about $1,250,000 and then provided that if the estate would justify it, she would double the bequests. We experienced great difficulty in trying to set aside the will. I made a memorandum of the bequests and thought it might interest you to hear some of them. She was very, very liberal. In the first place, she remembered a doctor with a bequest of $20,000 and she remembered a trained nurse with a bequest of $5,000, and then she remembered all the churches of the town and all the societies, and you can imagine that there was very great public sentiment in favor of the probate of the will, a great deal of local sentiment. For instance, she gave one sister $50,000, another sister $50,000, and a niece $200,000, and a niece's daughter $100,000, and a brother $50,000, and a cousin $25,000, another cousin $25,000, and the children of David and Mattie Rice $50,000, and a great many others. The newspapers exploited the will and everybody rallied to its support. Well, you can imagine the difficulty we had in finding anyone to testify that she was not competent to make a will, but we did find witnesses, especially at Waukesha, where she was for about a month before she died and where the interest in probating the will was not so great. The litigation showed that a draft of the will was made by Mr. Holt and was in his possession and that a copy of this *in extenso* had been made by Mrs. Rice, so it was wholly in her handwriting. It was witnessed by Mrs.

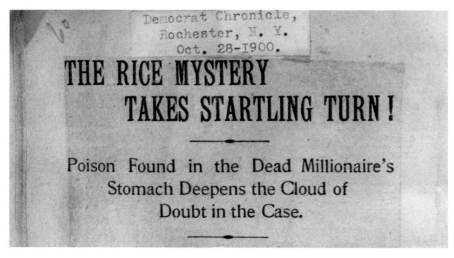

Democrat Chronicle,
Rochester, N. Y.
Oct. 28-1900.

THE RICE MYSTERY TAKES STARTLING TURN!

Poison Found in the Dead Millionaire's Stomach Deepens the Cloud of Doubt in the Case.

Holt's mother and by Mrs. Holt's sister. The will was probated and, on the evidence, I think it ought to have been probated. I never found any fault with the judgment, although there was testimony to show that she was not competent to make a will. Still, the preponderance of the testimony was in its favor. We did not appeal from that judgment. In the first place, we did not think it would do any good, and, in the second place, we took the position that inasmuch as Mr. Rice had become a widower in 1862 or 1863, his wife dying intestate and leaving no children, so much of his property as was owned at the time of the death of his first wife was his property and no interest passed by Mrs. Rice's will; furthermore, that no interest passed in the property that he acquired during the marriage with his second wife because on the very day that he married he went to New York, where the common law prevails and the wife had no rights in his property; that under the community law of Texas the wife had no interest in the property because of his domicile in New York. We advised him to file suit in the Federal Court, setting up claim to half of the community property, alleging that there was a cloud upon the title and that Holt had no interest as executor because Mr. Rice had always been domiciled in one of two common law states. Captain Hutcheson, Palmer's father, was associated with Colonel Holt in defending that suit in the Federal Court. Demurrers were presented to the bill and the legal questions that I have mentioned were

argued before Judge Bryant. He sustained our view, which was also supported by some three or four decisions that had been made in the very early history of the Supreme Court of Texas, and that is the law of the State today. Well, after the suit was instituted it became necessary to take Mr. Rice's testimony on the question of domicile to show that he had in fact resided in New York and New Jersey during all of these years. He was then about eighty years of age and was liable, of course, to die at most any time, and we went on and spent several months taking testimony. That was in the year '98 or '99.

A great deal of the testimony was taken. Mr. Holt went on and was present at the examination of all the witnesses, and while he was there he employed Mr. A. T. Patrick to assist him in procuring testimony and in the examination of the witnesses. I left New York in the late fall or early winter of 1899, expecting to take a great deal of testimony in Texas, as we did during the year 1900. By the fall of 1900 most of the testimony had been taken and we expected to try the case in the following November. I had not seen Mr. Rice since about September of 1899, although Mr. Parker had seen him. This was within two months before his death. Judge Lovett also had called to see him in his apartment and discussed the case and some of the facts of the case and told him when he thought the case would be tried in Galveston. This was within ten days of his death. That circumstance is important in connection with another feature of the evidence which I will mention later on.

One Monday afternoon, between three and four o'clock, September 24, 1900, I had a wire from Charles F. Jones, who was and had been for several years the valet of Mr. Rice—his handyman. In fact, Mr. Rice had no other servants and he lived alone with this servant. The message ran about this way:

"Mr. Rice died last night at eight o'clock under the care of a physician. Certificate of death weak heart, old age. Interment in Waukesha by the side of his wife. Funeral tomorrow morning at ten o'clock. When will you come?"

I wired immediately to Jones that N. S. Meldrum was in New York at a certain hotel; to see him and turn over the apartment and all papers to Meldrum pending his absence in Waukesha, as I assumed that he would go to Waukesha to the funeral. I 'phoned Mr. F. A. Rice, his brother, and afterwards showed him the telegram and my reply, and Mr. Rice said he would go to Waukesha that night to attend the funeral and join me in New York. I told him I would go on to New York. Between four and five that afternoon I received this telegram from Mr. Rice's bankers, Messrs. Swenson & Sons:

"Mr. Rice died last night under very suspicious circumstances. His body will be cremated tomorrow morning at nine o'clock. Interment at Waukesha."

Mr. Gerard was afterwards our Ambassador to Germany—during the war. We immediately wired Bowers and Sands to get in touch with the authorities and prevent the cremation of the body and preserve the *status quo* until we could get to New York. It developed that Mr. Gerard, with three detectives, went to Patrick's house that night and asked him about the check which he presented that day and he told them that he had a will in which he was named residuary legatee of Mr. Rice's estate. But they became very suspicious after talking with him and

Denver, Colo, Republican.

SEEKING SOLUTION OF GREAT RICE MYSTERY

PATRICK AND JONES AGAIN ARRAIGNED ON CHARGES OF FORGERY---NEW EVIDENCE DISCOVERED INDICATING THAT THE VALET PLANNED A WILL MAKING HIM RESIDUARY LEGATEE A YEAR AGO.

NEW YORK DISTRICT ATTORNEY AND DETECTIVES CONFIDENT THEY WILL UNRAVEL THE TANGLED SKEIN OF FORGERY AND PERHAPS UNCOVER A MURDER.

so officers were put in charge of the apartment and the next day, Tuesday, after funeral services the body was removed to the morgue and there was an autopsy and the stomach was removed from the body for analysis of its contents. They stood guard until I got to New York with Mr. F. A. Rice, Thursday morning. I, after breakfast, went up to the apartment with Mr. Rice and Mr. Meldrum. Now, you bear in mind that during all the time of this will litigation Mr. Patrick was acting as counsel for Mr. Holt, litigation which involved one-half of Mr. Rice's estate, and there was naturally a great deal of antagonism between Mr. Rice and Mr. Patrick. Furthermore, I knew that during all the taking of the testimony that Patrick and Mr. Rice had never met. So you can imagine my surprise when I went into the apartment to be met by Patrick and Jones. They both greeted me very cordially, especially Patrick, and said he was glad that I had come; that he was expecting me, and said: "By the way, I want to have a talk with you." I said: "All right, Patrick, but I would prefer to have either Mr. Rice here or Mr. Meldrum to be present at our conversation," and he said: "No, I prefer to see you alone." I said, "All right." We went into a back room and closed the door and through another door I saw the body of Mr. Rice resting. That door was then closed.

I never saw a man more composed than Patrick was—calm and deliberate. He called me "Jim" in those days. He said, "Jim, I expect you are surprised to see me in charge here. Well, in view of my relations with Mr. Rice I have an explanation to make and I want to make it." He said, "You know, the last two years I have been trying every way I could to settle this litigation between Mr. Rice and Mr. Holt; I advised Mr. Holt to take $750,000, and then $500,000, and then $250,000, all of which your firm declined, and finally offered us $50,000, which we would not think of taking. I made up my mind after you left to settle the suit, and I believed I was the man to settle. Knowing Mr. Rice as I had always known him, I realized I could never get into his presence if he knew that Patrick was coming there, and I resorted to this: I published in the *New York Tribune* of January 28th a notice in substance as follows: 'Will the heirs and friends of Elizabeth B. Rice please address Justice, 426 Lexington Avenue, New York,' hoping that it would come under Mr. Rice's eye. It did, and he wrote

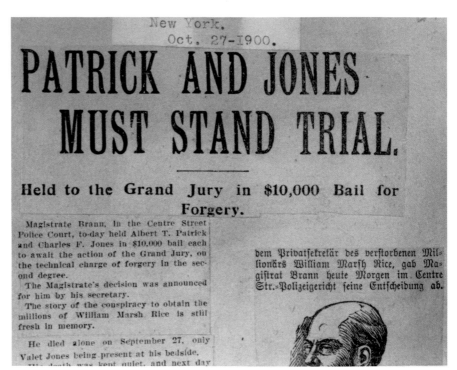

me to come and see him and referred to the notice that I had published in the *Tribune.* I called and sent in my card, J. B. Curtis, and was admitted, and spent the evening with Mr. Rice. I told him I had spent many years in Texas and we talked about Texas and other matters and I spent the entire evening with him. He asked me to call again and I did, two or three times afterwards, and spent the evening pretty much in the same way. Finally I made up my mind that I had gone far enough to tell him who I was, and I did so, and the old man became enraged and he cut up and ordered me out of the house, and I took my hat and started out and told him, 'Well, now, Mr. Rice, you must pardon me for what I have done but I had a purpose and that was to talk to you about settling this case.' I made a little talk to him, saying, 'You are old, and this litigation may continue indefinitely. It will never be settled during your lifetime. I cannot settle it with your lawyers, and I believe you and I can settle it,' and before I left he rather relented. He sat down and commenced talking about settling it, but we did not make much progress, however. He asked me to come back, and I did go back and we finally settled it, agreeing to settle

the litigation for $250,000, and I prepared the contract, and it was signed by him way last March." Now this was in September when we were talking. I said, "Did you notify Holt, your associate counsel, of your settlement?" He said, "No, Mr. Rice did not notify you, either. There is an explanation for this. He wanted to keep the settlement quiet. He did not want anybody to know about it. So I agreed not to divulge it, but we would go down to Texas in November and have the suit dismissed, and we would pay Holt the $250,000, and that would be the end of it." Well, I knew that Lovett had been talking with Mr. Rice about the case about ten days before. Patrick then said that there was another feature that he wanted to mention. These things seem very ridiculous, but they are exactly what Patrick told me. He said, "This little incident forecasts no justifiable criticism. Mr. Rice had lost confidence in you, and if you wish I will tell you the circumstances." I said, "Yes, I will be interested to know." He said, "He told me that on one occasion, while you were taking testimony, the hearing was adjourned for the lunch hour and you very cordially invited Holt to go to lunch with you and he accepted.

196

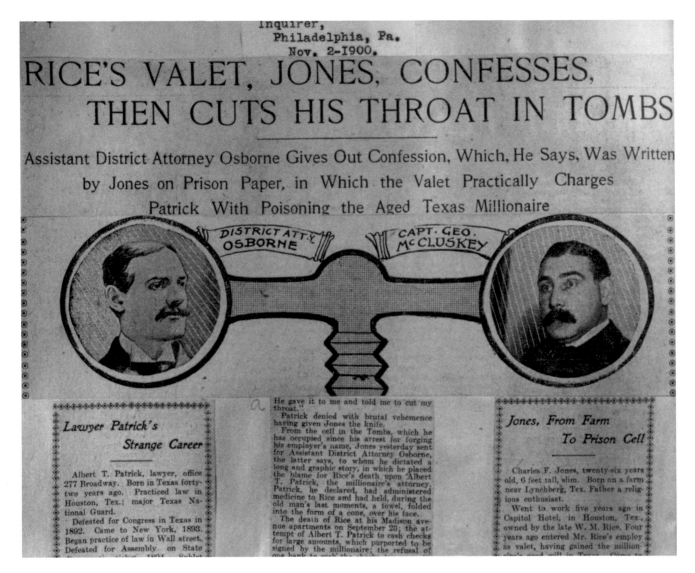

Inquirer,
Philadelphia, Pa.
Nov. 2-1900.

RICE'S VALET, JONES, CONFESSES, THEN CUTS HIS THROAT IN TOMBS

Assistant District Attorney Osborne Gives Out Confession, Which, He Says, Was Written by Jones on Prison Paper, in Which the Valet Practically Charges Patrick With Poisoning the Aged Texas Millionaire

DISTRICT ATT'Y. OSBORNE

CAPT. GEO. McCLUSKEY

Lawyer Patrick's Strange Career

Albert T. Patrick, lawyer, office 277 Broadway. Born in Texas forty-two years ago. Practiced law in Houston, Tex.; major Texas National Guard.

Defeated for Congress in Texas in 1892. Came to New York, 1893. Began practice of law in Wall street. Defeated for Assembly on State

He gave it to me and told me to cut my throat."

Patrick denied with brutal vehemence having given Jones the knife.

From the cell in the Tombs, which he has occupied since his arrest for forging his employer's name, Jones yesterday sent for Assistant District Attorney Osborne, the latter says, to whom he dictated a long and graphic story, in which he placed the blame for Rice's death upon Albert T. Patrick, the millionaire's attorney. Patrick, he declared, had administered medicine to Rice and had held, during the old man's last moments, a towel, folded into the form of a cone, over his face.

The death of Rice at his Madison avenue apartments on September 23; the attempt of Albert T. Patrick to cash checks for large amounts, which purported to be signed by the millionaire; the refusal of one bank to cash the check—

Jones, From Farm To Prison Cell

Charles F. Jones, twenty-six years old, 6 feet tall, slim. Born on a farm near Lynchberg, Tex. Father a religious enthusiast.

Went to work five years ago in Capitol Hotel, in Houston, Tex., owned by the late W. M. Rice. Four years ago entered Mr. Rice's employ as valet, having gained the million-

I told him there was nothing in it, but I could not eradicate it, and that had as much influence as anything about the settlement." Patrick continued, "Well I have seen the 1896 will that you prepared. Mr. Rice thought that it was a very unjust will. Of course, he did not when he made it, but he did afterwards. After we settled this litigation we became very chummy. In fact, nearly every letter that your firm would write up here to Mr. Rice, he would consult me about it, and I have letters which I can show in which he encloses letters from Baker, Botts, Baker & Lovett about certain matters and he would say, 'Mr. Patrick, what do you advise?' I have got any number of those letters, and the truth of the business is that I have been representing him professionally for the last six months." He said, "You would be surprised to know that I have prepared his will, wouldn't you?" and I said, "I certainly would." He said, "Well, I have—dated June 30th, last, but I did not overlook you in the preparation of it. You are one of the executors in the '96 will and you are an executor in the Patrick will." I said, "Patrick, I appreciate your thought of me, but I don't understand why, if Mr. Rice had lost confidence in me, he made me the executor in your will." He said, "That was my influence altogether, but I insisted with him that you and your firm would have to look after the business in

Texas, and he finally did it." I said, "Well, I appreciate that." He said, "There is only one thing that the old man and I ever disagreed about. He wanted me to go to Texas and give my personal attention to his affairs down there and I would not do it." He said, "The will provides for five percent on all receipts. You know that will be a pretty good 'sop' for the executors and I have made up my mind that I will not qualify as executor at all, and instead the court will simply divide the fees between the other executors, and more than that." I said, "Well, that is a good thought." He thought I saw the trend of his remarks to me, and I said, "By the way, Patrick, you know that this litigation of Holt's has been running now for about two years, and we have not been paid a cent for all of our services, and I would want it understood that we would have to be paid very liberally for those services, and as you are one of the executors I am just mentioning it now so that you may be thinking about it." He said, "Now, if there is anything to be considered it is the value of the services of a lawyer. New York lawyers do appreciate it, and I am a New York lawyer, and I will see that you will be not only fully but abundantly compensated," and I said, "Well now, that is very nice." So I said, "Where is the '96 will?" I was very anxious to get hold of that as I was afraid he had destroyed it. He said, "I have it around my house," and I said, "Where is your will?" and he said, "It is there, too. We can go down there directly and get them." We got up to go, and he said, "By the way, before we go let us attend to this body. It has been in here now since Sunday night and Mr. Rice left instructions for it to be cremated, and you gave instructions not to have it removed until you got here, and what are you going to do about?" I said, "What do you want to do?" He said, "I want to cremate it." "Where are you going to cremate it?" He said, "I have a letter of instructions from Mr. Rice." "Where is it?"

Evening Telegram,
New York,
Apr. 23. 1901.

PATRICK INDICTED FOR MURDER AND FORGERY

Grand Jury Finds True Bill Against Man Accused of Slaying Aged William M. Rice and Forging Latter's Name to Will Disposing of Millions

WITNESSES TO DOCUMENT MUST ALSO FACE TRIAL

Short and Meyers, Whose Signatures Appear on Disputed Paper, Are Indicted

forgery in connection with Mr. Rice's will," was taken from the Tombs at noon and went direct to the waiting room adjoining that occupied by the Grand Jury. Though they refused to testify before the Grand Jury yesterday, upon the advice of Cantwell & Moore, their attorneys, they were again invited to appear before that body. After waiting a few minutes, the three prisoners were met by a representative from their counsel's office, who held a short conference with them. They were told that, in

He showed it to me, and I said, "Well, I want to talk to Jones." I showed the letter to Jones, and said to Jones, "Did you write this letter?" and he said, "Yes, sir, I wrote it with a typewriter." "Mr. Rice dictate it?" "Yes, sir, he wrote it out in long hand and I copied it," and I said, "Where is the longhand copy?" "He destroyed it." "Did you see him sign it?" He said, "Yes, sir." It afterwards proved a forgery but it looked like his signature, so I talked to Fred Rice about it. I then went back to Mr. Patrick and told him that we would neither assent nor object to the cremation. Patrick then handed me the 1896 will, and I put it in my inside vest pocket. I really thought he had destroyed it. He showed that he reasoned in some respects very clearly about it. And then he showed me the 1900 will and I put that in my pocket, and he said, "You cannot take it," and I said, "Why, I am an executor. I have got just as much right to it as you have." He said, "No, I will not submit to you taking that will." "Well, I will not insist on it if you will give me a copy of it." So he said, "All right." He brought me out a carbon copy of it. I filled in the blanks and I wrote on the back that this is a true copy of the original. I asked him to sign it. He said he would not sign it. I asked him why. He said he did not see the will signed. To make a long story short, he said, "I will not sign." Meldrum and I signed it after comparing it with the original. Then he said, "I have got an assignment here of all his property to me," and he showed it to me. It was signed and witnessed. I said, "Why did you take that?" He said, "I thought I would just fortify myself, and then, again, principally because we have an inheritance tax in New York and you and I might agree not to probate the 1900 will and rely on the assignment and escape the tax." Mr. Rice had given instructions to permit me to enter his strong box. He said, "I have had that order revoked." On the morning following Mr. Rice's death, Patrick presented checks to Swanson & Sons and to the Fifth Avenue Trust Company making, altogether, $250,000. The Fifth Avenue Trust Company paid one of the checks. The others were not paid. I asked him to let me have those checks. He asked me what I wanted with them and I said, "Just as co-executor," and he turned them over to me and said, "When I left Mr. Rice's apartment the night of his death I took $10,000 in money and a number of securities." I said, "You might as well turn them over to me, too. I will take them down town and put them in a safety deposit vault." I think there were several hundred thousand, and he went with me, and we put them in a safety deposit vault.

The newspapers were full of accounts of the death of Mr. Rice, and the autopsy, and the presentation of these checks, and the fact that they were turned down, and everything of that kind. The newspaper reporters were around to find out what was going on, and, among others, the Chief of Police came down. He said that he understood that I had those checks. I told him I did, and he demanded them. I asked him what he wanted with them, and he said he wanted to have them examined. It seems that he did take them to some experts to have them examined. They said that they were tracings. In the meantime, Mr. Patrick and I had agreed to go to the strong box that Mr. Rice had and list the securities and then put them back. So we went down about five o'clock in the afternoon, after the bank had closed for the day. We were unable to find the key or combination, and it took about three

or four hours to open it. They had to drill through the steel plates. Meldrum went with me and we sat there for two or three hours, talking about various things until the box was opened. Finally, when the box was opened, Patrick came up and said, "I have a list of all those. You will find some Houston & Texas Central bonds there. You will find some Atcheson bonds. You will find the 527." They checked out just as he said. Then, as they went along and several others were checked off, his numbers did not harmonize at all. It developed afterwards that Jones had furnished him such information as he had. We made a list of them and put them in another box.

I remember that just as we left and got on the sidewalk a big six-foot policeman put his hands on my shoulder and asked, "Is this Captain Baker?" and he put his hands on Mr. Patrick and said, "You come with me, too." I said, "Can my friend here come with me?" and he said, "Yes, he can come, too." So we went to the Captain's office. The proceedings there were very short and to the point. He said, "Mr. Patrick, you are arrested for forgery. Officer, take him to the cell." He said, "Mr. Baker, you can go." Mr. Patrick said, "Well, I would like to 'phone my lawyer." He said, "All right, 'phone him." So Patrick and I parted, never to meet again, except across the table in the courthouse. The next day, Jones was arrested. I think that was about the 4th of November. There was a hearing before one of the Magistrates and they were bound over the sum of $10,000, which neither of them were able to give.

In the meantime, the experts were examining the stomach of Mr. Rice. There were several doctors and one expert chemist. The chemist reported that he found considerable mercury in the stomach. The physicians said that they could find no cause of death—the heart was good and all of the other organs seemed to be in excellent condition; that they could not detect anything, except that the lungs were very much inflamed, which indicated to them that some irritating substance had come into the lungs. After these reports came out, a charge of murder was preferred against both Patrick and Jones. They were both kept in prison.

One day while they were in prison, I received a note from a man who said, "I am just out of jail. I spent last night in the Tombs and just before I left I had a few words with Charlie Jones, the valet of Mr. Rice. He asked me to see you and tell you to come and see him." I went down town immediately after breakfast and got hold of our associates and the District Attorney. It was agreed that I should go up and see Jones. I took the District Attorney along, but he refused to see me except alone. When we met we talked about general matters, and I asked him what he wanted to see me about. "Well, I have changed my mind entirely, and I don't want to talk to you at all." So we parted. In about two or three days he sent word again that he would see me, and this time he said he

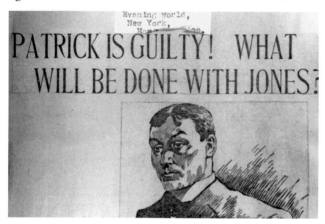

would see me with the District Attorney. We took down in longhand his statement, which was very interesting but which was not true. We could tell that. So Osborn, who was Prosecuting Attorney, said, "Well, Jones, this is just a bunch of lies, and this will never get you anywhere." In the meantime Jones had employed Gordon Battle, who is a rather prominent lawyer in New York today, and had made a statement in writing to Mr. Battle which was very different from the one he had made to Osborn, but which was no more true than the first one. Shortly after that Jones attempted suicide with a knife which he says Patrick furnished him under an agreement that they would both suicide simultaneously. He made an honest effort himself, but

Patrick did not. He got entirely well, but after that he sent for the District Attorney and said now that he wanted to make a third statement which would be the truth. Osborn said, "Now, Jones, I know more about the case than you do and there is no use telling me anything which is not the truth." "Well," Jones said, "I have made up my mind to tell the truth," and he sat down and made a statement. When the case came on for trial, Jones gave testimony in accordance with his last statement. Of course, his testimony was weakened by the fact that he had made two or three other conflicting statements, all of which he had signed and sworn to. When Osborn went into the case he said he must corroborate Jones' statement. He succeeded in doing so, and this is evidenced by the fact that the jury went out and were not gone more than one hour, one-half of which time they were eating, and in thirty minutes they returned a verdict of guilty. Now that is the part of the story that we are concerned with.

Now, Jones' story is this, and I will show you very briefly how he was corroborated by facts and circumstances: He said that Patrick came to see him under the name of "Smith" and finally told him who he was and told him that he was underpaid, and he wanted to settle that litigation and wanted to see Mr. Rice. He told him Mr. Rice would not see him. And then he said they concocted the conspiracy to make this will. He said, "I showed him the 1896 will." He said he showed that to Mr. Patrick and the latter said, "Now, Jones, we must have for our will the same witnesses as the Baker will—Weatherby and Hall—both of them working for Swenson & Sons. Do you suppose you can get Weatherby to fall into our scheme? Jones said, fortunately for him, very soon Weatherby came up to see Mr. Rice to borrow $7,000 to discharge a mortgage which he had down in Texas, and Mr. Rice refused to let him have it and, he said, "I thought that was a good time to go and see Weatherby." He said he made a proposition to Weatherby that if he would get a will, make himself executor and follow pretty much the will that I had prepared, he could get it signed, saying to Weatherby, "I can get it executed, because Mr. Rice is quite old. He sleeps a good deal during the daytime and it would be easy for me to slip the last sheet of a will in with a bunch of letters and have him sign it without reading it." He said that Weatherby repulsed him. Now, to corroborate that statement of Jones, we proved that Weatherby, who was a perfectly reputable citizen, went immediately to a notary public and had the notary write out just exactly what occurred between him and Jones, and he put it in his chest but never said anything to Mr. Rice. He said he did not say anything to anybody about it. So that was corroborative of this circumstance. Then, on June 30th Mr. Rice received from us five deeds. They bore that date (June 30th) and he executed them on that day. There was a man by the name of Morris Myers, who was a notary public and stenographer in Patrick's office, and a man by the name of Short, who was in the printing business. Patrick had had Short appointed a Commissioner of Deeds. Jones and Patrick had arranged that all papers which were acknowledged by Rice should be acknowledged either by Myers or Short. The Patrick will was dated June 30, 1900, the same day that Mr. Rice signed these five deeds. They did that so as to be able to show that these two witnesses were there on that day.

Then Patrick and Jones agreed that Patrick would write letters to himself in the name of Mr. Rice and that Patrick would furnish all the signatures if Jones would do the typewriting. He said that Patrick lived up to his part of it and furnished all signatures. Jones said he told Patrick, "I cannot mail these letters to you, for if the letters should come back Mr. Rice would open them and we would be exposed." Patrick said, "Well, I will tell you, you, at different times, every few days, mail me an envelope addressed to me at my place of business and you put blank paper in it, to make it

PATRICK SENTENCED TO DIE

By Recorder Goff,

IS TAKEN TO SING SING

Condemned Murderer of Millionaire Rice Hears His Fate With Same Jaunty Air That Has Marked Him Throughout—Motion for New Trial Embodying Numerous Counts Is Denied by the Court--Patrick Permitted to Take Leave of His Wife But Refuses to Talk to the Newspaper Men.

look like a letter, so that if it should come back to Mr. Rice there would not be any letter in it; then you write the letters and we will fix the date on the letters to correspond with the postmark on the envelopes and put them in the envelopes." Jones said they did that. On the trial Jones testified to that scheme and the District Attorney said, "You wrote those letters and sent them to Mr. Patrick?" He said, "Yes, sir." He said, "Where did you last see those letters?" and he said, "In the Tombs," and he said, "Who had them?" He said, "Mr. House, Mr. Patrick's attorney." "You said Mr. House, the man that is defending Mr. Patrick, he had those letters?" He said, "Yes, sir, twenty-five or thirty, maybe more than that." House did not say anything.

Jones further testified that early in March Mr. Rice was not very well and wanted a doctor, and Mr. Patrick had Dr. Curry to come and see him, who was Patrick's doctor and had been for several years, and he waited on him up to the time that Mr. Rice died.

Jones further testified, "We finally agreed that if Mr. Rice did not die pretty soon that we would have to use chloroform. Mr. Patrick wanted me to get the chloroform, and I asked him why he did not get it, and he said they kept a record of those things. I wrote then to my brother down in Goose Creek to send me four ounces of chloroform and two ounces of laudanum. My brother went down to Galveston and got the laudanum and chloroform and sent them to me." He testified as to the day he received it and about the hour, and then it was proved that in Galveston they had sold about that much laudanum and about that much chloroform and by the expressman, that they delivered a package at 501 Madison Avenue at the time Jones said he received it.

There were many other circumstances, most of which have now passed out of my mind. The trial lasted some two or three months and finally, near the end of the testimony for the prosecution, these facts came out, which convinced the jury and everybody who heard them that Patrick was guilty. Osborn said, "Jones, you have told three different stories about this matter, including the one that you have told the jury today. Now you say the other stories that you told to us and to Mr. Battle are not true and that the one you are telling today is true?" "Yes, sir." He said, "When did you ever tell this story that you have just told to the jury?" He said, "It was a few days after Mr. Patrick and I were in the Tombs." He said, "To whom did you tell it?" Jones said, "I told it to Mr. House." "You mean this man, attorney for Mr. Patrick?" and Jones said, "Yes, sir." "You told him the same story to which you have testified; that you murdered Mr. Rice and you did it at the instigation of Mr. Patrick and his influence? Who was present besides Mr. House?" Jones said, "Mr. Patrick was present." You could have heard a pin drop, and everybody instinctively was looking towards House, expecting him to arise and announce it as untrue. If he had, Patrick would have been acquitted, but House went on for a month and never opened his mouth. Patrick himself did not go on the stand and subject himself to cross-examination, so it always seemed to me that this circumstance was sufficient to satisfy anybody that Patrick was guilty of the murder of Mr. Rice.

Then, again, Patrick told me that every time he saw Mr. Rice he always saw him alone, and I said to

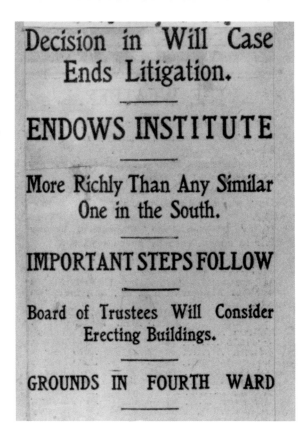

Decision in Will Case Ends Litigation.

ENDOWS INSTITUTE

More Richly Than Any Similar One in the South.

IMPORTANT STEPS FOLLOW

Board of Trustees Will Consider Erecting Buildings.

GROUNDS IN FOURTH WARD

him, "Patrick, if you expected anybody to believe that this will of yours was a valid will and you had become the counsel of Mr. Rice, why did you not call some of his friends or some of your friends to go before Mr. Rice and show them this will and have him admit in their presence as to the validity of the will?" He said, "Of course, I ought to have done that and so far as I know, to be frank with you, I don't know that anybody has." Of course, Jones testified that Mr. Patrick had never seen Mr. Rice.

Patrick was convicted, Jones turned state's evidence without any promise of the District Attorney of immunity.

Patrick's conviction was affirmed and he stayed in prison for about ten years. Afterwards he was given a full pardon by the Democratic Governor of New York. I understand he is somewhere in Oklahoma. He had a brother-in-law who lived in St. Louis who was many times a millionaire. He married one of Patrick's sisters, and it was believed that he furnished a great deal of the money for his defense, because he was defended by able lawyers. Jones afterwards came back to Texas and the last I heard of him he was in Goose Creek and some seven or eight years ago he disappeared as completely as if he had been swallowed up by the earth, and about that time Patrick made a motion for a new trial. In New York you never lose your right by lapse of time or otherwise to apply for a new trial. So after he had been in prison for ten years he filed a motion for a new trial. Jerome, who was the District Attorney, sent down here to us to send him affidavits of different citizens of Houston as to those who had made the affidavits on which the motion for a new trial was based. The latter affidavits consisted primarily of statements to the effect that Jones could not be found and that he had disappeared. They circulated the report up there that the Rice Institute had made away with Jones. We thought maybe they had murdered him. They sought to get a new trial based on these affidavits. It so happened that copies of these affidavits were sent to us and we got on the trail of a number of men. We found that three of the men had been in the penitentiary. We went to the penitentiary and got their records and things of that sort, and we sent all of this testimony upto Jerome. The first man that came along to testify on the motion for new trial had the name of "Skinny" Martin, and he testified about his conversation with Jones, and that Jones had told him that Capt. Baker had paid him $500 or $1,000 to testify against Patrick and that Patrick was innocent. Jerome told me about it. Jerome asked him, "Your name is Skinny Martin, you say?" "Yes, sir. They just call me Skinny for short." "Is not your name John Thomas?" "Yes, my name is John Thomas Martin." "Well, how long did you say you were in the penitentiary?" He said, "What did you say?" "I asked how long you had been in the penitentiary." He said, "Judge, I protest against any such question as that." The Judge said, "You answer the question." "Of course, I have never been there. That was my

brother." Jerome said, "Skinny, how old are you— 41, 10th of next January you will be 42?" "Yes, sir." "How high are you?" He said, "What do you ask me that for?" "Are you not five feet eight inches?" "Yes, I am about that." He said, "Skinny, have you not got a scar on your left leg?" He said, "I refuse to answer that." "Well," the Judge said, "Skinny, you better answer that." "Well," he said, "I don't know whether it is on that leg or not." "Well," he said, "Skinny, pull up your breeches," and he protested and the Judge made him. He said, "No, sir, I have not been in the penitentiary." "All right now, remember if you swear to a lie I will send you to the penitentiary for perjury." "That is all right; you can send me there if you want to." So when they got through with him they called a man that is here in town now by the name of Murray. Murray had been a guard in the penitentiary. Jerome had him hid out in the courthouse, and after Skinny got through he called him, and you should have seen Skinny's eyes when they put Murray on the stand and he was asked, "Do you know that man?" "Skinny Martin, yes, sir." He said, "Judge, I would know Skinny anywhere. I have known him for three years," and, to make a long story short, a few days after that Skinny was indicted for perjury and sent to the penitentiary for two years. It goes without saying that the application for a new trial was denied.